THE MOTIVATE SERIES

Macmillan Texts for Industrial Vocational and Technical Education

Electrical Installation
Principles and Practices

J.M. Hyde

MACMILLAN

First published 1994

Published by THE MACMILLAN PRESS LTD
London and Basingstoke
Associated companies and representatives in Accra,
Auckland, Delhi, Dublin, Gaborone, Hamburg, Harare,
Hong Kong, Kuala Lumpur, Lagos, Manzini, Melbourne,
Mexico City, Nairobi, New York, Singapore, Tokyo.

ISBN 0–333–60160–2

Printed in Hong Kong

A catalogue record for this book is available from the
British Library.

Cover illustration courtesy of Roger Ressmeyer, Starlight
Science Photo Library.

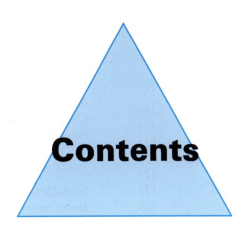

Contents

Contents

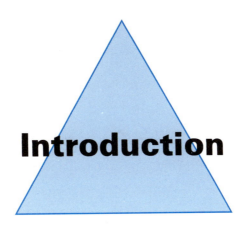

Introduction

As the demand for labour-saving devices in domestic, office and commercial premises, together with automation in industrial processes increases, the knowledge required by electricians is becoming more involved.

It is now a requirement that young people entering the electrical installation and maintenance industry carry out theoretical studies to gain certificates to at least approved electrician status, otherwise they will always have to work under the supervision of a qualified person.

This book contains ample material for study to enable a student to proceed to at least approved electrician status and it fully covers the requirements of a number of electrical installation syllabuses and courses.

In addition to theoretical knowledge, the practical aspect of the work demands that the electrician should be prepared to work in outdoor conditions and at heights and in awkward and confined spaces. Being able to diagnose faults on/in electrical installations, electrical machines and appliances and to carry out repairs, read wiring diagrams, layouts of equipment and specifications from architects and builders plans and to transfer the information to the actual building are vitally important skills in this area. This book has been written and developed with all the needs of students studying electrical installation fully in mind and will help students to study successfully and complete their courses.

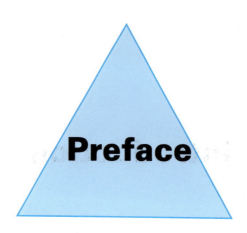

Preface

Governments or statutory bodies lay down regulations to safeguard the public against the potential dangers of electricity and to ensure its efficient use. Examples of these are

1. the electricity supply Regulations which mainly concerns the supply authorities;
2. Electricity Supply (Factories) Act which concerns the occupiers of the various buildings;
3. Mines and Quarries Act which applies to the use of electricity in the various types of mines and quarries;
4. Health and Safety at Work Act. These are **statutory** obligations on the occupiers in the use of electricity.

I.E.E. Regulations

These are regulations laid down by the Institution of Electrical Engineers for electrical equipment in buildings.

I.E.E. Site guidance and notes

These relate to the installation, testing, inspection and maintenance of electrical equipment in buildings. Although these are not compulsory by law, they are regarded as the standard of installation requirements by the supply authorities, insurance companies, local authority bodies, safety committees, and by candidates in advanced examinations.

Codes of practice (C.P.)

These deal with the manufacture and the installation of equipment. It is recommended that any contractor or designer working on installations with which he is not familiar should consult the forementioned documents for guidance.

The work outlined in this book is based on all the safe working practices laid down as far as they apply.

Manufacturers of electrical equipment, accessories and wiring systems have their own methods of production to meet the same specifications required of the finished product. If specialised knowledge is required, the instruction details or the manufacturers themselves should be consulted.
Note: For more detailed information direct reference should be made to the appropriate regulations.

The descriptions, wiring diagrams and sketches shown throughout the book are the basic essentials sufficient for the student to understand the working principles. They are of the standard which a candidate in a craft examination would be expected to reproduce in the time allotted.

Electrical installation practices are so varied it is difficult to cover all aspects in detail. Some questions in the more advanced examinations are phrased in such a way that the candidate must combine his own working knowledge with the standard information obtained from the textbook. Students are advised to familiarise themselves with a wide range of techniques and equipment in preparation for these questions.

The editors and publishers are grateful to the City and Guilds of London Institute for their co-operation in allowing extracts from past examination papers to be reproduced and to the I.E.E. for extractions from their wiring tables.

Safety, workshop and site operations

Introduction

Employers and employees have a duty to ensure that the place in which they work is free from dangers which are likely to affect the health and safety of themselves and others.

Safe working practices

Employer's obligations

Under the Health and Safety at Work Act 1974, the employer must:

1. ensure the health, safety and welfare of his employees;
2. provide and maintain safe equipment;
3. ensure the safety of employees in the use, handling, storage and transport of materials; and
4. provide information and training in health and safety as far as is necessary to enable his employees to carry out the work safely.

Employee's duties

The employee must:

1. take care not to endanger the health and safety of himself or others at work;
2. co-operate with his employer in carrying out the duties previously mentioned and to report any dangers of which his employer may be unaware; and
3. not interfere with anything that has been provided to ensure the well-being of himself and others.

Work areas

Workers should have free access to and from all floor areas, work-benches and machines and sufficient lighting to enable safe movement. Gangways, stairs, entrances and exits should be clearly marked, preferably by marked lines. These areas should be unobstructed, free from materials such as oil and grease and again, well lit.

In areas where there are extremes of temperature, accidents are more likely to occur. Therefore a more uniform working temperature should be maintained.

Power machines in workshops

> ▲ Machines do not stop when human beings or their clothing are caught up in the moving parts.

By far the most serious injuries and accidents occur where power machinery processes are being carried out. Although most processes are performed by operators, electrical personnel often find themselves working in these areas, carrying out installation and maintenance work or even operating the machines to repair apparatus and appliance components. It is therefore essential that electrical personnel are aware of the danger points and the procedure should an accident occur. There is little time to be lost in these situations.

The general safety aspects, access, lighting, gangways, obstacles, etc., have already been mentioned. The dangers of the machines will now be considered. See the machine danger points and guards sketches (Figures 1.1 – 1.4).

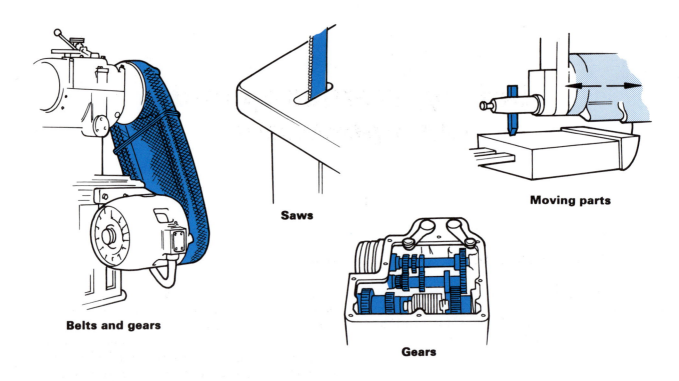

Figure 1.1 Machine danger points.

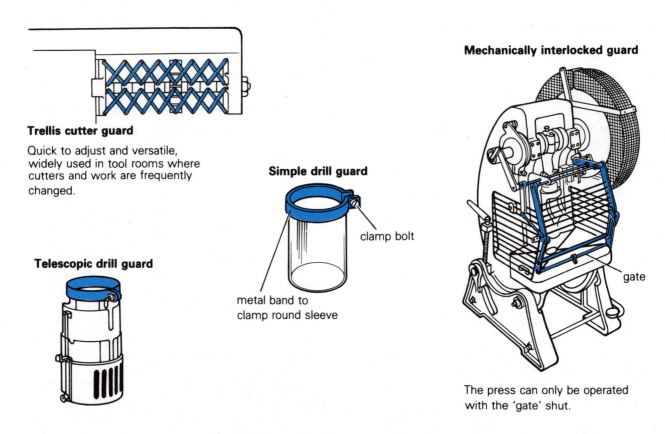

Figure 1.2 A mechanically interlocked machine guard.

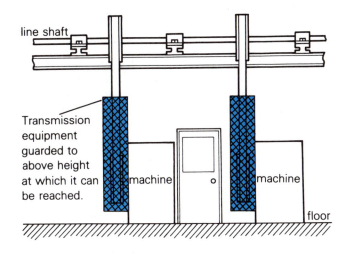

Figure 1.3 Guarding transmission equipment.

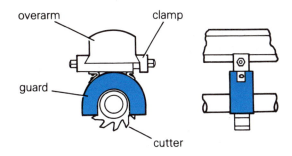

Cutter guard

Although simple to make, this type of guard can only suit a small range of cutter sizes.
A number of guards are required to suit a variety of work and cutter combinations.

Figure 1.4 Milling cutter guard.

Factories acts

It is a requirement that equipment which transmits power must be guarded in such a manner which makes it safe to **every person** on the premises. A procedure for stopping, electrical isolating and preventing unexpected or accidental restart of the machinery until **all** personnel are clear of the hazard is essential.

Chapter 8 shows an electrical wiring diagram where a series of **stop** switches with **mushroom heads** are installed in conspicuous and easily accessible positions in the machine workshop. These will **cut off** the supply to **all** machines.

The chapter also deals with I.E.E. regulations regarding the control and the protection of electric motors.

Clothing

In working areas, personnel should wear clothing which will provide protection from danger in the particular area in which they are working. In workshops where machinery is in use, the wearing of close-fitting overalls is required. Any loose clothing, such as hanging neck-ties, long sleeves, etc., can become entangled with moving parts. All clothing should be kept in a good state of repair.

Shoes

These should be of a type which provides protection against slippery conditions and which should be strong enough to protect the feet against injury. There are safety boots and shoes available of the industrial type, fitted with steel toe caps and sole plates, which help to protect the feet against penetration.

Gloves

These should be worn where there are risks when handling substances (from sharp or jagged materials etc.), or when continuous use of tools may cause damage to the hands. Care should be taken that the gloves do not cause slipping and dropping of the tools or materials. Various types of industrial gloves are available to suit local requirements.

It is advisable that while at work, rings, chains, etc., should not be worn, as these can cause accidents. Where substances and liquids likely to cause skin infection are to be handled, barrier cream should first be rubbed into the hands.

Headgear

Safety helmets should be worn in all areas where there is danger from falling objects, whether inside or outside buildings. Most building sites nowadays are classed as 'hard hat' areas, where it is compulsory for all personnel to wear safety helmets. Loose hair should be controlled when operating machine tools.

Safety glasses

Safety goggles or even face shields should be worn where there is likelihood of danger to the eyes, such as when using chisels, drills, grinding wheels, etc.

Note: When grinding wheels are being used, or materials are being handled from which abrasive, dust and chemical particles are released, the wearing of a face mask fitted with suitable filters may be necessary.

Special requirements

Where corrosive liquids are handled, for example by an electrician installing and maintaining batteries, the wearing of extra protective clothing is required, such as rubber aprons, rubber gloves, etc., to protect clothing and skin against burns. In these installations, good ventilation is necessary to reduce the build-up of inflammable and dangerous chemical vapours. Never allow naked flames near battery installations.

Where parts of the body are subjected to continuous pressure, such as when kneeling, pads may be strapped on to prevent discomfort.

Use of equipment and hand tools

The correct tools and equipment for a particular job should always be used. Do not improvise (that is, do not use pliers instead of spanners etc.). Improvisation is a common cause of accidents. Tools should always be maintained in good condition and cutting tools should have cutting edge-guards where necessary, to prevent accidental contact with material or personnel.

Use of portable machine tools

The most important feature of these is the flexible supply cable. Always ensure that it is in good condition, that there is no damage to the outer sheath and that the termination of the cable sheath is securely anchored in the cable grips provided. Regular tests on protective conductors as detailed in Chapter 4 should be carried out. The lead should be no longer than necessary or be stretched out across the floor, as it is liable to be damaged and be a danger to other people. The ideal arrangement is to have an extension lead coiled on a drum and to unwind the cable as required keeping it out of harm's way.

Note: beware of overheating when coiled if the cable is carrying heavy currents.

Electrical safety

> ▲ Read the following notes in conjunction with 'Transmission, distribution and consumer circuitry', Chapter 3. When any electrical circuit is to be worked on, it must be completely isolated from the supply and tests should be carried out to ensure that all poles of the circuit are dead.

At the position of the isolation, steps should be taken to ensure that the supply cannot be restored until required. An isolating switch may be provided with a lock position. If not, a securely fixed notice should be displayed on the isolator. When fuses are removed, say from a distribution board to isolate a circuit, they should be put in a safe position where they cannot be replaced without the knowledge of the person concerned. Ensure that no similar fuses are readily available. The circuit or equipment should always be isolated as near to the work position as possible, so that a visual check can be kept on any attempt to restore the supply. On high-voltage installations, a fully competent person must check all the isolation and safety precaution requirements before any work is carried out and a 'Permit to Work' certificate must be issued.

Note: When fuses are to be withdrawn or replaced in a circuit, always ensure that the circuit is isolated so that no arcing or explosion can occur as the contacts are broken or made.

> ▲ After carrying out the work always test for possible faults which may lead to excessive current flow before restoring the supply.

Fire precautions

The provision of suitable equipment such as carbon dioxide fire extinguishers (Figure 1.5) must be made to deal with fire outbreaks. The type and amount will depend upon the particular circumstances. The equipment should be clearly displayed, readily available and employees instructed in its use.

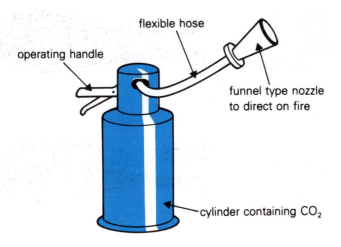

Figure 1.5 Carbon dioxide fire extinguisher.

First aid

First aid facilities

In every factory, workshop or site hut, a first aid box containing all the necessary treatment requisites must be provided. Workers should know where to go to obtain first aid materials and treatment. In larger premises, where more employees are engaged, every first aid box or cupboard should be placed in the charge of a person trained in first aid procedure. The person should be readily available during working hours and have his name and location displayed near the first aid cupboard. Very large establishments will require a first aid room under the charge of a qualified nurse.

Accident reporting

Proper records should be kept of all accidents which cause personal injury, especially where there is a danger of further complications, for example, infection.

The procedure to adopt in the event of an accident should be made widely known to employees and they should be encouraged to make full use of all facilities. Immediate treatment can often save employees from being away from work, needing lengthy treatment and imposing burdens on themselves and their employer.

First aid treatment

Electric shock

For detailed treatment, reference should be made to one of the authorised manuals on this subject, or instruction should be taken from qualified personnel. However, it may be necessary in some cases to carry out immediate emergency treatment to prevent possible loss of life.

- If the person is still in contact with the live conductor, he should be pulled or pushed away by his clothing or any insulating medium. Do not wait to find the switch and do not touch his skin.
- Remove him to a safe place, make him comfortable and warm and get assistance. If he is unconscious, check for breathing, loosen his clothing and place him on his side. Shout or signal for medical attention.

  If breathing has stopped, do not delay. Place casualty on his back, loosen neck clothing, remove false teeth (if any) and blow firmly into his mouth at repeated intervals, keeping his nose pinched. This may start him breathing again. It should be noted that this is emergency treatment only. Medical attention should be sought as quickly as possible.
- Arrangements should be made to get the casualty to hospital as soon as possible and full details of the accident should be reported to the relevant personnel.

When a person has been hurt and the type and extent of the injuries are unknown, he should be moved only to avoid further injury. Unskilled treatment may lead to further injury.

Burns
Cool the burnt skin with cold water and also spray water over any smouldering clothing. Do not remove any clothing unnecessarily, as it may remove damaged skin. Dress the wounds with burn dressings from the first aid box. Give sips of fluid, such as sweet tea. This will help calm the nerves. Again, seek qualified help. Report the accident immediately.

Cuts and abrasions
Clean with antiseptic and bandage to stop bleeding and infection.

Heavy bleeding

Lay the patient down to reduce blood pressure, elevating the bleeding spot. Expose the wound and try not to disturb any clots of blood. In serious cases apply pressure with a thick pad, apply a dressing and then bandage. If bleeding continues, apply extra bandages. If possible, a tight band on the artery above the wound will restrict the blood flow.

> Again, medical help should be sought as soon as possible and the reporting procedure carried out.

Suspected broken limb

As previously mentioned, the injured person should only be moved if absolutely necessary, if possible, the limb should be kept still by tying or strapping it to the other leg, or to the body in the case of an arm. Clothing or footwear should not be removed unless absolutely necessary and then with great care.

Electrical engineering fitting

Use of bench tools

Files

Files are made of specially-hardened steel and are used to remove metal from an object with accuracy. They are classified by their length, type of cut and shape.

File lengths vary from around 10 cm up to 40 cm, excluding the **tang**.
Note: The 'tang' end is to fit the wooden handle, which should never be left off the file.

The cuts can be

1. rasp or extra rough
2. rough
3. bastard
4. second cut
5. smooth
6. very smooth

They may be single- or double-cut, the latter having two series of cutting teeth at 45° to each other.

File shapes can also vary considerably; they can be

1. flat
2. half-round
3. round
4. square
5. triangular
6. knife

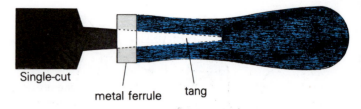

Figure 1.6 Types of engineer's files.

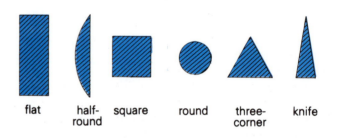

Figure 1.7 File shapes (cross-sections).

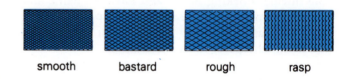

Figure 1.8 File cuts.

These file characteristics are shown in Figures 1.6, 1.7 and 1.8.

The nature of the removal operation will decide the type of file required. The work should be secured in a vice. Start with as rough a cut as possible to remove the metal quickly and finish off accurately with a smooth or very smooth cut.

One of the most common filing operations is the fitting of keys for machine pulleys, couplings and pinions. 'High' spots on these will be traced by the use of engineer's dye and then removed with a file until a full contact area fit is obtained.

Hacksaw

A hacksaw is used for cutting off tubes and materials. It consists of a permanent frame and handle with disposable blades, tensioned in the frame. When not in use, the blade tension should be removed by unscrewing the wing nut, to prevent frame distortion. Blades are in sizes of 250 mm and 300 mm and have teeth spacings of 14, 18, 24 and 32 teeth per 25 mm. The blade teeth are angled to cut on the forward (push) stroke.

For cutting larger sections of softer metals, a blade with a tooth spacing of 14 per 25 mm should be used. For cutting smaller sections and mild steel, a blade with a tooth spacing of 18 to 24 per 25 mm would be most suitable. For hard metals, alloy and carbon steels, a blade with a tooth spacing of 24 per 25 mm should be used, while for thin sheet, tubes, conduits and thin wall sections, 32 teeth per 25 mm would be the ideal choice, so that more teeth are in contact with the metal.

The work should be secured in the vice and long, steady strokes, using the whole of the blade should be used. For cutting sideways, the blade may be turned through 90° and secured in the frame.

Twist drills

These are used for cutting circular holes in metals and other engineering materials. They are made from carbon steel for general use, or from more expensive high-speed steel for machine and repetitious operations (Figure 1.9).

Twist drills range in size from 0.4 mm to 12.5 mm diameter in straight shanks, and up to 100 mm diameter in morse taper shanks. The straight shanks are mainly for use in portable drilling machines, fitted with an adjustable key-operated chuck. The morse tapers are for use in fixed pedestal-type machines fitted with a morse taper socket. Various morse taper sleeves are available to fit the drill taper shank size to the drilling machine morse socket. This method gives a firmer hold on the drill and greater accuracy in hole size.

In general, the larger the drill, the slower the speed of operation.

Sharpening twist drills

> The cutting edges of the drill must be correctly sharpened and shaped on a carborundum grinding stone. Incorrect sharpening can lead to an oversized hole being drilled and overheating of the drill.

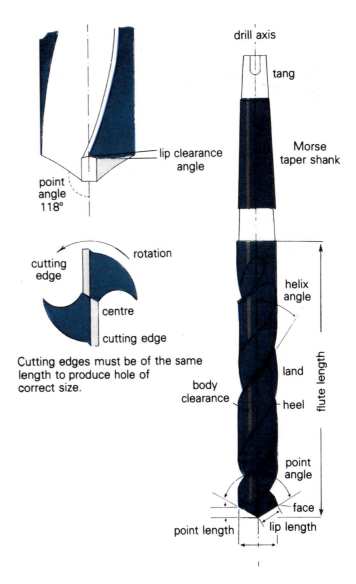

Cutting edges must be of the same length to produce hole of correct size.

Figure 1.9 (left) Parts of an engineer's twist drill. *Figure 1.10* (right) Sharpening of an engineer's twist drill.

There are four essential requirements when sharpening an engineer's twist drill.

1. The correct point angle of 118° must be retained.
2. The point angles must be equally divided (59°) to the drill axis.
3. The two cutting edges (known as lips) must be exactly the same length.
4. The edge or lip clearance must increase uniformly behind the cutting edge.

Figure 1.10 shows this in diagrammatic form.

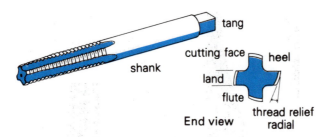

Figure 1.11 Parts of an engineer's tap.

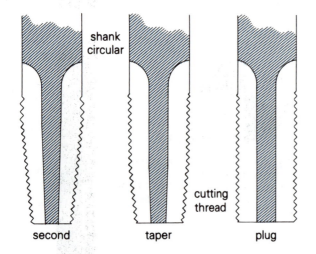

Figure 1.12 Types of engineer's taps.

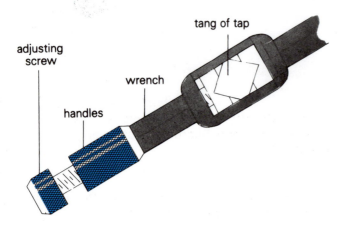

Figure 1.13 Tap wrench.

Cutting of screw threads

The fixing and fitting of engineering operations is done mostly by screw threads of nuts and bolts, or tapped holes in the equipment to which set screws or bolts are secured. The threads are either internal (female) and are cut with a **tap** (Figure 1.11), or they are external (male) and are cut with a **die**. Taps are made from high-carbon steel or high-speed steel and are made in sets of three: **taper**, **second taper** and **plug**. (See Figure 1.12.) When in use, the tap is held in a **tap-wrench** (Figure 1.13) to give the necessary leverage for turning. When cutting a thread, the wrench must be turned back half a turn for every full forward turn to clear the cut metal (swarf) from the teeth. It is important that the wrench is always kept at 90° to the hole axis, beginning with the taper and finishing with the plug tap. For a hole which is **blind**, that is, does not go through the material, care must be taken to sense when the plug tap reaches the bottom of the hole, to prevent the tap from breaking off in the hole. An application of cutting oil lubricant will ease the task and reduce wear on the tap.

> Always check that the correct drill size has been used before tapping, as too small a hole will cause tap breakage, while too large a hole will give a loose fit for the bolt thread.

Stock and die

These are used for the cutting of external threads or bolts and on tubes and conduits (Figure 1.14).

> When the thread on an electrical conduit is cut, the end of the tube must be filed or reamed internally to remove the frayed edge which otherwise would damage the cable insulation.

Some stocks and dies are fitted with a thread diameter adjusting screw, so that the threading operation can be done in stages. Other dies are in two semi-circular sections and can be adjusted to come closer together until the correct size diameter thread is achieved.

Measuring instruments

Engineer's rule

This is used for fine measurements and for checking the 'flatness' of a surface, it should have parallel edges which are perfectly straight and undamaged and divisions which are clear, sharp and easy to read.

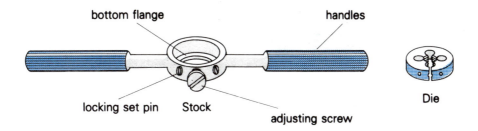

Figure 1.14 Engineer's stock and die.

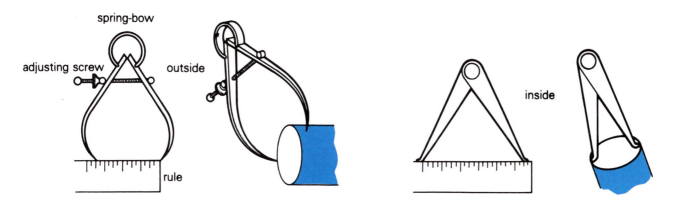

Figure 1.15 Engineer's callipers.

Callipers

These are used for the measurement of inside and outside diameters of circular holes and circular shafts and are useful, for example, when comparing a motor shaft diameter with its drive coupling bore size.

Callipers can be adjusted by feel or, in some better types, by a knurled nut on a fine thread. The measurement is then taken between the two legs of the calliper points on the engineer's rule. See Figure 1.15.

Micrometer

> This is used to take more exact measurements down to 0.01 mm. It is an instrument of extreme accuracy and must be treated with special care and kept in a case when not in use.

Micrometers are made in sizes up to 900 mm but normally have their adjustable range over 25 mm. The higher ranges are obtained by fitting accurately machined lengths of rod in the micrometer frame.

Reading the micrometer

1. Note the number of whole divisions on the horizontal sleeve.
   1 division = 1 mm
2. Note the number of any full half divisions.
   $\frac{1}{2}$ division = 0.5 mm
3. Now read the circular thimble number which is on the horizontal sleeve mark.
   1 division = 0.01 mm.

Micrometer reading shown in Figure 1.16.:
major divisions = 5 = (5 × 1) = 5 mm
minor divisions = 1 = (1 × 0.5) = 0.5 mm
thimble divisions = 21 = (21 × 0.01) = 0.21 mm
Reading = (5 + 0.5 + 0.21) = 5.71 mm

Try-square

Most surfaces are horizontal or vertical, that is, at 90° to each other. A try-square has two accurately machined blades which are spaced and securely fixed at 90° to each other, so that the accuracy of both horizontal and vertical surfaces can be checked and their angle of relationship to each other.

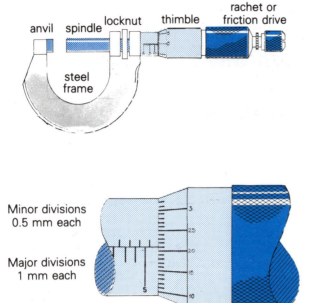

Figure 1.16 Engineer's micrometer reading.

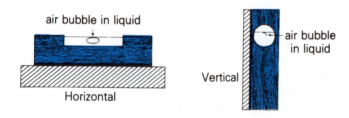

Figure 1.17 Use of a spirit level.

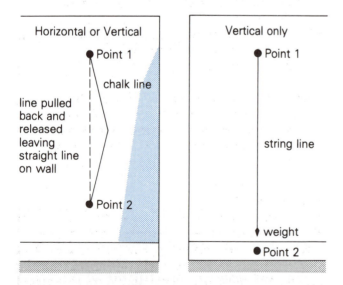

Figure 1.18 (left) Use of a chalk line.
Figure 1.19 (right) Use of a plumb line.

Spirit level

This is a flat, straight-edged instrument in which a chamber of liquid is housed. The liquid contains an air bubble which, when the spirit level is laid on the surface to be tested, will only come to rest in the exact centre of the chamber (which is marked by a line), if the said surface is horizontal. Some spirit levels are fitted with a second air bubble chamber at 90° to the flat surface. When this flat surface is placed on a vertical surface, the bubble will come to the centre when that surface is vertical. See Figure 1.17.

Scriber

Used for marking lines on work surfaces, it has a hardened needle point which can be drawn along the straight edge of a rule or try-square. Usually these lines are drawn at 90° to each other and at points where they intersect, some drilling or other operation is carried out on the metal.

Centre punch

This is used for making indentations on metal surfaces to enable any lines or points to be seen more easily. It is also used to indent position on metals to be drilled to form a start centre for the drill.

Simple marking tools

The following implements are simple tools to assist marking out for electricians on site.

Line or string

This can be covered with chalk or similar material. Each end is held in position at points on a wall where a conduit or cable is to run. The centre of the string line is then pulled away from the wall and when released it will return and leave a straight line between the two points, thus enabling the cable to be fixed perfectly straight, giving a neat appearance. See Figure 1.18.

Plumb line

A string line similar to the previous tool, but suspended vertically by the attachment of a pointed weight. This method ensures that point No. 2 is a true vertical below point No. 1 and is useful for switch point drops and vertical cable runs in buildings. See Figure 1.19.

Water level tubes

These comprise two glass tubes which have a centre mark. They are joined by a flexible rubber or

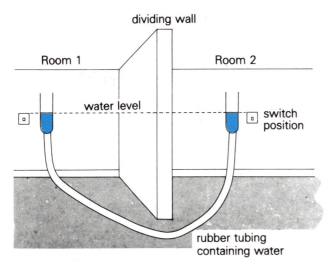

Figure 1.20 Use of a water level tube.

plastic tube of suitable length and filled with water. When the water is at the same level in each glass tube, those levels are perfectly horizontal to each other, that is, at the same height. See Figure 1.20.

This device is useful in buildings where, during construction, the floor is not made up in all rooms to the same level.

> Fixing points for equipment are required which will all need to be at the same height when the building is finished.

Properties of materials

> All materials used in engineering possess properties which make them the most suitable choice for the purpose for which they are to be used.

Ductility
This is the property which enables a material to be drawn out into longer lengths of smaller section, that is, drawing out of bar section into wire – such as mild steel, copper, wrought iron.

Malleability
The property which enables a material to be pressed, formed or beaten into a given shape without breaking. For example, lead can be shaped to any position when cold; mild steel and wrought iron can be heated and shaped without fracture.

Strength
The ability to withstand external loads and forces without damage.

Elasticity
The property which enables a material to return to its original dimensions after distortion as shown by rubber for example.

Hardness
The ability of a material to withstand use without blunting its surfaces. For example, carbon-steel, high-speed steels and most engineering tools previously mentioned.

Hardness is increased by the introduction of other materials such as silicon and carbon during the manufacturing process.

Toughness
The ability of a material to withstand force and bend or change shape without breaking. The process of hardening materials by the introduction of carbon or silicon, or heat treatment, such as in the making of files and drills, can reduce their toughness and they become **brittle** and will break easily when subjected to force.

Cast iron is an example of a brittle material; although hard, it breaks easily.

Thermal conductivity
The ability of a material to conduct heat. Copper and brass are good conductors of heat.

Electrical conductivity

> Electrical conductivity is the ability of a material to allow the free passage of electrons (electric current). These materials are used for cable conductors. Copper and aluminium are examples of electrical conductors.

Thermal insulation

> Thermal insulation is the ability of a material to prevent the conduction of heat where heat retention is required. Fibre glass, asbestos, mica and refractory materials are all thermal insulators.

Electrical insulation

The property which does not allow the easy transmission of electrical current (electrons). Glass, paper, rubber, PVC, porcelain and paxolin are all used for electrical insulation purposes.

Magnetism

Metals which contain iron (Fe), that is, ferrous metals, such as steels and irons, are normally magnetic materials. Metals which do not contain iron, that is, non-ferrous metals, such as lead, copper and aluminium are normally non-magnetic.

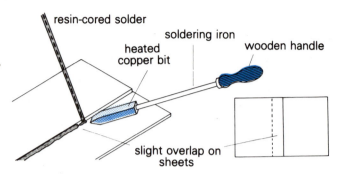

Figure 1.21 Jointing of two light gauge copper sheets.

Soldering and soldering methods

This is the method of joining non-ferrous metals by the use of a heat process and solder, where the solder does not have to reach the melting point of the metals to be joined. This means they are not fused together as in brazing or welding.

The solder is a composition of lead and tin and the melting point is determined by the ratio of the two. For electrical joints and terminations of copper conductors, 60 per cent cent tin to 40 per cent cent lead content solder is used. This has a melting point of around 200°C. A suitable soldering flux is also required in the process.

Soldering equipment

Soldering iron

This consists of a block of copper (known as a **bit**) which is heated up to the melting point of the solder. At this temperature, the solder stick may be applied to the copper block and a layer of liquid solder will be coated on the copper bit. This is a process known as **tinning the bit**. At the same time, a flux paste or liquid should also be applied to the copper bit and to the surfaces which are to be joined. The purpose of this flux is to prevent an oxide film forming on the surfaces, which stops the solder from adhering to them and to create an even flow of solder.

> The copper bit of the iron and the surfaces to be joined must be perfectly clean and free from any oxide film before the soldering operation commences.

The heated copper bit may now be applied to the prepared surfaces to bring them up to the melting temperature of the solder, while, at the same time, more flux and solder are applied. When the temperature is correct, the tinned surfaces and the solder will flow together freely, and when cooled will form a solid unit of some strength. See Figure 1.21.

> If the temperature is too low, the solder will not flow freely and the joint will be weakened. This is referred to as a **dry** joint. When too high, oxidisation will quickly occur and destroy the 'tinned' surfaces, so they will not unite.

Flux

This can be of 'killed' spirits, but this has a corrosive effect on the joint. For electrical purposes, a resin flux is used which may be applied separately in the form of a paste, or be combined in the solder itself as in a resin-core solder. The copper bit of the soldering iron can be heated externally by a gas ring or blowlamp, or it may contain an electric heating element, in which case it will need to be connected to a supply. The power rating of these is such that the required temperature is not exceeded.

Blowlamp or torch

This is a heat source fuelled by paraffin or butane gas which produces a clean, pressurised flame which may be used as the heating medium for the soldering operation.

The paraffin-fuelled type of blowlamp needs preheating to vaporise the paraffin and is then pressurised by a hand-operated pump. See Figure 1.22. The butane gas type is pressurised by its own gas cylinder and needs no preheating (Figure 1.23). It is more convenient but more expensive to operate. Blowlamps are used for the joining of large conductors and the fitting of terminal 'lugs' or cable sockets to the conductor. See Figure 1.24.

First, the cable insulation is protected by heat resistant tape to prevent heat damage and the socket, or surfaces to be joined are heated to the required temperature by the blowlamp. The solder stick is then dipped into the flux and applied to the socket or termination and the conductor. The conductor is then dipped into the solder in the socket and removed, making sure that the conductor is tinned. The conductor is then re-entered and the solder made up to the full level. It is then allowed to cool and solidify, forming a sound join.

Pot and ladle
This makes use of an iron pot and ladle. The solder is melted in the pot over a gas ring or coke fire. The joint or termination joint or termination is pasted

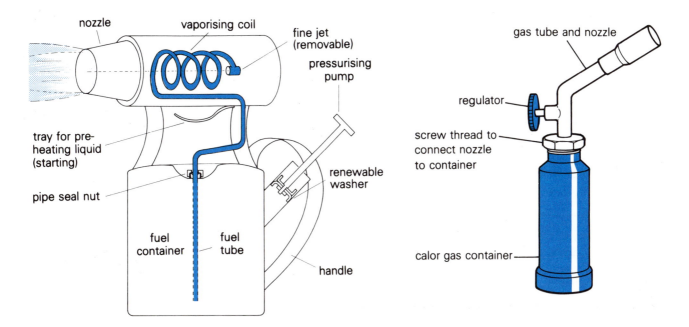

Figure 1.22 Parts of a paraffin blow lamp.

Figure 1.23 Butane gas blow torch.

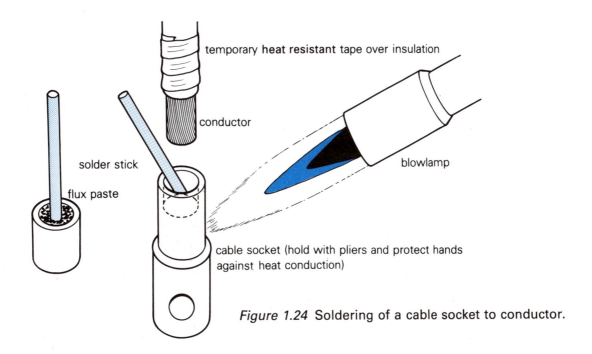

Figure 1.24 Soldering of a cable socket to conductor.

with flux and the liquid solder is poured repeatedly over the surfaces until they are brought up to the melting solder temperature. At this point, the surfaces and solder will form one mass and solidify on cooling. If possible, the melting pot should be placed under the joint to catch the falling melting solder, which may be reheated and used again. See Chapter 4.

Soldering of brass and aluminium

Brass
The soldering of brass can be carried out in a similar manner to that described for copper.

Aluminium
This requires the use of a different composition of solder which consists of 53 per cent lead, 45 per cent tin with 2 per cent zinc. The flux is a powdery substance based on borax. The soldering temperature is around 350°C which is rather critical because of the charring of the flux above that value. Solidification takes place at around 200°C.

> Any insulation which has been damaged by the heat process of soldering should be removed and made good with suitable insulating tapes, sleeves or compounds.

It is good practice to protect the insulation during the operation by the use of asbestos tapes which can be removed when the soldering is complete. See Chapter 4.

On-site working

The quality of an electrician in most cases can be judged from his appearance and tool kit, particularly when he is working in premises occupied by his or his firm's clients.

His clothing should be neat and tidy with no loose ends hanging around.

> The tools should be sufficient and of the correct types to carry out efficiently the job in hand.

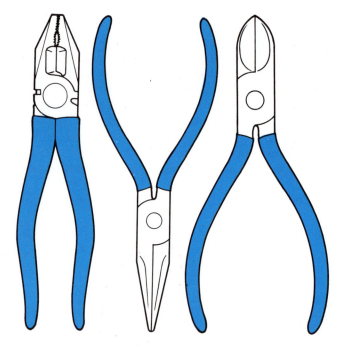

Figure 1.25 (left) Electrician's general pliers.
Figure 1.26 (centre) 'Long nose' pliers.
Figure 1.27 (right) Diagonal or 'side' cutters.

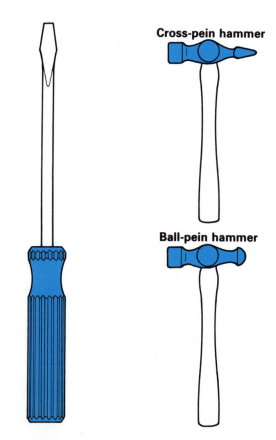

Cross-pein hammer

Ball-pein hammer

Figure 1.28 (left) Screwdriver.
Figure 1.29 (right) Type of hammers.

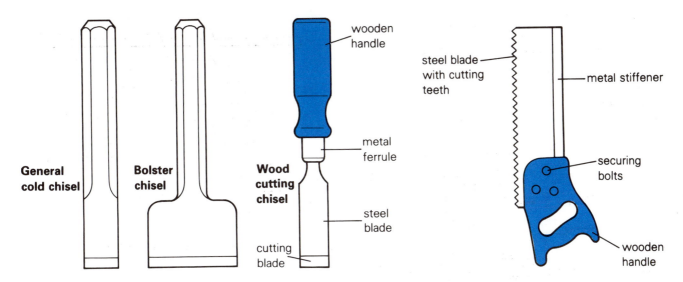

Figure 1.30 Types of chisels.

Figure 1.31 Tenon saw.

He should not have to make do or improvise, for example, he should not drill larger holes or cut more of the building fabric away than is necessary to accommodate the cables, conduits and accessories just because those are sizes of the tools he happens to have brought with him.

An electrician's basic tool kit for general installation work would consist of the following:

1. general pliers around 200 to 230 mm (8″ to 9″) long for the purpose of cutting cables and twisting or bending conductors for entry into terminations (Figure 1.25);
2. long nose pliers to trim and to guide conductors into terminations too small or inaccessible to the general pliers (Figure 1.26);
3. side or diagonal cutters to trim insulation and conductors of smaller size fixed and flexible cables (Figure 1.27);
4. cable insulation stripper with various hole sizes although a sharp knife used correctly can be used;
5. variety of screwdrivers from small terminal ones up to larger sizes, both 'crosshead' and 'single' groove types up to No. 12 screws (Figure 1.28);
6. crimping tools for termination of conductor into ferrules or lugs without soldering.

Note: All the above should have insulated handles for possible use on live conductors.

7. a set of 'open end' and 'box' type spanners suitable for terminations by nuts and bolts;
8. adjustable pipe grips or gas pliers to rotate or secure pipework or 'rounded' parts;
9. hacksaws, both junior and normal size, to cut larger conductors and pipe work;
10. hammers both **ball pein** and **flat pein** (Figure 1.29);
11. measuring tape and rule;
12. spirit level for use on horizontal or vertical surfaces.

Since a lot of the operations are carried out on building fabrics the kit should contain a certain quantity of builder's tools to prepare for the running and fixing of cables and the securing of the various electrical accessories particularly on existing buildings.

These would include:

13. cold chisels for the cutting of thermal blocks and brickwork (Figure 1.30a);
14. bolster chisel for cutting of channels to house conduits and channels, and lifting of floorboards (Figure 1.30b);
15. wood chisels to cut and shape joists, ceiling and floor materials (Figure 1.30c);
16. tenon saw again to cut joints and floorboards (Figure 1.31);
17. wood drills or gimlets for drilling of joists;
18. various size masonry drills for the fixing of rawlplugs for No. 4 to No. 12 screws;
19. larger masonry drills from 10 to 25 mm diameter up to 0.5 m long to cut through thermal blocks and brickwork to pass cables through;
20. power drill with variable speeds and hammer action to operate most of the above tools (Figure 1.32 shows a drill stand to enable a portable electric drill to be used as a pedestal drill on a workbench);

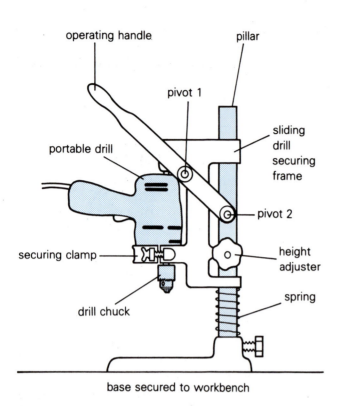

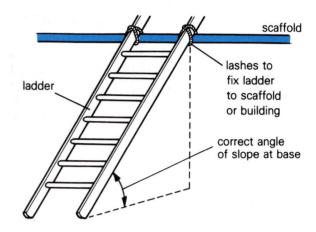

Figure 1.34 Slope and support of ladders.

Figure 1.32 Drill stand to enable a portable electric drill to be used as a pedestal drill on a workbench.

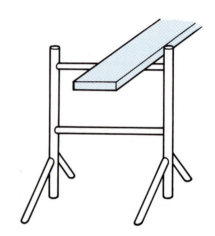

Figure 1.35 General trestle.

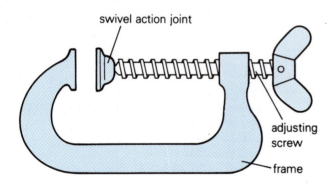

Figure 1.33 G' clamp for securing materials while carrying out work operations.

21. securing clamp for securing materials while carrying out work operations (Figure 1.33).

Larger tools items which require heavy transporting and are normally provided by the employer would consist of:

1. stand and platform vices, pipe benders, stocks and dies for conduit and trunking work, see Chapter 4;

Figure 1.36 Mobile tower.

2. ladders (Figure 1.34), steps, trestles (Figure 1.35), planks, mobile platforms (Figure 1.36), all used for work access as shown below;
3. possibly a small transportable secure hut or such to house materials and tools.

> The electrician must study the job in hand and then decide the tool requirements, that is, does the wiring system require special tools outside the basics, say, for treatment of terminations such as stripping and sealing of MIMS or lead or aluminium cables.

There is now a large selection of power tools for the various installation processes but they are very expensive so the contractor has to decide whether or not he can justify the capital outlay to get the return from the work he undertakes.

In these times of competitive pricing, power tools can greatly speed up the work and hence reduce labour costs. The decision on whether to buy will depend on the size of the contracts that are tendered for. A contractor will have to limit his outlay on equipment to an amount his finances will stand.

Electrical installation for very large projects such as hospitals, superstores and large industrial complexes, will be restricted to a very few large contractors who have the financial backing, equipment and personnel to complete the work in the allotted time. However, even they may sub-contract out sections of the work such as high voltage signs, high voltage cable jointing, securing systems and electronics.

An introduction to contract planning is given in Chapter 11.

Note: The term **first fix** stated on the charts relates to the power distribution, such as positioning of transformers, switchgear and running of cables during the construction of the building, usually when the roof is in position. This removes the need to cut and chase finished masonry, woodwork and plaster.

Second fix relates to the fixing of accessories to finished surfaces like ceilings and walls, and their terminations. The two operations must be timed to 'fit in' with the operations being carried out by the other services contractors, so that there is no hold-up in the timetable for the completion of the project. There will possibly be a clause stating that there will be a penalty for any delay unless it was unforeseen.

> Ensure that material and labour are on site at the required time.

Planning and procedure of site work

The electrician must get to know exactly the requirements of the job in hand.

On smaller installations this information can be obtained by discussion with the client where the electrician can help in the planning. On larger installations, he will need to have a plan of the apparatus, accessories, lighting and power ratings, or may prepare one himself from the client's specification.

He can then proceed as follows.

1. Decide on the type of wiring to use.
2. Determine the switchgear required at the supply incoming point.
3. Calculate the sizes of cables required.

See later chapters for help with these.

4. From the plans and location diagrams and a study of the building structure the electrician can plan the cable routes, methods of protection and securing them. This will vary as to whether or not the building is in course of erection or it is a finished building. If it is the former he will run the cables as in the first fix which can be carried out as soon as the building is weatherproof. If it is a completed building or an extension or, say, a rewire, he will try to make use of existing routes and protection for the new cables such as using the conduits or channels buried in plaster and holes drilled in brickwork and joists. He may even use the existing cables as **draw in** wires for the new cables, which will simplify matters.
5. The next step: from reference to the plans and the use of a scale rule or from the building itself he can calculate the lengths of the various size cables required. He should now be in a position to order or obtain all materials required.

Procedure to carry out the work

> ▲ The electrician must wear clothing and headgear to protect against potential dangers such as falling objects, sharp edges, trenches, oil and greasy areas.

Where he has to work at heights or in precarious areas he must ensure that he has correct equipment and, as with the use of tools, he must not improvise to gain access. Conditions should be made as comfortable and secure as possible.

As mentioned for lengthy kneeling operations use a mat or wear kneepads. When using ladders ensure they are in good condition, securely tethered and used at the correct slope angle. On extension ladders see that the catches are fully engaged. The wearing of thick sole boots will ease the feet and prevent slipping on the rungs. Make sure that step ladders are fully extended and do not stand on the top step unless they are of the platform type.

> When working for lengthy periods at heights, the use of trestles and planks or a mobile tower can be helpful and time saving. If working on outside scaffolds see that guard and toe rails are in place.

Cutting and channelling for conduits and cables

As previously mentioned these operations call for a knowledge of building construction and materials. Be careful, note load bearing areas and restrict fabric removal to a minimum. On finished buildings it means in most cases the lifting of floor boards with care not to damage them. Cut the tongue with a tenon or circular power saw, driving the fixing nails below the surface and then prise the board with a bolster chisel on each side.

> When a board is to be cut it must be done so that the two pieces butt together in the centre of a joist.

Where cables are run at right angles to the joist, the joist must be drilled not less than 50 mm from the floor board fixings to avoid damage from nails.

When passing cables through walls, drill with a masonry drill or cut carefully with a cold chisel just sufficient for the cable protection used to protect against rough masonry. On switch drops and wall fixtures a channel would be cut with a bolster chisel either by hand and hammer or the use of a power tool such as a 'Kango'. In all positions where there is potential damage to cables, protection should be

provided. When routing cables in hidden positions such as under floor boards, they should be clipped along joists and passed through at right angles.

> Cable drops from ceilings and rises from the floor should be vertical to the accessories, not run diagonally, and preferably fitted with protective covers.

Fixing to walls and ceilings

Ensure ceilings are secure enough to support the luminaire, fix to joist or secure a plinth between them (Figure 1.37). On some buildings the use of plaster boards fixed to wooden framework is used for interior walls, a process known as **cladding**. These will not secure loads directly. Special fixings which grip the plasterboard when the screws are tightened are used, sometimes referred to as **butterfly** fixings (Figure 1.38).

Final note

Before starting the work on a new installation the electrician should obtain the following information from the supply authority.

1. The nature of the supply they are to provide, that is, T.P.N. or S.P.N., since this will govern the method of the distribution of the loads.
2. Methods of earthing and, if known, the external loop impedance (Z_E).

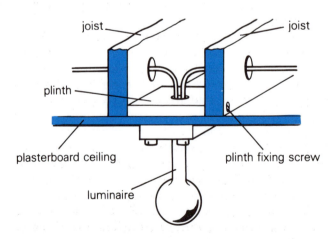

Figure 1.37 Support of luminaire (light fitting) on a plasterboard ceiling.

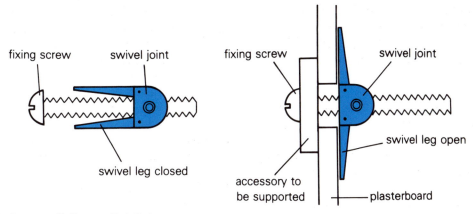

Figure 1.38 Hollow wall (butterfly) fixings.

3. Size of bonding conductors to other services.
4. Requirements for size and lengths of cables (tails) for them to connect to meter and earth terminal.
5. The above can normally be provided when the installer has completed an **application form** (which lists details of the installation) for the supply of electricity to a new installation.

■ CHECK YOUR UNDERSTANDING

Workshop practice

● First aid facilities and CO_2 fire extinguishing equipment must be provided in workshops and large site huts.
● All power machines must be guarded and provided with emergency stopping.
● 'Permit to work' forms must be obtained when there is the possibility of 'live' circuits or apparatus to be worked on.
● There must be free access to work areas at all times.
● All accidents must be reported and recorded.
● For marking out and measurements of materials use rules, scribes, centre punches, calipers, squares, gauges, micrometer.
● Cutting of materials requires shears, hacksaws, files, drills, grinding wheels.
● Internal screw threads are cut with wrenches and taps. External screw threads are cut with stocks and dies.
● Soldering processes use blowlamps or gas torches for heating with suitable fluxes and solders for the jointing medium.
● Crimping and riveting are 'cold' compression methods of jointing.

Site practice

● Electricians' general tools are required for cable installation operations plus fabric cutting and accessory fixing tools.
● Access to work areas requires steps, ladders, trestles, platforms, mobile towers.
● First fix is the installation of cables and accessory enclosures, carried out when building is weatherproof.
● Second fix is the fitting of accessories and luminaires when interior surfaces are completed.
● The application form for the supply of electricity giving all information of the installation must be submitted to the supply authority on completion.

REVISION EXERCISES AND QUESTIONS

1 Whilst working on a site with others you hear a shout and go to investigate. You find someone lying on the ground, not moving nor apparently breathing, holding in his hand a flexible lead, connected to a socket.
　i) List the correct order of **three** actions which should be taken.
　ii) List **five** items of information which should be included in a report.
　iii) What action should be taken regarding the lead?
2 i) Explain three types of aids to ease the work operations to be carried out at a ceiling height of 4 m.
　ii) State the precautions to be observed on the use of your choice.
3 i) What is meant by an internal **studded** or **cladded** room dividing wall?

ii) Make a sketch of a fixing device for wiring accessories to its surface.

4 In the **rewire** of an existing building, explain what features of the old installation, with details, you could possibly make use of to facilitate the new wiring.

5 List precautions to bear in mind when:
   i) cutting the fabric of a building to install the wiring; and
   ii) having to fix a heavy suspended lighting fitting from a plaster board ceiling.

6 State
   i) the precautions and for what reasons they are to be taken when removing fuses on a potentially heavy current circuit,
   ii) a) the type of extinguisher used for electrical fires,
       b) how it is recognised from other appliances,
       c) what is the best initial treatment for skin burns.

7 i) List the danger points associated with power machines in a workshop.
   ii) State methods of reducing these dangers.
   iii) Explain with the aid of a circuit diagram how an accident-involved machine can be stopped quickly without having to locate it.

8 i) State when it is necessary to obtain a 'permit to work' form on electrical equipment.
   ii) State the reasons for the permit.

9 i) Make a neat sketch of a micrometer and label each component.
   ii) Draw a separate sketch with divisions showing a reading of 13.83 mm.

10 List the procedure to be taken on finding a person unconscious from apparent electric shock.

11 Name **six** essential tools in a maintenance engineer's tool-kit and state a typical example of the work for which each would be used.

12 Describe, with the aid of a sketch, the method of terminating an insulated cable with a soldering socket or 'lug' for connection to a terminal screw.

13 i) Explain how similar heights on the walls of a building can be obtained before the floors are laid.
   ii) For what purpose would this be necessary?

14 What steps would need to be taken to ensure safe working on an item of electrical equipment in a factory?

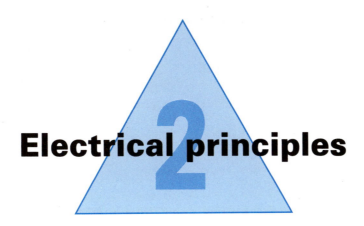

Electrical principles

Introduction

This chapter describes the principles of electricity and how they apply in different d.c., a.c., electrical and magnetic circuits. It should be read in conjunction with Chapter 3.

Atomic theory of current flow

Matter or material is made up of molecules, which consist of atoms. These **atoms** consist of a central core of protons which are positive charges of electricity and they are surrounded by an equal number of **electrons** which are negative charges.

In the normal state the electrons move around the central protons and do not come detached.

When a p.d. (potential difference) or voltage is applied between the ends of the material some of the electrons become detached and move on to the next atom and so on. This means that there is a movement of electrons along the material. With **insulating materials** the electrons do not move easily, whereas with **conductors** they move more freely.

The theory is that electricity is this movement of electrons in materials.

> The conventional flow of current is assumed to be in the opposite direction to the electron flow, for example
> current flows from +ve to −ve
> electrons flow from −ve to +ve
> and theory of polarity and calculations are based on current directions of flow.

The **coulomb** (symbol Q) (abbr. C) is the quantity of electricity. It consists of 6.3×10^{18} electrons.

The **ampere** (symbol I) (abbr. A) is the unit of current flow. For a given material

$$I = \frac{Q}{t} \, (A)$$

$$Q = It \, (C)$$

where t = time in seconds, so
Q = ampere-seconds

In practice the larger unit, the ampere-hour (symbol A h) is used = 3.6×10^3 coulombs.

Power (symbol *P*)

The current flow multiplied by the pressure (voltage) creating the flow is the **power** (symbol P) in the circuit.

$$P = I \times V \text{ watts (abbr. W)}$$

Energy is the product of power and time.

Energy = joule (abbr. J) or watt-seconds

> In practice and for tariff purposes, the larger unit of energy, the kilowatt-hour (abbr. kW h) is used.
> kW h = $1000 \times 60 \times 60 = 3.6 \times 10^6$ J

Resistance (symbol *R*)

The opposition to flow of current in a circuit or material is termed **resistance** and is measured in

ohms (abbr. Ω) and the name **Ohm's law** is given to the formula

$$R = \frac{V}{I} \ (\Omega)$$

Now

$$P = V \times I \qquad\qquad (1)$$

and

$$V = I \times R \qquad\qquad (2)$$

Substituting this in equation (1) gives

$$P = I \times R \times I = I^2R$$

also

$$I = \frac{V}{R}$$

Substituting this in equation (1) gives

$$P = V \times \frac{V}{R} = \frac{V^2}{R}$$

So by transposition given any **two** of the values P, V, R and I, the remaining two can be determined.

Resistivity or specific resistance (symbol ρ)

The resistivity value depends upon the type of material. To calculate the value of the **resistance** of a circuit or material three factors must be known:

1. value of ρ,
2. area (a),
3. length (l).

The formula

$$R = \rho \ \frac{l}{a} \ (\Omega)$$

where ρ is given in ohm per metre (Ω/m), l is length in m and a is area in m². The value of ρ for copper is 1.7×10^{-8} Ω/m.

EXAMPLE 1

Calculate the resistance of a copper wire 100 m long having an area of 10 mm².

$$R = \rho\frac{l}{a} = \frac{1.7 \times 10^{-8} \times 100}{10 \times 10^{-6}}$$

$$= \frac{1.7 \times 10^{-8} \times 10^2 \times 10^6}{10} = 0.17 \ \Omega$$

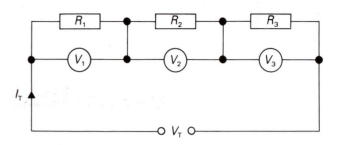

Figure 2.1 Resistors connected in series.

Resistors connected in series (Figure 2.1)
Value of total resistance

$$R_T = R_1 + R_2 + R_3$$

Value of current

$$I_T = \frac{V_T}{R_T}$$

Volts drop (V_1) across $R_1 = I_T \times R_1$
Volts drop (V_2) across $R_2 = I_T \times R_2$
Volts drop (V_3) across $R_3 = I_T \times R_3$
Total power in circuit $P \ = V_I \times I_T$
Power in each resistor $\quad = I_T \times V_1, \quad I_T \times V_2,$
$$\qquad\qquad\qquad\qquad I_T \times V_3$$

EXAMPLE 2

In Figure 2.1 $R_1 = 5 \ \Omega$, $R_2 = 10 \ \Omega$ and $R_3 = 15 \ \Omega$ Determine (i) total resistance, (ii) current, (iii) p.d. across each resistance and (iv) total power.

The voltage $T_T = 15$ V

i) $R_T = 5 + 10 + 15 = 30 \ \Omega$

ii) $I \ = \frac{V_T}{R_T} = \frac{15 \ V}{30 \ \Omega} = 0.5 \ \Omega$

iii) p.d. across $\quad R_1 = 0.5 \times 5 = 2.5$ V
$\qquad\qquad\qquad R_2 = 0.5 \times 10 = 5$ V
$\qquad\qquad\qquad R_3 = 0.5 \times 15 = 7.5$ V

iv) Total power $P \ = 15 \times 0.5 = 7.5$ W
or

$$P = \frac{V^2}{R_T} = \frac{15^2}{30} = 7.5 \ W$$

or

$$P = I^2R = 0.5^2 \times 30 = 7.5 \ W$$

Resistors connected in parallel (Figure 2.2)
Note: V_T is supplied to **all** resistors, but I_T splits up and is shared by **all** resistors.

To calculate the total resistance R_T the reciprocal formula is used

$$\frac{1}{R_T} = \frac{1}{R_1} + \frac{1}{R_2} + \cdots\cdots$$

EXAMPLE 3

In Figure 2.2 R_1 is 5 Ω and R_2 is 10 Ω and $V_T = 45$ V.

Calculate (i) R_T, (ii) I_T, (iii) I_1 and (iv) total power.

i) $\dfrac{1}{R_T} = \dfrac{1}{5} + \dfrac{1}{10} = \dfrac{3 + 1.5}{15} = \dfrac{4.5}{15}$

ii) $R_T = \dfrac{15}{4.5} = 3\frac{1}{3}$ Ω

   $I_T = \dfrac{45}{3\frac{1}{3}} = 13.5$ A

iii) $I_1 = \dfrac{45}{5} = 9$ A

   $I_2 = \dfrac{45}{10} = 4.5$ A

iv) Total power $= 45 \times 13.5 = 607$ W

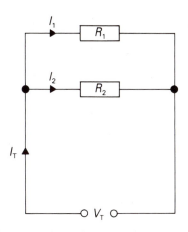

Figure 2.2 Resistors connected in parallel.

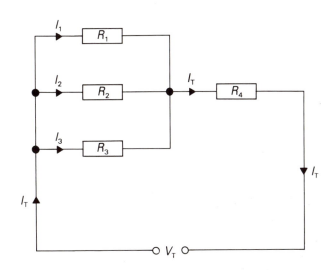

Figure 2.3 Resistors connected in series–parallel.

Resistors in series – parallel circuits (Figure 2.3)

EXAMPLE 4

In Figure 2.3 the resistors R_1, R_2 and R_3 are each 9 Ω, R_4 is 6 Ω and V_T is 18 V. Calculate (i) total resistance R_T, (ii) current in each resistor, (iii) p.d. across each resistor, and (iv) total power.

Note: When resistors of **equal** value are connected in parallel the total value of their resistance equals

$$\frac{\text{one value}}{\text{number of resistors}}$$

This can be verified from the use of the reciprocal formula. Therefore the value of R_1, R_2 and R_3 connected in parallel $= \dfrac{9}{3} = 3$ Ω

This value is in series with R_4.

i) $R_T = 3 + 6 = 9$ Ω

   $I_T = \dfrac{V_T}{R_T} = \dfrac{18}{9} = 2$ A

ii) $I_1 = \dfrac{6}{9} = 0.67$ A, $I_2 = \dfrac{6}{9} = 0.67$ A,

   $I_3 = \dfrac{6}{9} = 0.67$ A

iii) p.d.s across R_1, R_2 and $R_3 = I_T \times$ *combined value* $= 2 \times 3 = 6$ V

   p.d. across $R_4 = 2 \times 6 = 12$ V

iv) $P = V_T \times I_T = 18 \times 2 = 36$ W

Variable resistors or potential dividers

These are resistors which are fitted with a sliding contact so that the resistances may be varied and hence the voltages across them are varied (Figure 2.4).

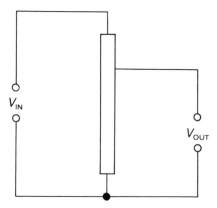

Figure 2.4 Variable resistor or potential divider.

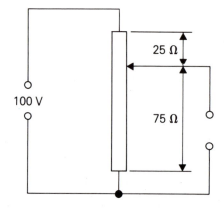

Figure 2.5 Example 5.

EXAMPLE 5

If a resistor of total value 100 Ω is fitted with a sliding contact which is moved to a point one quarter of the way along its length, calculate the voltage at that point if the voltage across the whole resistor is 100 V (Figure 2.5).

$$I \text{ across whole resistor} = \frac{100 \text{ V}}{100 \text{ Ω}} = 1 \text{ A}$$

Voltage across ¼ section (25 Ω) = 1 A × 25 Ω
$$= 25 \text{ V}$$
Voltage across ¾ section (75 Ω) = 1 A × 75 Ω
$$= 75 \text{ V}$$

Temperature coefficient of resistance

This is the ratio of change of resistance in a material or conductor per °C change of temperature from 0°C. It is represented by the Greek letter alpha (α).

The relationship between temperature and resistance is given by the formula

$$\frac{R_1}{R_2} = \frac{1 + \alpha t_1}{1 + \alpha t_2}$$

where R_1 (Ω) = resistance at t_1 (°C),
R_2 (Ω) = resistance at t_2 (°C).

EXAMPLE 6

A certain wire has a resistance of 40 Ω at 10°C. Calculate the value of its resistance when the temperature has risen to 90°C, given that the value of α for the wire is 0.0062 per °C at 0°C.

From the formula $\dfrac{40}{R_2} = \dfrac{1 + (0.0062 \times 10)}{1 + (0.0062 \times 90)}$

$$= \frac{40}{R_2} = \frac{1.062}{1.558}$$

$$R_2 = \frac{40 \times 1.558}{1.062}$$

$$= 58.17 \text{ Ω}$$

Nearly all metals increase in resistance with temperature rise.

A few materials such as carbon decrease in resistance with temperature rise. These are said to have a negative coefficient.

They are made use of to limit the current in a circuit when the temperature is low; sometimes referred to as a thermistor.

Alternating current (a.c.) circuits

Inductance (symbol *L*)

In addition to its resistance, when a coil of wire is wound on an iron former or core it possesses **inductance**.

The coil and its core are sometimes referred to as a **choke** or **inductor**. The value of the inductance is measured in **henrys** (abbr. H). On a purely inductive circuit the current will lag the voltage by an angle of 90°. See the **phasor** diagrams (Figure 2.6).

The opposition to the current flow due to inductance is termed **inductive reactance** (symbol X_L), and its value is $2\pi fL$ (Ω) where f is the frequency of the supply in cycles per second, called **hertz** (abbr. Hz) and L is the **inductance** in henrys. For calculation purposes a choke can be treated as R and X_L in series. Now the current in R is **in-phase** with V, the current in L **lags** V by 90°. So that the total opposition to current flow in the choke termed **impedance** (symbol Z) = $\sqrt{R^2 + X_L^2}$.

EXAMPLE 7

A coil or choke which has a resistance of 30 Ω and an inductance of 0.1. H is connected to a 110 V 50 Hz supply. Calculate (i) X_L, (ii) Z and (iii) I.

i) $X_L = 2\pi fL = 314 \times 0.1 = 31.4\ \Omega$

ii) $Z = \sqrt{R^2 + X_L^2} = \sqrt{(30)^2 + (31.4)^2} = 43.4\ \Omega$

iii) $I = \dfrac{V}{Z} = \dfrac{110}{43.4} = 2.53\ \text{A}$

The only power being consumed by the choke is in its resistance and this is calculated from the formula I^2R (W).

Power factor (pf)

The *power factor* (pf) of the choke
$$= \frac{\text{total power watts}}{\text{supply } V \times \text{supply } I} = \frac{W}{VI}$$

it is also the cosine of the phase angle between V and I.

Note: From the phasor diagram, Figure 2.6, the cosine is also equal to R/Z which again gives the value of the pf.

EXAMPLE 8

Using the above information calculate (i) the power in the circuit of Example 7 and (ii) the power factor.

i) Power $P = I^2R = (2.53)^2 \times 30 = 192\ \text{W}$

ii) $pf = \dfrac{W}{VI} = \dfrac{192}{110 \times 2.53} = 0.69$

check on $pf = \dfrac{R}{Z} = \dfrac{30}{43.4} = 0.69$

See phasor diagram, Figure 2.6.
Note: If the respective values of R and L are drawn to scale on the phasor diagram, values of Z and pf can be measured.

Capacitance or capacitors in a.c. circuits

Capacitance is measured in **farads** (abbr. F). The opposition to the flow of current in this circuit is termed **capacitive reactance** (symbol X_c) and its value is $1/2\pi fC$ where C is in farads.

The current in a purely capacitive circuit or capacitor will lead the voltage by 90°.

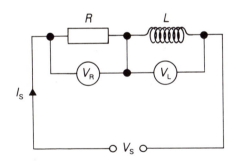

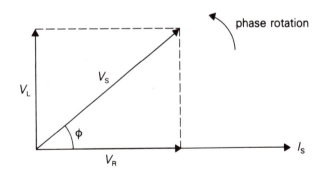

Phasor diagram of voltages and currents

I_S = supply current, V_S = supply voltage
V_R = V across resistance = ($I_S \times R$) in phase with I_S
V_L = V across inductance = ($I_S \times X_L$) leads I_S by 90°
V_S = voltage across R and L = V_Z and leads I_S by cos ϕ

Figure 2.6 Circuit containing R and L in series.

This means the current in an inductor is in opposition to the current in a capacitor (180° apart).

> When the two values are equal, that is, when $X_L = X_C$ the only opposition to the current flow is the resistance of the circuit.
>
> The value of the frequency at which this occurs is known as the resonant frequency and its value is calculated from the circuit condition when the inductive reactance is equal to the capacitive reactance.

That is, when

$$2\pi fL = \frac{1}{2\pi fC}$$
$$(2\pi f)^2 LC = 1$$
$$2\pi f \sqrt{LC} = 1$$
$$f = \frac{1}{2\pi \sqrt{LC}}$$

Because maximum current will flow at this frequency it is referred to as a **current acceptor circuit** (Figure 2.7).

Circuit containing R, L and C in series (Figure 2.8)

From the above the total opposition to current flow

$$Z = \sqrt{R^2 + (X_L \sim X_C)^2}, \text{ where } \sim = \text{difference.}$$

EXAMPLE 9

If a resistor of 5 Ω, an inductor of 0.08 H and capacitor of 150 μF are connected in series to a 50 V, 50 Hz supply, calculate

 i) the impedance of the circuit,
ii) the current,
iii) the pf,
iv) the power.

$$X_L = 2\pi fL = 314 \times 0.08 = 25 \ \Omega$$
$$X_C = \frac{10^6}{2\pi fC} = \frac{10^6}{314 \times 150} = 21 \ \Omega$$

Note: The 10^6 is to convert farad to microfarads ($1F = 10^6 \ \mu F$).

$$Z = \sqrt{5^2 + (25 - 21)^2} = 6.4 \ \Omega$$
$$I = \frac{V}{Z} = \frac{50}{6.4} = 7.8 \ A$$
$$P = (7.8)^2 \times 5 = 304 \ W$$
$$pf = \frac{304 \ W}{(50 \times 7.8) \ VA} = 0.78$$
$$\text{check } pf = \frac{R}{Z} = \frac{5}{6.4} = 0.78$$

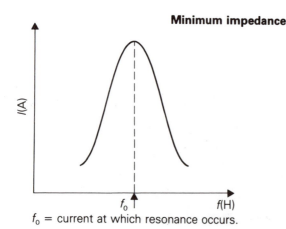

Minimum impedance

f_0 = current at which resonance occurs.

Figure 2.7 Variation of current with frequency in an L–C series circuit (current acceptor).

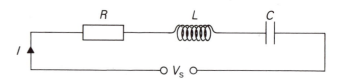

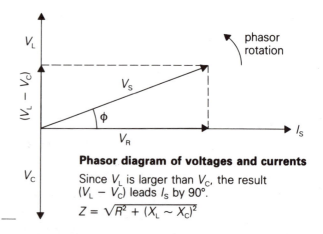

Phasor diagram of voltages and currents

Since V_L is larger than V_C, the result $(V_L - V_C)$ leads I_s by 90°.

$$Z = \sqrt{R^2 + (X_L \sim X_C)^2}$$

Figure 2.8 Circuit containing R, L and C in series.

Note again by drawing to scale all the above values may be measured.

Capacitor and inductor in parallel (Figure 2.9)
At resonant frequency the current will simply oscillate in L and C and very little current will be taken from the supply, just sufficient to make up the loss due to the resistance in the circuit.

Therefore the supply current will be at a minimum. For this reason, this circuit is referred to as a **current rejector** (Figure 2.9).
Note: in Figures 2.7 and 2.9 circuits are used for frequency selection on radio transmission.

Induced e.m.f. in inductive circuits
Circuits which contain coils of wire wound on iron formers possess inductance which when current flows sets up magnetic fluxes. When this flux changes it creates a **back e.m.f.** (electromotive force) due to the flux 'cutting' the turns of wire on the coil.

The value of this e.m.f. $(E) = \dfrac{NI}{t}$

where N is the number of turns on the coil, I is the flux change (Wb) and t is the time (s).

It can create much higher voltages than the voltage which caused the current flow in the first place. This effect is particularly noticeable on, say, discharge lighting circuits where in some cases **arcing** is noticeable at the switches, or when, say, carrying out tests using a battery and 'buzzer' for continuity.

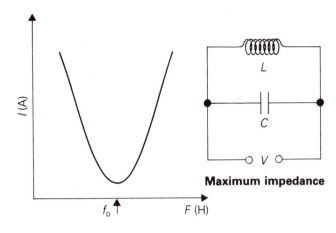

Maximum impedance

Figure 2.9 Circuit containing L and C in parallel (current rejector).

Inductors in parallel
$$\frac{1}{L_T} = \frac{1}{L_1} + \frac{1}{L_2} + \frac{1}{L_3} + \cdots$$

Capacitors in series
$$\frac{1}{C_T} = \frac{1}{C_1} + \frac{1}{C_2} + \frac{1}{C_3} + \cdots$$

Capacitor in parallel
$$C_T = C_1 + C_2 + C_3 + \cdots$$

EXAMPLE 10

The choke (inductor) in a discharge lighting circuit has 750 turns and a flux of 0.075 Wb is set up when current flows. When the light is switched off the flux falls to zero in 1/20 s. Calculate the value of the induced e.m.f.

$$E = \frac{750 \times 0.075}{0.05} = 1125 \text{ V}$$

Note: It is the action of the starter lamp momentarily interrupting the current that 'sets up' the voltage necessary to cause initial ionisation of the gas. See Chapter 6.

Inductors in series

Total inductance $L_T = L_1 + L_2 + L_3 + \cdots$

EXAMPLE 11

Three capacitors of 2, 3 and 5 μF each are connected in (i) parallel and (ii) series. Calculate the total value of the capacitance in each case.

i) $C_T = 2 + 5 + 3 = 10$ μF

ii) $\dfrac{1}{C_T} = \dfrac{1}{2} + \dfrac{1}{5} + \dfrac{1}{3}$

$\qquad = \dfrac{15 + 6 + 10}{30} = \dfrac{31}{30}$

$C_T = \dfrac{30}{31} = 0.967$ μF.

Note: When connected in series the total capacitance is less than the smallest capacitor.

Capacitors are connected in series in order to decrease the voltage across each capacitor and keep it down to the working voltage of the capacitor.

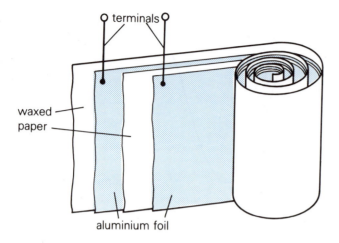

waxed paper

aluminium foil

Figure 2.10 Construction of a capacitor.

Capacitor information

Figure 2.10 shows the basic construction of a capacitor. The value of the capacitance is directly proportional to the area of the plates and indirectly proportional to the distance between them.

In order to get the maximum area into the smallest space a **layer** of conductor material and a layer of insulation (**dielectric**) are sandwiched and then rolled to form a tubular shape. They are then mounted on, but insulated from, a supporting frame. All the rolls are then internally connected in parallel with each other to produce a maximum area and hence a maximum capacitance. On industrial installations the whole assembly will be contained in a large steel fabricated case.

The insulation between the plates is referred to as the **dielectric**.

The capacitance value of a capacitor

$$C = \frac{E_0 E_r \, A \, (\mathrm{m}^2)}{d \, (\mathrm{m})} \text{ farads (F)}$$

Note: Where there are a number of plates (n) the total area between them = ($n - 1$).
where E_0 = **permittivity of space** = 8.85×10^{-12},
  E_r = **permittivity of dielectric material**,
  A = area of plates,
  d = distance between them.

Electrolytic capacitor
These are used mainly on d.c. supplies, the plates polarise and an oxide gas is given off which forms the dielectric. The dimensions of these are even smaller, there are some electrolytics which can be used on a.c. supplies. However, the installer must be careful to check manufacturer's data.

Before connection the working voltage of the capacitor must also be noted, this is normally given as the inverse peak voltage which is approximately three times the r.m.s. (stated) value of the a.c. supply.

Note also that capacitors store a charge which is retained for lengthy periods after disconnection although in most cases an internal discharge resistor is connected across the terminals to prevent unexpected shock from otherwise live terminals.

EXAMPLE 12

A capacitor has the equivalent area of two parallel plates each 100 cm by 8 cm. Calculate the capacitance if the dielectric material is 0.1 mm thick and its E_r = 2, given that $E_0 = 8.85 \times 10^{-12}$.

$$C = \frac{E_0 E_r \, A \, (\mathrm{m}^2)}{d \, (\mathrm{m})}$$

$$= \frac{8.85 \times 10^{-12} \times 2 \times (2-1) \times (100 \times 8) \times 10^{-4}}{1 \times 10^{-4}} \text{ F}$$

$$= 8.85 \times 16 \times 10^{-10} \times 10^6 \, \mu\mathrm{F}$$
$$= 8.85 \times 16 \times 10^{-4} \, \mu\mathrm{F}$$
$$= 0.01416 \, \mu\mathrm{F}.$$

Effects of an electric current

There are three effects that a flow of current will produce:

1. heating,
2. chemical effects,
3. magnetic effects.

1. The friction created by the movement of the electrons causes a generation of heat in the material known as **resistive heating** (as opposed to **magnetic** or **electrostatic heating** set up by alternating currents). The resistive heating is made use of in elements of fire bars, electric stoves, etc.
2. The passage of a current can split up the molecules in liquids and solids, a process known as **electrolysis**. This forms the basis to produce an e.m.f. by a battery and the deposition of one metal on another known as electroplating.
3. The current flow in a conductor or coil sets a **magnetic field flux** or force around it which is more pronounced when an iron (ferrous metal)

core is present. The strength of the force (symbol F) depends upon the value of the current and the number of turns on the coil

$$F = \text{ampere-turns (A.T)}$$

An iron magnetic circuit is shown in Figure 2.11.

Magnetic circuits

These for calculation purposes can be likened to electrical circuits where

reluctance (S) corresponds to **resistance,**
magnetic flux (Φ) is measured in **weber** (Wb), corresponds to **current,**
magnetising force (magnetomotive force) (m.m.f.) A.T corresponds to **voltage.**

So that for a magnetic circuit

$$\Phi = \frac{(F) \text{ ampere-turns}}{(S) \text{ reluctance}} \text{ (Wb)}$$

where for the electrical circuit

$$I = \frac{(V) \text{ e.m.f.}}{(R) \text{ resistance}} \text{ (A)}$$

Further, as the value of resistance for an electric material is calculated from the formula

$$I = \rho \frac{l}{A}$$

The value of reluctance for the magnetic material

$$S = \frac{l \, (m)}{\mu A \, (m^2)}$$

where μ is the value of **permeability**. It is made up of the permeability of air (μ_o) and of **relative permeability** for the given material (μ_r).
The value μ_o is given as $4\pi \times 10^{-7}$, while the value for μ_r for the given material must be 'looked up' in tables.
From this the value of $\mu = \mu_o\mu_r$

$$\mu = 4\pi \times 10^{-7} \times \mu_r$$

EXAMPLE 13

An iron core has a mean length of 0.4 m and a cross-section area of 10 mm², calculate the reluctance if μ_r for the iron is given as 2000 (see Figure 2.11).

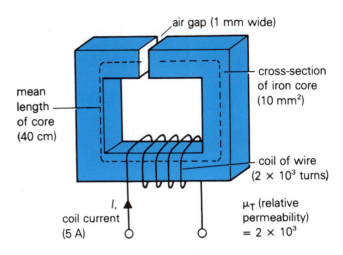

Figure 2.11 Iron magneto circuit with air gap.

$$\begin{aligned}
\text{Reluctance } S &= \frac{l \, (m)}{\mu_o\mu_r A \, (m^2)} \\
&= \frac{4 \times 10^{-1}}{4\pi \times 10^{-7} \times 2 \times 10^3 \times 10 \times 10^6} \\
&= \frac{4 \times 10^{-1} \times 10^7 \times 10^{-3} \times 10^6}{80\pi} \\
&= \frac{4 \times 10^9}{80\pi} = 1.6 \times 10^7
\end{aligned}$$

EXAMPLE 14

If the same coil from Example 13 is wound with 1000 turns of wire which carry a current of 5 A, calculate the value of (i) flux and (ii) flux density in the ring.

$$\begin{aligned}
\text{i) } \Phi \, Wb &= \frac{A.T}{\text{reluctance}} \\
&= \frac{5 \times 10^3}{1.6 \times 10^7} \\
&= 3.125 \times 10^{-4} \, Wb
\end{aligned}$$

$$\begin{aligned}
\text{ii) flux density} &= \frac{1 \, (m^2)}{\text{area of ring } (m^2)} \times \text{ring } \Phi \\
&= \frac{1}{10 \times 10^{-6}} \times 3.125 \times 10^{-4} \\
&= 1 \times 3.125 \times 10 \\
&= 31.25 \text{ tesla}
\end{aligned}$$

EXAMPLE 15

If an air gap 1 mm wide is cut into the core of the above iron ring, calculate the change of flux due to this (see Figure 2.11).

Reluctance of airgap $= \dfrac{1 \times 10^{-3}}{4\pi \times 10^{-7} \times 1 \times 10 \times 10^{-6}}$

$= \dfrac{1 \times 10^{-3} \times 10^{7} \times 10^{6}}{4\pi \times 10}$

$= \dfrac{1 \times 10^{10}}{40\pi} = 8 \times 10^{7}$

The 1 mm reduction in the length of the iron circuit due to the airgap may be neglected, so the reluctance remains virtually the same at 1.6×10^{-7}.
Note: This 1 mm cut is in series with the ring.
   So that the total reluctance = iron + airgap

$= (1.6 \times 10^{7}) + (8 \times 10^{7})$
$= 9.6 \times 10$

New flux $= \dfrac{5 \times 10^{3}}{9.6 \times 10^{7}} = \dfrac{5}{9.6} \times 10^{-4}$

$= 0.52 \times 10^{-4} \text{ Wb}$

Practical examples of faults on magnetic circuits

From these examples it can be seen that air gaps in magnetic circuits will increase the reluctance by a great amount.

   Since A.T = $\Phi \times$ reluctance

if the reluctance increases, then to maintain the same flux the A.Ts must increase in the same proportion and since the turns of the coils are fixed it means the current will be greatly increased to a value which probably will 'burn out' the coil.

> It is therefore essential that the air gaps in machines, solenoids and all equipment which uses magnetic fluxes be maintained at the values of the design. This means any dirt, distortion or wear on pivots etc. must be attended to (see Figure 2.12). The first symptoms of the above will be overheating of the coil, usually the 'smell' of the coil insulation.

Permeability

When iron is subjected to alternating current supplies so that the direction of the current and hence the polarity of the magnetisation is constantly changing, see Figure 3.4, the magnetic flux change of direction lags behind the current change of direction.
   This **lag** is called **hysteresis**, which results in an energy loss in the iron core in the form of heat.

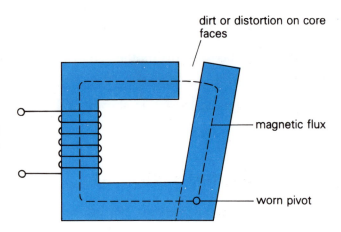

Figure 2.12 Faults in a practical magnetic circuit.

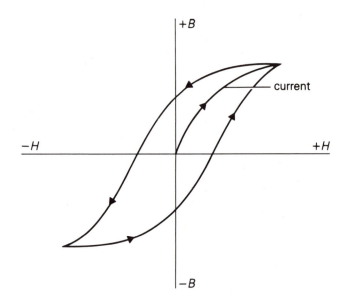

Figure 2.13 B–H curve or hysteresis loop.

   The amount of loss can be shown by an hysteresis loop on a flux density (B) (tesla) to a magnetising force base (H) (Figure 2.13). The larger the area inside the loop, the greater the loss.

> In practice the energy loss is reduced by making cores for a.c. machines of thin sheets of a special iron called stalloy.

Note: For permanent magnets which need to retain their magnetic flux in one direction the area of the loop will be large.
   For alternating magnetism applications where the fluxes need to be lost quickly, the area of the loop will need to be small.

Magnetic fields

When a conductor carrying a current is situated in a magnetic field a **force** is set up on that conductor. The direction of the force is governed by the polarity of the field and the direction of the current in the conductor.

The screw rule

This states that if a right-handed screw is turned so that it moves in the same direction as the current, then its direction of rotation is the direction of the magnetic field. The direction of current in the conductor is denoted by the symbols

⊕   current flow into the page of the book
⊙   current flow away from the page of the book

In a magnetic field due to a magnet the direction will be from N to S.

So in Figure 2.14 the two fluxes of field concentrate above the conductor and a downward force is exerted.

The strength or magnitude of the force (F)

$$F = Bl\,I \text{ newtons}$$

where B = **flux** density (Wb per m²),
      l = **length** of the conductor (m),
      I = **current** in the conductor (A).

Left-hand rule

Figure 2.15 illustrates a method of working out the current direction in a moving conductor. The above action forms the basis of the electric motor.

Also, when there is a movement of a conductor situated in a magnetic field an e.m.f. or voltage is generated in that conductor. The polarity of the e.m.f. and hence the direction of current when a circuit is completed is governed by the direction of the magnetic field and the direction in which the conductor is moved, as shown in Figure 2.15.

Right-hand rule

The right-hand rule again uses the thumb, first and second fingers to indicate directions.

The magnitude of the e.m.f. generated is

$$E = BlV \text{ (volts)}$$

The above action forms the basis of the electric generator.

Magnetic fields around conductor

When current-carrying conductors are placed near to each other, the magnetic fields set up around

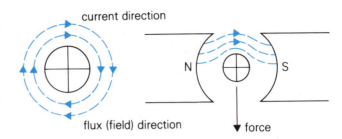

Figure 2.14 Force on a conductor in a magnetic field.

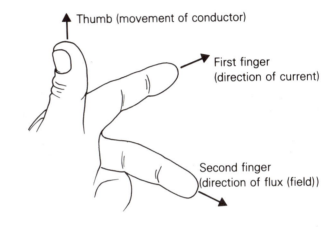

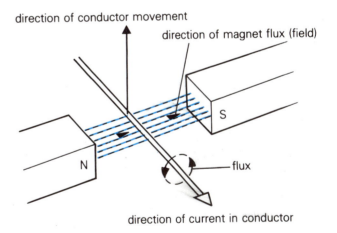

Figure 2.15 Left-hand rule for movement of conductor.

them exert a force between them. If the currents are flowing in the **same** direction the force tends to **pull** the conductors together, that is, an **attraction** force and when the currents are in the **opposite** direction, the force pushes them apart, that is, a **repulsion** force. See Figure 2.16.

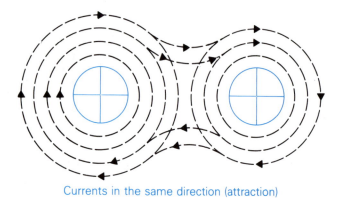

Currents in the same direction (attraction)

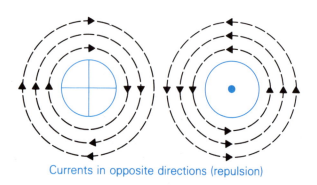

Currents in opposite directions (repulsion)

Figure 2.16 Magnetic fields around conductors.

The magnitude of the force

$$= \frac{2\pi \times 10^{-7} (\mu_0) \times I_1 \times I_2 \, (A)}{d \, (m)} \text{ newton}$$

where I_1 and I_2 are the current in each conductor (A), and d is the distance between them (m).

The definition of the unit of current the **ampere** is obtained from this.

> The ampere is that current which if maintained in two parallel conductors would produce a force of $2\pi \times 10^{-7}$ newtons per metre length between them.

EXAMPLE 16

Two heavy current duty conductors (**busbars**) are situated 0.05 m apart. A short circuit fault occurs and, before the excess current protection device operates, a current of 10 000 A flows in each.

Calculate the magnitude of the force between the conductors.

$$F = \frac{2\pi \times 10^{-7} \times 10^4 \times 10^4}{5 \times 10^{-2}}$$

$$= \frac{2\pi \times 10^3}{5}$$

$$= 1256 \text{ newton}$$

Note: This would be likely to pull the conductors off the supports.

Electro-magnetic induction

Transformer action

If two separate coils are placed on an iron core and one of them is energised from an a.c. supply it will produce an alternating flux in the core. This flux will link with the second coil and induce an e.m.f. (voltage) in that coil.

This is the basic action of the transformer where the energised coil is called the **primary coil** and the other is the **secondary coil**. See Figure 2.17 for single phase, Figure 2.18 for three-phase construction and Figure 2.19 for three-phase connections.

Transformer ratios

The **voltage ratios** will be in the same proportion as the turns ratios of the coils, so that

$$\frac{N_P}{N_s} = \frac{V_P}{V_s}$$

where N_P = primary turns,
N_s = secondary turns,
V_P = primary voltage,
V_s = secondary voltage.

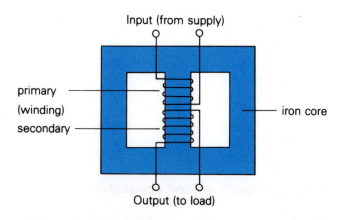

Figure 2.17 Single-phase transformer.

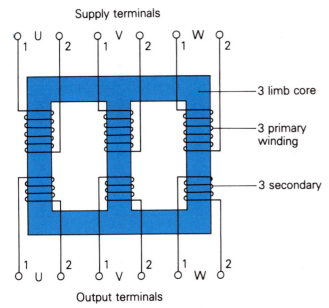

Supply terminals

- 3 limb core
- 3 primary winding
- 3 secondary

Output terminals

Input windings are normally connected in delta. Output windings are normally connected in star, so that the neutral can be connected to the star point to produce a line voltage and a phase voltage on the 3-phase 4-wire supply.

Figure 2.18 Three-phase transformer.

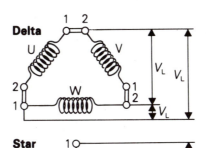

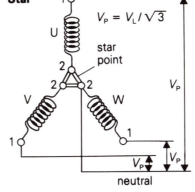

Note: There are six ends of coils for each winding for connection to a 3-phase supply. They may be connected in star or in delta depending on voltages required.

The windings must be correctly phased for connection. 1 is the start of winding; 2 is the finish of winding.

Figure 2.19 Three-phase transformer connections.

EXAMPLE 17

If the primary winding of a transformer has 200 turns and the secondary has 300 turns, calculate the secondary voltage if the primary is connected to a 150 V a.c. supply.

$$\frac{N_P}{N_s} = \frac{V_P}{V_s}$$

$$V_s = \frac{N_s V_P}{N_P} = \frac{300 \times 150}{200}$$

$$= 225 \text{ V}$$

Current ratios
The **current ratios** between the two coils will be in inverse proportion to the voltage ratios.

$$\frac{I_P}{I_s} = \frac{V_s}{V_P}$$

EXAMPLE 18

If the above transformer supplies a load of 25 A, calculate the current in the primary winding.

$$I_P = \frac{V_s I_s}{V_P} = \frac{225 \times 25}{150} = 37.5 \text{ A}$$

Transformer power losses
These can be divided into two parts

1. iron (Fe) loss, and
2. copper (Cu) loss.

Iron loss
Iron loss occurs because of the alternating magnetic fluxes in the core, these were mentioned in the section on permeability.

This iron loss can be divided again into two parts.

1. **Eddy currents** These are small a.c. voltages set up in the core which produce circulating currents and cause loss in the form of heat in the core.
2. **Hysteresis** This, as already mentioned is lag of flux behind the magnetising force which again sets up loss in the form of heating the core.

Copper loss
This is due to the windings resistance (I^2R) in both windings. Although these combined (Fe and Cu)

losses are relatively small, say 1 per cent of the transformer rating, on large transformers, say on a 1 MV A (megavolt-ampere) transformer, it can be a considerable power loss, that is, 1 per cent of 1 MV A = 1 per cent × 10⁶ V A = 10 kW

Since there are no rotating parts on which to fit fan blades, other means of cooling have to be employed.

The most common method of cooling is to fit pipes on the outside of the case, so that the insulating oil in which the windings are immersed can circulate. On very large power installations they are also placed out the building so that the atmosphere can help in the cooling.

Determination of losses and efficiency

The iron loss is fairly constant at all loads. This means that a test can be carried out without loading the transformer, it is known as an **open circuit test** (Figure 2.20).

Open-circuit test
The primary winding is connected to the correct voltage rating supply, while the secondary is left open-circuited.

A **wattmeter** connected to the input supply will now indicate the power consumption due to the iron loss only, since the currents in the windings are minimal.

Short-circuit test
The copper loss will vary as the square of the load current, it is the I^2R loss in both windings. A test for this, again without loading the transformer, is called the **short-circuit test** (Figure 2.21). The secondary winding is connected to an **ammeter** to measure the current in the windings. The primary winding is connected to a variable supply so that the voltage can be adjusted until the ammeter reads full load current.

Note: There will be a very small voltage on the primary winding since the ammeter is almost a short circuit on the transformer.

Again a wattmeter connected in the supply will indicate the power consumed.

The **efficiency** of a transformer is calculated from

$$\text{efficiency} = \frac{\text{power output}}{\text{power output} + \text{losses}}$$
$$= \frac{\text{power output}}{\text{power output} + (\text{Fe} + \text{Cu}) \text{ losses}}$$

See Figures 2.20 and 2.21 for basic construction, connection and tests.

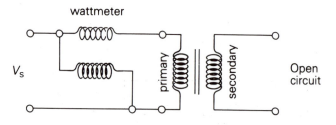

Figure 2.20 Open circuit test on transformer.

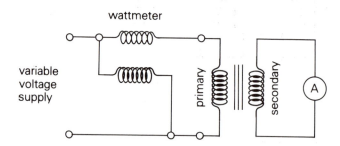

Figure 2.21 Short circuit test on transformer.

EXAMPLE 19

A 100 kV A transformer supplies a load of 0.8 pf. The transformer iron losses are 5 kW and the copper losses at full load are 8 kW. Calculate the efficiency of the transformer when working at (i) ¼, (ii) ½, (iii) ¾ and (iv) full load.

The power output at full load = 100 kV A × 0.8 pf
= 80 kW

The iron loss is constant at all loads.
The copper loss is proportional to the square of the load

$$\text{efficiency} = \frac{P \text{ output}}{P \text{ output} + (\text{iron} + \text{copper}) \text{ loss}}$$

i) Efficiency $= \dfrac{20 \text{ kW}}{20 + 5 + (1/16 \times 8)} = \dfrac{20}{25.5}$
$= 78.4\%$

ii) $= \dfrac{40 \text{ kW}}{40 + 5 + (1/4 \times 8)} = \dfrac{40}{47}$
$= 85\%$

iii) $= \dfrac{60}{60 + 5 + (9/16 \times 8)} = \dfrac{60}{69.5}$
$= 86.33\%$

iv) $= \dfrac{80}{80 + 5 + (8)} = \dfrac{80}{93}$
$= 86\%$

EXAMPLE 20

In the transformer in Example 19, calculate the line output current from the transformer at full load if the output is three-phase 11 kV.

Three-phase $P = \sqrt{3} V_L I_L \cos \phi$

$$I_L = \frac{P}{\sqrt{3} V_L \cos \phi}$$

$$= \frac{80}{1.732 \times 11 \times 0.8}$$

$$= 5.23 \text{ A}$$

Autotransformer

This has a single winding with a tap-off connection for primary and secondary windings (Figure 2.22) below.

Similarly to the double winding transformer, the voltage ratios are equal to the turns ratios.

In the common portion of the winding the 'in' and 'out' currents are in **antiphase** so they oppose each other, hence the current is the difference between the two: $(I_1 - I_2)$ or $(I_2 - I_1)$ whichever is the greater.

This makes the Cu loss much less and leads to better efficiency particularly where the ratio between input and output voltages is low.

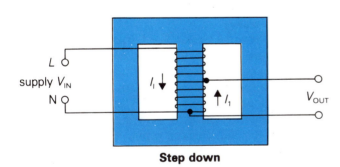

Step down

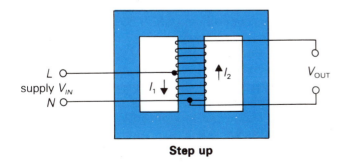

Step up

Figure 2.22 The autotransformer.

Because it is a common winding there are dangers of short circuits between input and output, for this reason the regulations restrict its use.

> - A step up may not be used where it is not solidly earthed to a supply.
> - It must be supplied through a linked switch to disconnect all poles.
> - On a single phase supply the neutral must be the common conductor.
> - It should be contained within the equipment it supplies.

The main uses for the autotransformer are sodium vapour lamps and motor starters.

■ CHECK YOUR UNDERSTANDING

- Current flow is movement of electrons $Q = It$ (coulombs).
- Power in resistive circuits $= V I = V^2/R = I^2R$ (watts).
- Resistance R $= \rho \dfrac{l \ (\text{m})}{a \ (\text{m}^2)}$ (Ω) where ρ = resistivity of the material.
- Total resistance (R_T)

Series circuit $R_T = r_1 + r_2 + r_3 \ldots$

Parallel circuit $\dfrac{1}{R_T} = \dfrac{1}{r_1} + \dfrac{1}{r_2} + \dfrac{1}{r_3} + \cdots$

- Resistance change with temperature

$$\frac{R_1}{R_2} = \frac{1 + \alpha t_1}{1 + \alpha t_2}$$

where α is the temperature coefficient of resistance of material.

- A.c. circuits

Reactance $X_L = 2\pi fL$, $X_c = \dfrac{1}{2\pi fc}$ (Ω)

Impedance $(Z) = \sqrt{R^2 + (2\pi fL \sim 1/2\pi fC)^2}$ (Ω)

Resonant frequency $(f_0) = \dfrac{1}{2\pi \sqrt{LC}}$ (Hz)

Series circuit is the current acceptor, parallel circuit is the current rejector.

- Induced e.m.f. in a coil $E = \dfrac{NI}{t}$

● Capacitance $C = \dfrac{E_0 E_r A (m^2)}{d(m)}$ (F)

● Effects of an electric current: heating, magnetic effects, chemical effects.

● Magnetic circuits

Reluctance $(S) = \dfrac{l \ (m)}{\mu_0 \mu_r A \ (m^2)}$

Flux $\Phi = \dfrac{A.T}{S}$ weber (Wb)

● Magnetic fields

Force $(F) = B \, l \, I$ newtons (N),

newton $= \dfrac{kg}{9.81}$

B = flux density (Wb/m²) (tesla)

Force between parallel conductors (F)

$F = \dfrac{2\pi \times 10^{-7} \ (\mu_0) \times I_1 I_2 \ (A)}{d \ (m)}$ (N)

● Transformer ratios $\dfrac{N_P}{N_s} = \dfrac{V_P}{V_s} = \dfrac{I_s}{I_P}$

Losses: iron (Fe) = eddy current and hysteresis (constant)

copper (Cu) = $I^2 R$ in windings (variable)

Efficiency $= \dfrac{\text{power output}}{\text{power output} + (\text{Fe} + \text{Cu}) \text{ losses}}$

REVISION EXERCISES AND QUESTIONS

---

1 Calculate the reluctance of a magnetic circuit which has an area of 1 cm² and is wound with 25 turns of wire if a current of 12 A sets up a flux density of 0.25 T.

2 Explain how the efficiency of a transformer can be determined without fully loading it.
Show diagrams to illustrate your answer.

3 An autotransformer for a sodium vapour lamp steps up the voltage from 250 to 500 V. If the current on the secondary side is 2 A, i) make a diagram of this arrangement, ii) determine the current and direction in each section of the winding and mark it on the diagram, iii) state a possible danger in the use of the autotransformer.

4 A conductor 22 cm long 'cuts' a magnetic field at speed of 36 m/s. If the induced e.m.f. is 3.2 V what is the flux density of the field?

5 A 240 V 100 W lamp filament operates at a temperature of 2200°C. At switch on in a

temperature of 20°C it takes an initial current of 4 A.
Determine the temperature coefficient of the filament material.

6 Iron loss in transformers can be divided into two parts:
   i) name these and state briefly how the loss is caused in each case.
   ii) State how (a) iron loss, and (b) copper loss are affected by the load supplied by the transformer.

7 i)   Explain with aid of a sketch the basic construction of a capacitor for use on an a.c. supply.
   ii) How does the
        a) area of plates,
        b) distance between the plates
        affect the total capacitance?
   iii) If a capacitor is rated at 800 V peak inverse, what is the value of the maximum a.c. supply it can be connected to?

8 A 240 V 60 W tungsten filament lamp operates at 2000°C. Calculate the current at switch on when the temperature is 20°C. Assume α for tungsten to be 0.005°C at 0°C.

9 i)   Explain how the use of laminated iron cores reduce the losses in alternating current equipment.
   ii) What is the meaning of alternating current? (See Chapter 3.)
   iii) State the relative values of
        a) peak, (b) r.m.s., (c) average for a sine wave,
        d) inverse peak. (See Chapter 3.)

10 Calculate the flux density in the iron ring if the mean length is 16 cm and it has a μ_r of 1030.

11 The copper coils of a certain machine take a current of 2 A from a 500 V d.c. supply when first switched on with the temperature at 15°C. Calculate the current when the machine has been running for some time and the temperature of the coils is 45°C. Take the value of α for copper as 0.0043°C at 0°C.

12 A contactor coil on a 240 V 50 Hz supply when tested by an ohmmeter gives a reading of 300 Ω. When operating on a 240 V 50 Hz supply the coil takes 0.12 A.
   i) Determine (a) the coil impedance (Z),
       (b) the coil inductance (L).
   ii) Calculate the reactance (X_L) at a frequency of 25 Hz.

13 i) State the danger of touching the terminal of a capacitor even when disconnected from the supply.

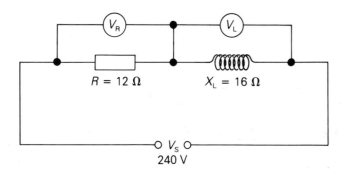

R = 12 Ω X_L = 16 Ω

V_S
240 V

ii) What steps are taken by the manufacturers to minimise this danger?

14 For the circuit shown, $R = 12\ \Omega$, $X_1 = 16\ \Omega$. Calculate

  i)   a) impedance (Z), (b) current (I),
         c) voltage across each component $(V_R)(V_{XL})$.
  ii)   Show a phasor diagram between I_s, V_s, V_L and V_{XL}.
  iii)   From the phasor or otherwise determine
         a) phase angle between I_s and V_s,
         b) power factor (*pf*).

Transmission, distribution and consumer circuitry

Introduction

Figure 3.1 shows the generation, transmission and distribution stages from the raw fuel input to the power station to the electricity supply at the consumers' premises. The key to the diagram is as follows:

1. input fuel to power station (coal, oil or nuclear fuel);
2. power station containing boiler plant, prime mover (steam turbine) and the electric generator;
3. supply from the generator at 25 kV three-phase;
4. generator transformers and switchgear;
5. primary distribution at 400 or 275 kV three-phase on overhead lines;
6. primary outdoor substations situated on the outskirts of industrial areas, containing high voltage switchgear and transformers;
7. secondary distribution at 132 kV or 33 kV overhead or underground dependent upon the nature of the area;
8. local electric supply authority substation;
9. high voltage cables at 11 kV three-phase underground direct to large consumers' premises or to further substations;
10. further local authority supply substations;
11. final distribution underground at 415 V three-phase four-wire or
12. 240 V single-phase two-wire.

Note: In rural areas for economic reasons supplies at the lower voltage will be taken directly to consumers' premises on overhead lines from the local authority substations. Up to the no. 7 stage, the primary transmission at very high voltage is under the control of the authority which specialises in the work. The installation electrician is mainly concerned with the wiring and maintenance of equipment on the consumers' premises and this chapter deals with this aspect.

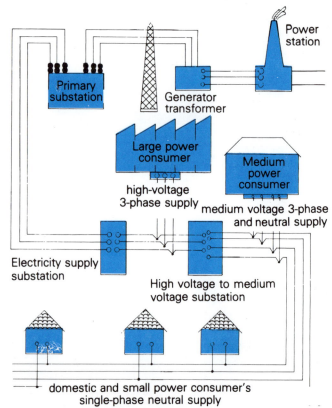

Figure 3.1 Stages in transmission and distribution of electric power.

The electric circuit

Figure 3.2 shows a water pump creating a water **pressure**. The pipework offers a **frictional resistance** to the water **flow**. The larger the pipe, the lower the resistance and hence the greater the flow from the same pressure. Also, if the pump pressure is increased, the greater is the flow for a given pipe size. This means that the flow is dependent upon the pressure and the pipe resistance.

In Figure 3.3, the pump is replaced by an electric generator creating an electrical pressure, the pipe is replaced by an electrical conductor and the water flow by a flow of electric current.

In this circuit, the current flow is dependent upon the electrical pressure and the circuit resistance in exactly the same manner as the water circuit.

An important factor in distribution is the fact that the conductor resistance causes a voltage drop and heating along the cable run. This is explained later.

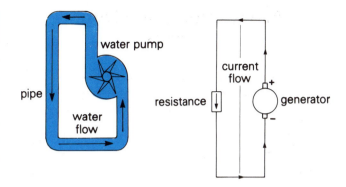

Figure 3.2 (left) A water system circuit.
Figure 3.3 (right) An electric circuit.

Ohm's law

The pressure, resistance and current are connected by a formula known as Ohm's law, which states that the current in a circuit is inversely proportional to the circuit resistance. Expressed mathematically in symbol form

$$I = \frac{V}{R}$$

where I = current in amperes (A),
V = pressure in volts (V),
R = resistance in ohms (Ω).

From this equation, it is seen that the current flow can be controlled or regulated by variation of the circuit voltage or the circuit resistance.

An increase in voltage increases the current flow.
An increase in resistance decreases the current flow.

Electrical power

The unit of power (P) is the watt.

It requires both voltage and current to deliver power to a consumer's installation and the power is the product of these
$P(\text{watts}) = V \times I$

Electrical energy

The unit of electrical energy takes into account the length of time for which the power is being used and is the unit on which electricity charges are based. The unit is called the joule (J) and the following definition can be made:

1 joule of energy is consumed when a power of 1 watt is used for a time of 1 second, that is, 1 joule = 1 watt-second.

In the electrical power installation, the larger unit, the kilowatt-hour (kW h) is used for electricity charges or tariffs. This is when 1 kW of power is used for a time of 1 hour.
Note: 1 kW h = 3 600 000
$$= 3.6 \times 10^6 \text{ joules}$$

Alternating and direct current

In the description of a simple circuit it was assumed that the current was flowing in one direction all the time. This is called a **direct current**, referred to as **d.c.** For power systems of distribution, an **alternating current**, referred to as **a.c.** is used. This means that the current flows for a time in a forward direction and then reverses to flow in the opposite direction. This is explained more simply in Figure 3.4.

The complete cycle is known as a **sine wave**. The wave form above and below the zero line shows the variation of the current with time. One cycle is one complete set of changes and the number of cycles which occur in one second of time is known as the **frequency** of the electricity supply. This unit of frequency, or number of cycles per second is known as the **hertz** (Hz).

Therefore, with a supply frequency of 50 Hz, one cycle would have a duration of 1/50 of a second, in which time it would pass through the zero position twice. If the frequency is much lower than this, these zero points, at which there is no current flow, would cause lights to flicker. Because of this and other reasons, the standard supply frequency in the U.K. is 50 Hz.

As stated, the current and the voltage are changing from instant to instant.

> The stated or declared value of an alternating current or voltage is that value which would have the same heating effect as a direct current or voltage of the same value.

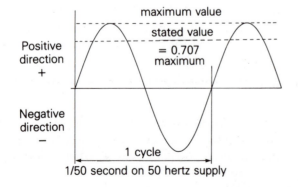

Figure 3.4 Sine wave of alternating current.

The advantage of a.c. transmission is that the voltage can be stepped up or down quite economically by a **transformer**. If a consumer requires a d.c. supply for a certain process he must install the necessary rectifying equipment to convert the a.c. supply to d.c.

From the formula $P = V \times I$ (watts), it will be seen that for a given power supply, the higher the voltage the lower the current and, since conductor sizes are determined by the current they have to carry, the smaller the conductor required.

> To transmit a power of 1 000 000 watts which is 1000 kilowatts (kW) or 1 megawatt (MW) at a supply of 100 V, would require a current of 10 000 A, whereas, if the supply was stepped up to 10 000 V, it would require a current of only 100 A.

In addition, the switching is more economical because of lower currents and the fact that when the alternating current is at the zero point, the arc is self-extinguishing.

Supply voltages

Nearly all transmission supplies are **three-phase**, that is, there are three live conductors where the currents in each phase have displacement of 120° respectively.

At the local authority substation or the larger consumers' premises, a fourth conductor is connected to the supply system to provide a three-phase four-wire supply. This conductor is known as the neutral and hence the supply is sometimes referred to as a **triple-pole-neutral** (T.P.N.) supply. The idea of this neutral conductor is to provide the consumer with a **single-phase** supply at a lower and safer voltage for lighting and smaller current-rated appliances. This neutral conductor is also connected at the transformer position to the general mass of earth to provide protection against earth leakage current. Figure 3.5 shows a theoretical diagram of the windings on the secondary side of a consumer's supply transformer at the local authority supply substations in Figure 3.1.

In the U.K., the voltage in each of the three-phase windings on the transformer is 240 V and, because the voltages in each are 120° apart, the

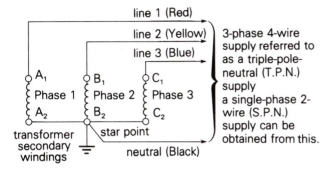

Figure 3.5 Secondary winding of supply transformer.

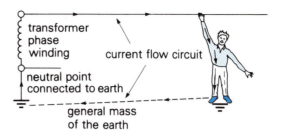

Figure 3.6 How an electric shock occurs.

voltages between any two phases or live conductors is $240 \times \sqrt{3} = 415$ V, which is referred to as the **line voltage**. The voltage between any one live conductor and the neutral is 240 V, which is referred to as the **phase voltage**. The supply conductors are identified by colours RED, YELLOW and BLUE (phases) and BLACK (neutral).

Electric shock

A study of Figure 3.6 shows that if a person standing on the general mass of earth touches one live conductor only, his body will complete a circuit and allow a current to flow and he will experience an electric shock.

> The severity of an electric shock is determined by the amount of the current flow which, in turn, is governed by the circuit resistance and the voltage.

Since the voltage is fixed the determining factor is the resistance value and this will vary mainly with the state of the earth or ground. If the soil is wet, then its resistance is less and the shock greater. If the ground is dry or the person is standing on some form of insulator, the degree of shock is much less.

> The body can sense a current of around 1 milliampere (1 mA), a current of 20 mA or so could prove fatal by contraction of the heart muscles.

EXAMPLE 1

A person standing on the general mass of earth touches a phase conductor on a 240 V supply. If the resistance of the circuit is 48 000 Ω, which is mainly his body resistance, calculate the current flow in his body.

From Ohm's law

$$I = \frac{V}{R} = \frac{240}{48\ 000} = \frac{0.1}{20} \text{ A}$$
$$= 0.005 \text{ A} = 5 \text{ mA}$$

Consumer supplies

From Figure 3.1 it can be seen that medium-sized buildings such as smaller factories, office blocks and larger shopping premises, are supplied with three-phase conductors and a neutral, that is, a T.P.N. supply at the supply intake position.

From here, the consumer or his electrician will arrange suitable switchgear and distribution to the various current-consuming loads. The circuits which are taken directly to the loads are known as **subcircuits**. The heavier loads will be connected to the three-phase T.P. or the three-phase and neutral (T.P.N.) supply providing them with 415 V or 415/240 V. The smaller loads are supplied from any one phase and the neutral supply, referred to as **single-pole and neutral** or S.P.N. at 240 V.

The single-phase loads are connected in such a way that they are as near as possible divided equally over the three phases and the neutral, referred to as **balancing** the loads (Figure 3.7). This is for reasons of economy which are explained later.

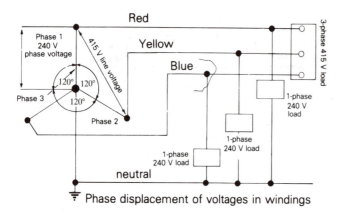

Figure 3.7 Connections for three-phase and single-phase loads.

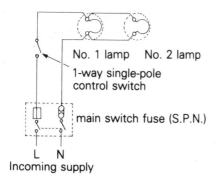

Figure 3.8 A simple form of switchgear for lamps in parallel.

Switchgear at consumers' intake terminals

For full details of switchgear refer to I.E.E. Regulations for Electrical Equipment in Buildings. Regulations detail the switchgear required. This includes:

1. means of isolation, that is, switching of all conductors connecting the installation to the supply;
2. means of circuit protection, that is, automatic disconnection of the installation when the current exceeds the normal full load value, which would cause overheating and lead to fire; and
3. protection against leakage of current to earth, again to disconnect automatically when excess current flows to earth which would, if left to leak, result in shock and fire damage.

The simplest form of switchgear would consist of a switch and a fuse as in Figure 3.8.

With a few exceptions, the current rating of the fuse should not exceed the current rating of the cable it protects.

The I.E.E. Regulations state that the consumer's main switch must be able to disconnect all the conductors (poles) from the supply, and the fuse or other excess current device must be connected in the phase conductors only.

No fuse, excess current device or single-pole switch should be connected to the neutral or the earthed conductor, as it can, under faulty conditions, cause exposed metalwork connected to earth to become live, giving rise to a very dangerous situation.

Details of circuit protection are given in Chapter 5.

Simple lighting circuits

Lamps in parallel

Two lights are to be controlled from one switch position. A theoretical circuit diagram of this arrangements, including the switchgear at the consumer's intake terminals, is shown in Figure 3.8.

The lamps are each connected between the live (phase) and the neutral conductors so that they each receive the full supply (240 V) voltage. This is known as connecting the points in **parallel** with each other and since the lamps and other single-phase appliances are rated at the standard 240 V voltage, this is the normal method of connecting lamps and appliances.

Because the neutral conductor is at earth potential (not live) it is only necessary in this circuit to connect the control switch in the phase conductor. It is connected in series to interrupt the supply to both lamps by opening the circuit.

As previously mentioned, this circuit is referred to as a subcircuit and the total load, that is, the number and the power rating of lamps which can be connected to one subcircuit, is stated in the I.E.E. Regulations.

For a domestic lighting subcircuit, the fuse rating is 5 A (coloured white). Therefore, if the lamps have a rating of 100 W each and the supply voltage is 240V, from the power formula

$$P(\text{watts}) = V \times I$$

Maximum number of lamps on one circuit

$$= \frac{5 \times 240}{100}$$

When more lighting loads are to be supplied on the same installation, further subcircuits would have to be used which would require the installation of more fuse-ways at the incoming terminals.

Lamps in series

In a few cases it becomes necessary to connect lamps in series as shown in Figure 3.9.

It will be seen that instead of each lamp receiving the full supply voltage, the voltage is shared amongst all of the lamps in the series circuit. Furthermore, a break or open circuit in any one lamp would completely break the current flow and all the lamps would go out. An example of this form of wiring is in Christmas tree lighting where there may be 20 lamps, each rated at 12 V thus totalling 240 V connected to the 240 V supply.

> When lamps are connected in series, the voltage across them and hence the brightness will be inverse to their power ratings, that is, the higher the power rating the lower the voltage and hence the brilliance, the lower the rating the higher the voltage and therefore the brilliance.

EXAMPLE 2

Two lamps, rated at 240 V 60 W and 240 V 100 W respectively, are connected to a 240 V supply. Calculate the voltage across each (see Figure 3.9).

Using Ohm's law and power formula:
At 240 V the current taken by the 60 W lamp

$$I = \frac{W}{V} = \frac{60}{240} = \frac{1}{4}\,A$$

Similarly, the current taken by the 100 W lamp

$$= \frac{100}{240} = \frac{5}{12}\,A$$

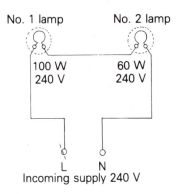

Figure 3.9 Lighting circuit of lamps connected in series.

From this, the resistance of the 60 W lamp

$$= \frac{V}{I} = \frac{240}{1/4} = 960\ \Omega$$

Similarly, the resistance of the 100 W lamp

$$= \frac{240}{5/12} = 576\ \Omega$$

When connected in series, the total resistance of the circuit is equal to the sum total of all the resistances so connected.

Total resistance $= (960 + 576) = 1536\ \Omega$

Circuit current $\quad I = \dfrac{V}{R} = \dfrac{240}{1536} = 0.156\ A$

Voltage across the 100 W lamp $= I \times R$
$$= 0.156 \times 576$$
$$= 90\ V$$

Voltage across the 60 W lamp $= I \times R$
$$= 0.156 \times 960$$
$$= 150\ V$$

Try other examples for series circuits where the voltage and power rating of the lamps are given.

BS 1363 socket outlet circuits

In order to supply the consumers' portable appliances by means of flexible cables, it is necessary to install socket outlets in convenient positions throughout the installation. The appliances can then be connected to the socket by a plug connected to the end of the flexible cable. The standard used for most installations is a three-terminal type live–neutral–earth socket rated at 13 A. The plug contains a fuse in the phase terminal to protect the flexible cable against excess current and these fuses can be obtained in 3 A, 5 A and 13 A ratings. These socket outlets are connected in parallel with each other to form a subcircuit and this circuit must be supplied from a separate subcircuit outlet.

I.E.E. Regulations quote two methods of wiring socket outlet circuits and detail the number of sockets that may be supplied by each method.

The first method is the radial circuit in which the sockets are supplied as in Figure 3.10.

The second method is the ring circuit in which the conductors are taken from the consumer unit to each socket in turn, but after the last socket, the conductors are returned to the same connection in the consumer unit, as in Figure 3.11.

Domestic distribution design

A domestic installation consisting of the following is to be wired in PVC twin and earth cable.

1. 8 lights, each controlled by 1 switch, and 2 lights, each controlled by 2 switches.
2. An immersion heater rated at 3 kW.
3. An electric cooker, total rating 12 kW, plus a socket outlet on the cooker control unit.
4. 12 × 13 A socket outlets.

The floor area is 95 m² and the voltage supply 240 V. By referring to the I.E.E. Regulations, the number of subcircuits required can be decided. It will be found that a minimum of three subcircuits will be required if the immersion heater is supplied from the socket outlet circuit. Although this is permitted, it is not good practice because it restricts the use of the other sockets.

Therefore, four subcircuits are to be used which will require the use of a four-way distribution fuse board for circuit protection and a double-pole switch as a means of isolation. For neatness and best use of space, the four fuses, the neutral bar, earth terminal and double-pole switch are all contained within a single unit known as a **consumer unit**.

The fuse ratings and the size of cables for each circuit must now be decided.

Fuse ratings

1. Lighting circuit
Each of the filaments lamps is deemed to be rated at 100 W so the total load is

$$10 \times 100 = \frac{1000 \text{ W}}{240 \text{ V}} = 4.2 \text{ A}$$

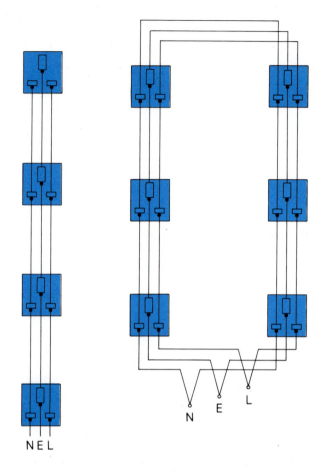

Figure 3.10 (left) Radial socket outlet circuit.
Figure 3.11 (right) Ring socket outlet circuit.

From the wiring tables, the minimum cable size is 1 mm² and the fuse size will be 5 A.

2. Immersion heater circuit

$$\text{Current demand of immersion heater} = \frac{3000 \text{ W}}{240 \text{ V}}$$
$$= 12.5 \text{ A}$$

Minimum size cable will be 1.5 mm² and the fuse size is 15 A.

3. Cooker circuit
For the cooker circuit loading, the I.E.E. Regulations allow a diversity factor to be applied as follows.

First 10 A + (30% of the remainder) + 5 A for the socket outlet

$$\text{Total load} = \frac{12\,000 \text{ W}}{240 \text{ V}} = 50 \text{ A}$$

Assumed current demand = 10 + (30% of 40) + 5
= 27 A

Minimum cable size will be 4 mm² and fuse size 30 A.

4. Ring circuit

Regulations state that one ring circuit is required for every 100 m² of floor area, which may supply any number of socket outlets. It also states that the minimum size of PVC twin and earth cable is 2.5 mm² with fuse protection of 30 A for the ring.

After a study of the Regulation requirements, it will be seen that the equipment at the consumer's intake terminal will be a four-way consumer unit provided with one 5 A, one 15 A and two 30 A

fuse-ways. Since the manufacturer applies a diversity factor to their main switch rating, it will be a standard 60 A double-pole switch.

In addition to this consumer unit, further switchgear and metering equipment are installed by the supply authority. Figure 3.12 shows a complete distribution and the theoretical wiring diagram. For simplicity at this stage, the earthing has been omitted (see Chapter 5).

Voltage drop

In all the above cable selections, only the current rating of the cable has been considered.

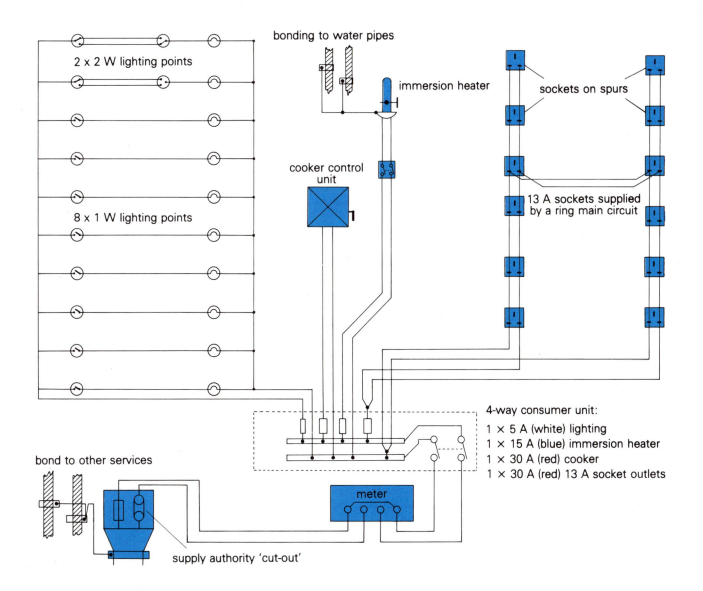

Figure 3.12 Theoretical diagram for domestic lighting and power.

Remember that the cable conductor has resistance and when it is carrying current, a drop in voltage will occur along its length of run.

Voltage drop = conductor current (A) × conductor resistance (Ω)

Because of this voltage drop, the voltage at the load is less than the incoming supply voltage. In view of this, the I.E.E. Regulations state that conductor sizes must be such that the voltage at any point on an installation does not drop by more than 4 per cent of the incoming voltage at the consumers' terminals. For an installation where the incoming voltage is 240 V, the maximum permissible volts drop is 9.6 V.

The 16th edition of the I.E.E. Regulations have increased the voltage drop on a consumer's installation from 2.5 per cent to 4 per cent of the incoming supply voltage.

Note: In addition to this the supply authority is permitted a tolerance of 6 per cent on the declared value of the incoming voltage.

The combination of these give a limit of 10 per cent voltage difference. This will appreciably affect the output of the consumers' machines and appliances.

Remember

$$\text{power } P = \frac{V^2}{R}$$

this means that the power will fall inversely as the square of the voltage where the resistance R remains constant.

EXAMPLE 3

An electric heater is rated at 3 kW on a 240 V supply. Calculate the power output if the supply falls by 10 per cent to 216 V.

$$\text{New power rating} = \frac{(216)^2}{(240)^2} \times 3 \text{ kW} = 2.43 \text{ kW}$$

Figures 3.13 to 3.15 show wiring diagrams for the conversion of a one-way to a two-way circuit, lighting in a long corridor and the use of an appliance simmerstat.

Note: An earth terminal must be provided at every terminal point of the wiring.

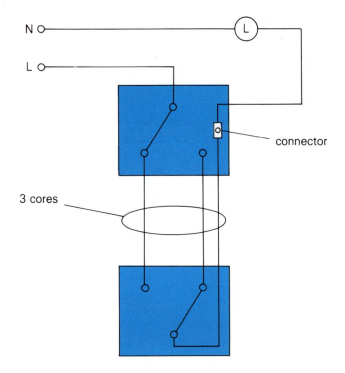

Figure 3.13 Conversion of one-way to two-way switching with three-core cable.

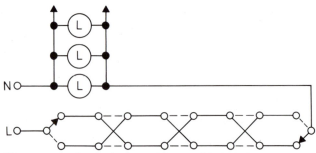

Note: an earth terminal must be provided at every terminal point of the wiring.

Figure 3.14 Lighting in a long corridor with several entrances and exits. Dotted lines show alternative switch positions.

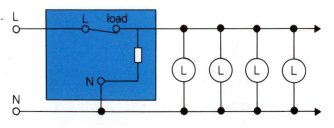

Figure 3.15 Use of a simmerstat for variable timing of lights.

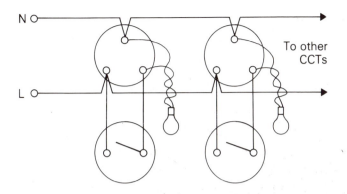

Figure 3.16 Three-plate ceiling rose method of 'lopping in' at terminals.

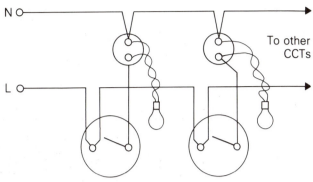

Figure 3.17 Looping method at switch position.

All joints in conductors on installations must be electrically and mechanically sound and available for inspection. The cable protection sheath must also enter the connection enclosure.

The normal method of achieving this is to joint at the accessory terminals known as **looping in** (see Figures 3.16 and 3.17).

It is also permitted to use joint or junction boxes but it is not easy to make them available without being 'eyesores'.

On all modern domestic installations the consumer's main switchgear for excess current protection, distribution and isolation is a consumer unit located at the incoming supply position.

All the circuit conductors are brought back to the unit for connection to the supply voltage.

All **phase** conductors are connected to their respective **fuses** or CB.

All **neutral** conductors are connected to the **neutral** block.

All c.p.c.s are connected to the **earth** block.

Although the neutral and earth blocks are of a solid brass bar, the circuit neutrals and c.p.c.s must be connected in the same order on the respective block as the live conductors are to the fuses or CBs. This is to enable any circuit to be completely disconnected from the supply without having to 'trace out' which conductors are which. In the sketch of the six-way unit note that the downstairs lighting circuits conductors are all connected to the respective No. 1 position at the terminations and so on.

These consumer units can also be obtained fitted with an **r.c.d.**s (residual current device) so that the whole of the installation is protected against any unbalance in L and N current which an earth leakage fault would produce. Figure 3.18 shows the internal wiring of a six-way consumer unit.

Heating effect

Because of the conductor resistance, there is also a heat effect on the conductor:

Heat = $(I^2 \times R)$ watts

This heat will have an effect on the cable insulation and, if excessive, will cause it to break down. The I.E.E. tables publish the maximum current that each type and size of cable can carry.

From these, it will be seen that the current rating depends upon the following factors:

1. ambient temperature (surrounding temperature);
2. types of protective equipment used (fuses and circuit breakers);
3. grouping of the circuits (the number of circuits running together in one enclosure, such as trunking or conduit);
4. disposition (position relative to other conductors and surfaces);
5. type of cable insulation and sheath.

I.E.E. Regulations deals with current ratings and voltage drops for cables and flexible cords based on 30°C.

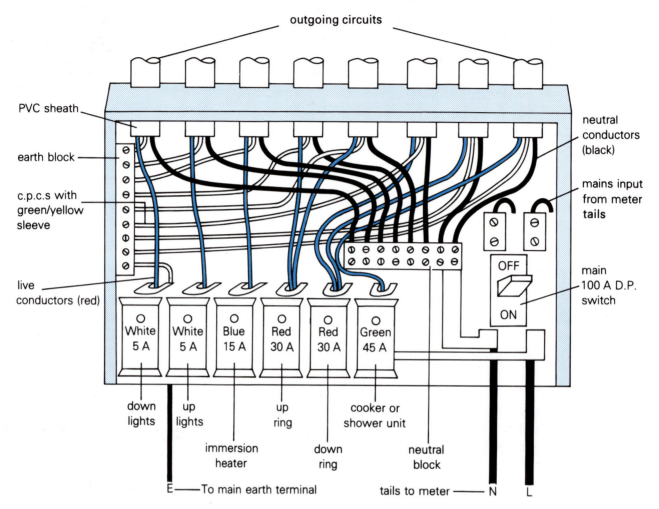

outgoing circuits

PVC sheath

earth block

c.p.c.s with
green/yellow
sleeve

live
conductors (red)

neutral
conductors
(black)

mains input
from meter
tails

OFF

ON

main
100 A D.P.
switch

White 5 A	White 5 A	Blue 15 A	Red 30 A	Red 30 A	Green 45 A

down
lights

up
lights

immersion
heater

up
ring

down
ring

cooker or
shower unit

neutral
block

E——To main earth terminal

tails to meter —— N   L

Figure 3.18 Internal wiring of a six-way consumer unit.

Procedure for selecting a cable

1. Choose the type of cable most suitable for that particular installation, bearing in mind the cost.
2. Determine the most suitable size of cable as follows.
   A) Calculate the design current of the circuit, I_B.
   B) Choose the type and the current rating, I_N of the circuit protective device.
   C) Divide I_N by the ambient temperature correction factors (C_a) if necessary. Note that the tables for current ratings are based on an ambient temperature of 30°C.
   D) Further divide by the grouping correction factor (C_g) if necessary.
   E) Divide again by the thermal insulation correction factor (C_i) if necessary when in contact with thermal insulation on one side and when completely surrounded by thermal in-

sulation. These correction factors are given in Appendix 4, I.E.E. Regulations. The result is the minimum current rating of the cable I_z. The standard size above this value is chosen from the relevant table in Appendix 9, I.E.E. Regulations.

Note: If the circuit protective device is a rewireable semi-enclosed fuse (BS 3036) a different table of ambient temperature correction factors applies as given in I.E.E. tables and there must be a further division of I_z by a factor of 0.725. Where circuit protective devices are H.B.C. (BS 88 or BS 1361) or circuit breakers (BS 3871) this note does not apply.

3. Finally, check that the voltage drop for the cable run is not too high. If it is, then the cable size will have to be further increased.

Volts drop = mA (given in tables in Appendix 9) × design current (A) × length of run (m)/1000.

I.E.E. Regulations Table 7A1. Single-core PVC-insulated cables, non-armoured, with or without sheath (COPPER CONDUCTORS)
Ambient temperature: 30°C. Conductor operating temperature: 70°C CURRENT-CARRYING CAPACITY (amperes): BS 6004, BS 6231, BS 6346

Conductor cross-sectional area	Reference method 4 (enclosed in conduit in thermally insulating wall etc.)		Reference method 3 (enclosed in conduit on a wall or in trunking etc.)		Reference method 1 (clipped direct)		Reference method 11 (on a perforated cable tray horizontal or vertical)		Reference method 12 (free air)		
									Horizontal flat spaced	Vertical flat spaced	Tre-foil
	2 cables, single-phase a.c. or d.c.	3 or 4 cables three-phase a.c.	2 cables, single-phase a.c. or d.c.	3 or 4 cables three-phase a.c.	2 cables, single-phase a.c. or d.c. flat and touching	3 or 4 cables three-phase a.c. flat and touching or trefoil	2 cables, single-phase a.c. or d.c. flat and touching	3 or 4 cables three-phase a.c. flat and touching or trefoil	2 cables, single-phase a.c. or d.c. or 3 cables three-phase a.c.	2 cables, single-phase a.c. or d.c. or 3 cables three-phase a.c.	3 cables tre-foil three phase a.c.
1	2	3	4	5	6	7	8	9	10	11	12
mm^2	A	A	A	A	A	A	A	A	A	A	A
1	11	10.5	13.5	12	15.5	14	–	–	–	–	–
1.5	14.5	13.5	17.5	15.5	20	18	–	–	–	–	–
2.5	19.5	18	24	21	27	25	–	–	–	–	–
4	26	24	32	28	37	33	–	–	–	–	–
6	34	31	41	36	47	43	–	–	–	–	–
10	46	42	57	50	65	59	–	–	–	–	–
16	61	56	76	68	87	79	–	–	–	–	–
25	80	73	101	89	114	104	126	112	146	130	110
35	99	89	125	110	141	129	156	141	181	162	137
50	119	108	151	134	182	167	191	172	219	197	167
70	151	136	192	171	234	214	246	223	281	254	216
95	182	164	232	207	284	261	300	273	341	311	264

Note: Where the conductor is to be protected by a semi-enclosed fuse to BS 3036, see Item 6.2 of Preface to Appendix 4, 16th Edition. The current-carrying capacities in columns 2 to 5 are also applicable to flexible cables to BS 6004 Table 1(c) and to 85°C heat resisting P.V.C. cables to BS 6231 where the cables are used in fixed installations.

EXAMPLE 4

A subcircuit is to supply a 3 kW heater. It is decided to use single-core copper PVC insulated cables run in a PVC conduit. The supply is 240 V, the ambient temperature is 30°C, the length of run is 20 m and the circuit is protected by a miniature circuit breaker. Determine

i) the design current of the circuit (I_B),
ii) the ratings of the miniature circuit breaker (I_N),
iii) the smallest permitted cable size.

i) $I_B \dfrac{W}{V} = \dfrac{3000}{240} = 12.5$ A

ii) Nearest standard size (above) circuit breaker = 15 A.

iii) From I.E.E. Table 7 AI, two 1.5 mm² single-core cables in conduit can carry 17.5 A and since no correction factors apply, this size is sufficient in current rating.

Check voltage drop
Maximum permissible voltage drop is 4% × 240 = 9.6 V.
From Table 7 B2, the actual voltage drop for this cable run = (Voltage drop (per A per m) × I × l) = 29 mV × 12.5 A × 20 m = 7250 mV = 7.25 V
This is the correct size.

EXAMPLE 5

A three-phase induction motor is to be supplied by a three-core PVC armoured cable with aluminium conductors from a T.P.N. distribution fuse board. The fuse board is supplied by a submain cable some distance from the main incoming supply substation. The motor cable is to be clipped closely with two other cables to a cable tray, which passes through an area where the ambient temperature is 40°C. The length of this run is 60 m and H.B.C. fuses (BS 88) are to be used.

I.E.E. Regulations Table 7B2. Voltage drop: (per ampere per metre). Conductor operating temperature: 70°C

Conductor cross-sectional area 1	Two-core cable d.c. 2		Two-core cable single-phase a.c. 3			Three-or four-core cable three-phase a.c. 4		
mm²	mV		mV			mV		
1	44		44			38		
1.5	29		29			25		
2.5	18		18			15		
4	11		11			9.5		
6	7.3		7.3			6.4		
10	4.4		4.4			3.8		
16	2.8		2.8			2.4		
		r	x	z	r	x	z	
25	1.75	1.75	0.170	1.75	1.50	0.145	1.50	
35	1.25	1.25	0.165	1.25	1.10	0.145	1.10	
50	0.93	0.93	0.165	0.94	0.80	0.140	0.81	
70	0.63	0.63	0.160	0.65	0.55	0.140	0.57	
95	0.46	0.47	0.155	0.50	0.41	0.135	0.43	
120	0.36	0.38	0.155	0.41	0.33	0.135	0.35	
150	0.29	0.30	0.155	0.34	0.26	0.130	0.29	
185	0.23	0.25	0.150	0.29	0.21	0.130	0.25	
240	0.180	0.190	0.150	0.24	0.165	0.130	0.21	
300	0.145	0.155	0.145	0.21	0.135	0.130	0.185	
400	0.105	0.115	0.145	0.185	0.100	0.125	0.160	

Using I.E.E. tables determine the minimum size of cable that should be used if the power input to the motor is 23 kW, it is working at a power factor of 0.8 and a 4 V drop in the cable is to be assumed. The incoming supply is 415 V.

Sub-station	$\dfrac{(16.6-4) = 12.6 \text{ V drop}}{\text{submain cable}}$	Fuse board

Fuse board	$\dfrac{60 \text{ m} \quad 4 \text{ V drop}}{\text{motor cable}}$	Motor

Design current $I_B = \dfrac{P \text{ (W)}}{\sqrt{3}\, V_L \cos \phi}$

$\qquad = \dfrac{23 \times 1000}{1.732 \times 415 \times 0.8}$

$\qquad = 40 \text{ A}$

Current rating (I_N) nearest standard fuse size is 60 A. Correction factors: 0.7 = grouping factor; 0.87 = ambient temperature factor.

Hence cable current rating $I_z = \dfrac{60}{0.7 \times 0.87} = 98.5 \text{ A}$

From I.E.E. tables a 50 mm² three-core cable has a rating of 105 A.

Check voltage drop
From tables, actual volts drop in motor cable

$= \dfrac{1.3 \times 40 \times 60}{1000} \text{ V}$

$= 3.12 \text{ V}$

Since a 4 V drop is allowed, this cable size would be suitable.
Note: Maximum permitted volts drops between substation and motor: $= 4\% \times 415 = 16.6$ V.

This means a maximum volts drop of $16.6 - 4 = 12.6$ V is allowable on the submain cable.

EXAMPLE 6

A 6 kW storage heater is to be wired from a 240 V supply by two single core PVC insulated cables drawn into a conduit which is clipped to a wall.

If the ambient temperature if 45°C and the circuit protective device is a semi-enclosed fuse BS 3036. Determine
i) load current,
ii) fuse rating,
iii) correction factors,
iv) current rating of cable,
v) cable size,
vi) volts drop on the circuit as the length of run is 30 metres.

i) Load current $= \dfrac{(6 \times 1000)\ \text{W}}{240\ \text{V}} = 25\ \text{A}$

The following information is obtained from the I.E.E. tables.

ii) Nearest fuse size above 25 A = 30 A.
iii) Ambient temperature factor = 0.84.
     Semi-enclosed fuse = 0.725
iv) Current rating of cable

$= \dfrac{\text{protective device rating}}{\text{rating correction factors}}$

$= \dfrac{30\ \text{A}}{0.84 \times 0.725} = 50\ \text{A}$

v) Cable size = 10 mm²
vi) From the formula mV per ampere per metre

$$\text{Volts drop} = \frac{4 \times 25 \times 30}{1000} = 3\ \text{V}$$

EXAMPLE 7

A 240 V domestic stove is fitted with four 2 kW rings, one 3 kW oven and one 1.5 kW grill.
The control unit has a 13 A socket outlet. It is to be wired with a PVC sheathed twin and earth cable from an eight-way consumer unit fitted with m.c.b.s.
The cable is grouped with seven others of similar type and runs partly in the loft where there is fibre glass insulation touching one side of the cable. Determine

i) load current,
ii) rating of protective device,
iii) rating factors to be applied,
iv) current rating of the circuit cable,
v) size of cable required.

$\text{Total load} = \dfrac{(4 \times 2) + (1 \times 3) + 1 \times 1.5)\ \text{kW}}{240\ \text{V}}$

$= 52\ \text{A}$

i) **Note**: For a domestic stove a diversity to this may be applied. See Table 3.
   First 10 A + (30% of remainder) + 5 A for socket outlet = 10 + (30% × 52) + 5 = 27.6 A
ii) Nearest size of m.c.b. (above) = 30 A
iii) Rating or correction factors (a) 0.5 grouping, (b) 1 for m.c.b., (c) 0.75 for thermal insulation, (d) 0.94 for ambient temperature.
iv) Circuit current rating

$= \dfrac{30\ \text{A}}{0.5 \times 1 \times 0.75 \times 0.94}\ 85\ \text{A}$

v) Nearest cable size (above this) = 16 mm².
Note: Again information for (ii), (iii), (v) is from I.E.E. tables.
Note how the application of correction factor greatly increases the size of cable required for given load.

However, it is rarely that all these conditions occur at the same time. By carefully choosing the cable route and the type of protective device, the cable sizes can be reduced.

In order to assist and simplify the calculation the 16th edition have published values of current ratings, cable sizes, types of protective device, means of earthing and lengths of circuits for conventional radial and ring circuits using 13 A socket outlets.

The condition for the use of these values are as follows.

1. The installation is earthed by a T.N.C.S. system. This is where the metallic sheath or armour of the supply cable is used as the earth return conductor and whose value of Z_E is not less than 0.8 Ω.
2. It is earthed by T.N.S. (P.M.E. combined N and E return) whose value is not less than 0.35 Ω.
3. Sheathed cable is used, clipped or embedded in plaster.
4. Cables are run in a conduit or trunking.
5. The ambient temperature does not exceed 30°C.
6. Grouping is limited to four circuits for semi-enclosed fuse or six circuits for m.c.b.s.

For more details see I.E.E. Regulations, Table 7. Under the above requirements any unlimited number may be installed.

Notes on application of rating factors

1. **Diversity** By application of these factors to the respective circuits, the current ratings of switchgear and cables and hence the cost may be considerably reduced.

I.E.E. Regulation Table 1B.   Allowances for diversity

Purpose of final circuit fed from conductors or switchgear to which diversity applies	Type of premises		
	Individual household installations, including individual dwellings of a block	Small shops, stores, offices and business premises	Small hotels, boarding houses, guest houses, etc.
1. Lighting	66% of total current demand	90% of total current demand	75% of total current demand
2. Heating and power (but see 3 and 8 below)	100% of total current demand up to 10 amperes + 50% of any current demand in excess of 10 amperes	100% f.l. of largest appliance + 75% f.l. of remaining appliances	100% f.l. of largest appliance + 80% f.l. of second largest appliance + 60% f.l. of remaining appliances
3. Cooking appliances	10 amperes + 30% f.l. of connected cooking appliances in excess of 10 amperes + 5 amperes if socket outlet incorporated in unit	100% f.l. of largest appliance + 80% f.l. of second largest appliance + 60% f.l. of remaining appliances	100% f.l. of largest appliance + 80% f.l. of second largest appliance + 60% f.l. of remaining appliances
4. Motors (other than lift motors which are subject to special consideration)		100% f.l. of largest motor + 80% f.l. of second largest motor 60% f.l. of remaining motors	100% f.l. of largest motor + 50% f.l. of remaining motors
5. Water heaters (instantaneous type)*	100% f.l. of largest appliance + 100% f.l. of second largest appliance + 25% f.l. of remaining appliances	100% f.l. of largest appliance + 100% f.l. of second largest appliance + 25% f.l. of remaining appliances	100% f.l. of largest appliance + 100% f.l. of second largest appliance + 25% f.l. of remaining appliances
6. Water heaters (thermostatically controlled)	No diversity allowable[+]		
7. Floor warming installations	No diversity allowable[+]		
8. Thermal storage space heating installations	No diversity allowable[+]		
9. Standard arrangements of final circuits in accordance with Appendix 5	100% of current demand of largest circuit + 40% of current demand of every other circuit	100% of current demand of largest circuit + 50% of current demand of every other circuit	
10. Socket-outlets other than those included in 9 above and stationary equipment other than those listed above	100% of current demand of largest point of utilisation + 40% of current demand of every other point of utilisation	100% of current demand of largest point of utilisation + 75% of current demand of every other point of utilisition	100% of current demand of largest point of utilisation + 75% of current demand of every point in main rooms (dining rooms etc.) + 40% of current demand of every other point of utilisation

  * For the purpose of this Table an instantaneous water heater is deemed to be a water heater of any loading which heats water only while the tap is turned on and therefore uses electricity intermittently.

  [+] It is important to ensure that the distribution boards are of sufficient rating to take the total load connected to them without the application of any diversity.

I.E.E. Regulations Table 9A.   Final circuits using 13 A BS 1363 socket outlets

| Type of circuit | Excess current protection device | | Minimum conductor size (mm²) | | Maximum floor area served (m²) |
| | | | Copper rubber or PVC cables | Copper m.i.m.s | |
	Rating (A)	Type			
Ring	30 or 32	Any	2.5	1.5	100
Radial	30 or 32	Cartridge fuse or circuit breaker	4	2.5	50
Radial	20	Any	2.5	1.5	20

2. **Grouping** Careful study of the cable runs must be made to avoid grouping a lot of cables together. This will reduce cable size.
3. **Temperature** Again by routing cables, where possible, away from high ambient temperature it will mean a reduction in cable size.

Note: If items 2 and 3 have to be applied together, for example where a lot of cables are grouped in a high temperature, a very large increase in cable sizes is required. This can double or even treble the size that would be required if it was only the current to be considered.

4. **Type of excess current protection** This will considerably reduce the cable size and result in savings of costs particularly on the longer lengths of cable runs.
5. **Thermal insulation** Again careful choice of cable runs must be made to avoid the cables being completely surrounded. From the above it can be seen that the selection of cables routes are of utmost importance in order to save costs.

Diversity factor
This factor takes into account the fact that all the total connected loads supplied by a cable will not be in use at the same time.
Note: Socket outlet circuits and domestic cookers have this factor applied.
It can be defined as:

$$\frac{\text{current under normal load conditions}}{\text{total connected load current}}$$

The main application of the diversity factor is to submain cables which supply distribution boards to which several outgoing subcircuits are connected.

Another example from the I.E.E. Regulations, which gives guidance on the application of the diversity factor, states that in assessing the current demand of a distribution board which supplies six 30 A socket outlet ring main circuits, the following diversity factor may be applied:

Full current of the first circuit plus 50% of the remaining circuits.

Hence current demand $= 30 + (50\% \times 150)$ A
$= 105$ A

This results in considerable savings in installation materials and labour costs. See I.E.E. Regulations B1 for more detail.

Distribution on larger installations

When the sustained power demand of an installation is in excess of around 12 kW, it becomes necessary for the incoming supply to be of the three-phase four-wire (T.P.N.) type in order to reduce the currents and hence cable sizes, on both the supply and consumer sides. The nature of this supply and its distribution have been previously explained. It is important that the load currents are equally divided over the three phases, that is, they present a balanced demand to the incoming supply. Another reason is that in a T.P.N. supply, the neutral conductor only carries the out of balance current.

If there is perfect balance, the neutral carries zero current representing a saving in conductor size and power loss.

EXAMPLE 8

A T.P.N. supply has the following currents all operating at unity power factor in its phase conductors:

RED – 200 A, YELLOW – 100 A, BLUE – 150 A. Determine the current in the **neutral** conductor.

Since the power factors are similar, and the currents are 120° apart, then the lowest value can be subtracted from all three without affecting the balance. This leaves only two currents of 100 A and 50 A with a phase angle of 120° between them. Draw these to scale. (These can be drawn to scale in a phasor diagram, and the resultant of the parallelogram formed will be the value of the neutral current.) See Figure 3.19.

Note: If the power factors of the currents are not similar, this simplified method does not apply.

The design of individual items of equipment to operate on T.P.N. and T.P. supplies is such that the currents in each phase are equal, that is, the load is balanced. It is the responsibility of the installation designer to ensure that the S.P.N. loads are balanced as near as practicable over the T.P.N. supply.

> As a safety measure, the I.E.E. Regulations state that when S.P.N. loads are supplied by different phases of the supply and 415 V is present, the areas served must be more than 2 m apart. Where this is not possible, a warning notice must be displayed stating that the line voltage (415 V) is present.

Study the I.E.E. Regulation which applies to the presence of the line voltage.

Power factor

At this stage, it will be helpful to introduce the term **power factor** (pf). Simply explained, it is the factor which takes into account the fact that not all the current being carried by the cables in an a.c. circuit delivers power to the load.

The total current is made up of two components:

(a) the **power component** kW, and
(b) the **reactive component** kilovolt-amperes (kvar).

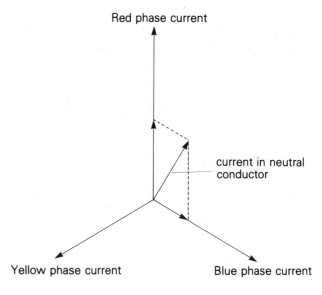

Figure 3.19 Phasor diagram of T.P.N. supply.

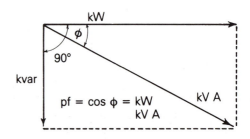

Figure 3.20 Derivation of power factor.

The phase angle between these two is 90° so that

$$\text{total kV A} = \sqrt{(\text{kW})^2 + (\text{kvar})^2}$$

See Figure 3.20.

> The power factor is defined as the ratio of power (kW) to the product of voltage and current in the circuit
>
> $$\text{pf} = \frac{\text{kW}}{\text{kV A}}$$

Its value is equal to the cosine of the phase angle between the voltage and the current, referred to as cos ø. The power in a single-phase (S.P.N.) circuit:

$$P = V_L I_L \cos \phi \text{ (watts)}$$

$$I_L = \frac{P}{V_L \cos \phi} \text{A}$$

The power in a three-phase (T.P.N.) circuit:

$$P = \sqrt{3}\ V_{\text{L}} I_{\text{L}} \cos \phi \text{ (watts)}$$

$$I_{\text{L}} = \frac{P}{\sqrt{3}\ V_{\text{L}} \cos \phi}\text{A}$$

where P = power in watts,
          V_{L} = line voltage,
          I_{L} = line current,
          $\cos \phi$ = *pf* of circuit being supplied.

Calculate a few examples of the appropriate line current of three-phase and single-phase loads at various power ratings and pf values.

For a given value of power consumption by a circuit or equipment the current rating will change with the change in power factor.

EXAMPLE 9

A machine takes a power of 20 kW. If the supply voltage is 250 V. Calculate the current it will take when it is operating at a pf of (i) 0.5, (ii) 0.75 and (iii) unity (1).

$$P = V\ I\ pf\ (\cos \phi)$$

i) $I = \dfrac{P}{V\ pf} = \dfrac{20 \times 1000}{250 \times 0.5} = 160\text{ A}$

ii) $I = \dfrac{20 \times 1000}{250 \times 0.75} = 107\text{ A}$

iii) $I = \dfrac{20 \times 1000}{250 \times 1} = 80\text{ A}$

Note: It is the power component of the current which is required by the load to do the work. The reactive component simply oscillates between the supply and the load causing I^2R loss in the supply cables.

A.c. equipment which possesses inductance, that is, coils of wire, are rated in V A or kV A. It will be seen in Chapter 10 that the pf of a circuit can be improved by connecting capacitors in the circuit, usually in parallel with the equipment itself.

The basic theory of inductance and capacitance is explained in Chapter 2.

> **Advantages of a three-phase supply system**
> - Because of the higher voltage it will reduce current for a given load.

> - It will produce a rotating magnetic field when connected to a three-phase motor stator winding.
> - With the introduction of the neutral (N) conductor on the supply transformer it enables two separate systems (a) single-phase and neutral (S.P.N.) and (b) three-phase neutral T.P.N. to be obtained.

Economy

EXAMPLE 10

Two motors each have a 12 kV A rating.
No. 1 is a 240 V S.P.N. motor connected to the single-phase supply;
No. 2 is a 415 V T.P. motor connected to the three-phase supply.
Calculate the sum total current in all supply conductors of both supplies (Figure 3.21).

For no. 1

$$I = \frac{V\,A}{V} \times 2 = \frac{12\,000}{240} \times 2 = (50 \times 2)\text{ A} = 100\text{ A}$$

For no. 2

$$I_{\text{L}} = \frac{V\,A}{\sqrt{3}\ V_{\text{L}}} \times 3 = \frac{12\,000}{1.732 \times 415} \times 3$$

$$= (16.7 \times 3)\text{ A} = 50\text{ A}$$

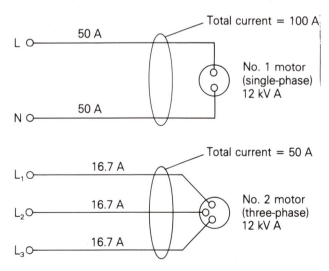

Figure 3.21 Reduction of conductor sizes in three-phase and single-phase supplies.

Note: When three S.P.N. loads of equal rating (that is, balanced load) are supplied from a T.P.N. system there is a 50 per cent reduction in total supply current for the same load demand.

Loads of different power factors

> The total load demand of loads operating at different values of power factor cannot be calculated by arithmetic addition. The loads must be added vectorially by the use of phasor diagrams.

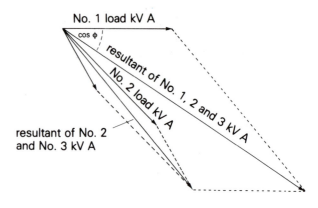

Figure 3.22 Phasor diagram of three loads at varying power factors.

EXAMPLE 11

The following three loads are connected to a 415 V three-phase supply:

  i) 40 kW operating at **unity** pf,
 ii) 50 kV A operating at 0.8 pf **lagging**,
iii) 30 kV A operating at 0.6 pf **lagging**.

If these three loads are connected as subcircuits to a distribution board, determine the line current in the submain cable supplying the board.

These three supply kV A loads may be drawn to scale and phase angle values and the resultant kV A value and phase angle measured. See Figures 3.22 and 3.23.

Or, alternatively, they may be calculated by the following method:

No. 1 load kV A $= \dfrac{kW}{pf} = \dfrac{40}{1} = 40$

$$
\begin{aligned}
\text{Power or horizontal component} &= 40 \cos \phi \\
&= 40 \times 1 \\
&= 40 \text{ kW}
\end{aligned}
$$

$$
\begin{aligned}
\text{Reactive vertical component} &= 40 \sin \phi \\
&= 40 \times 0 \\
&= 0
\end{aligned}
$$

No. 2 load kV A = 50

$$
\begin{aligned}
\text{Power or horizontal component} &= 50 \cos \phi \\
&= 50 \times 0.8 \\
&= 40 \text{ kW}
\end{aligned}
$$

$$
\begin{aligned}
\text{Reactive or vertical component} &= 50 \sin \phi \\
&= 50 \times 0.6 \\
&= 30 \text{ kvar}
\end{aligned}
$$

LAG

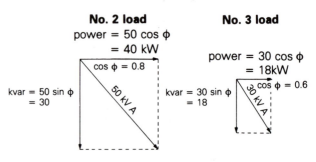

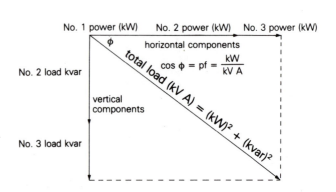

Figure 3.23 Determination of total kV A.

No. 3 load kV A = 30

$$
\begin{aligned}
\text{Power or horizontal component} &= 30 \cos \phi \\
&= 30 \times 0.6 \\
&= 18 \text{ kW}
\end{aligned}
$$

$$
\begin{aligned}
\text{Reactive or vertical component} &= 30 \sin \phi \\
&= 30 \times 0.8 \\
&= 24 \text{ kvar}
\end{aligned}
$$

LAG

All the power, or horizontal components can now be added arithmetically:

Therefore, total power component
$$= (40 + 40 + 18) = 98 \text{ kW}$$

Again, the reactive or vertical components can be added arithmetically:

Therefore the total reactive component
$$= (0 + 30 + 24) = 54 \text{ kvar}.$$

$$\text{Total load kV A} = \sqrt{98^2 + 54^2}$$
$$= 112$$

$$\text{Line current } I_{\text{L}} = \frac{kVA \times 1000}{\sqrt{3}\ V_{\text{L}}} = \frac{112 \times 1000}{1.732 \times 415}$$
$$= 156 \text{ A}$$

High voltage intake procedure to large buildings

Heavy industry is normally supplied at either 11 kV or 33 kV three-phase 50 Hz.

Hospitals and medium-sized industrial buildings are usually supplied at 11 kV three-phase 50 Hz.

Depending upon the size of the installation, one or more supply feeder cable will be bought into one or more substation. The substation is built to house the H.V. equipment, step-down transformers and the consumers' lower voltage switchgear. The substation will also contain meters and protection equipment (circuit breakers, fuses, etc.).

Figure 3.24 shows a typical substation layout of the switchgear and transformers for a medium-sized industrial or hospital building.

The actual intake position would be decided in conjunction with the supply authority. The most economic position would be as near to the centre of the loads as possible in order to reduce the length of the cable runs and hence power loss and the voltage drop. Cables are often contained in earthenware pipes within the substation, or in concrete ducts in the floor, cast *in situ*. See Figure 4.12.

Substation construction

The substation should be of fireproof construction, well ventilated and dry. Adequate space should be allowed for moving equipment about and provision should be made to limit the spread of fire in the event of the escape of burning oil. An adequate method of achieving this is to place oil-filled equipment above a pit filled with ballast or graded chippings which tend to absorb leaking oil.

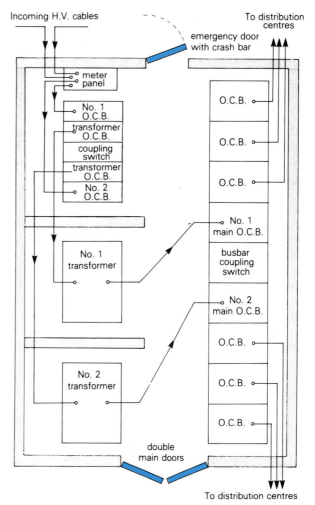

Figure 3.24 Typical substation layout: high voltage, three-phase incoming supply, lower voltage three-phase and neutral (T.P.N.) to distribution centres.

The floor should slope away from switchgear (the gradient being not less then 1 m in 100 m) towards a sump so that in the event of water getting into the substation, it will run away from switchgear. The sump must not be connected with the town drainage, which could lead to problems of flooding or the build-up of sewer gas. Windows should be located high up the walls and glass should be unbreakable. Doors should be of solid construction and kept locked, keys should be retained by a responsible person and the supply authority. Emergency doors must be fitted with crash barriers.

A notice to explain the correct treatment for electric shock should be displayed. Emergency lights and automatic fire extinguishers (CO_2) should be available. (See the Factories Act sections 30, 31 and 32.)

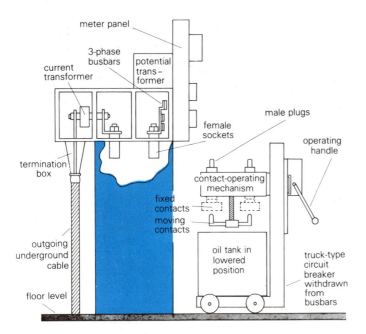

Figure 3.25 Construction of a high voltage oil-immersed circuit breaker.

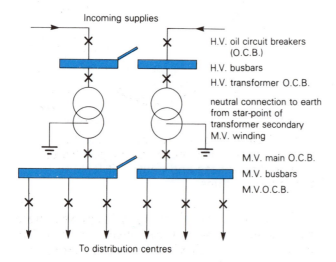

Figure 3.26 Two-feed ring main distribution system.

Substation equipment

High voltage switchgear
Figure 3.25 shows the basic arrangement of a typical high voltage oil-immersed circuit breaker which is constructed so that live parts are screened by earthed metal. Individual units can be bolted together so as to form a compact bank of switchgear. To remove the truck containing the oil-immersed switchgear, the switch-off button is pressed, the interlocking lever is put in the isolated or earthed position and the tank lowered by the winding handle. Maintenance may now be carried out on the switchgear. To replace, the tank is raised, the truck is rolled into position and the circuit breaker raised on to the busbars. The interlock is held in the closed position and the circuit breaker is reset. It should be noted that operating contacts in mineral insulating oil is much more effective than in air at atmospheric pressure, since the oil has a much higher dielectric strength. This means that for a given gap between contacts, air breaks down and becomes conductive at a considerably lower voltage than oil. Therefore, by using oil in a tank, the contacts need less space to extinguish the arc and therefore the tank is more compact.

Note: Because of excessive arcing produced by a d.c. current, oil would become severely carbonised and therefore oil circuit breakers are not used for d.c. supplies.

High voltage air-break circuit breaker
Special air-break circuit breakers have been developed for high voltage circuits. For voltages of 11 kV and above, air-blast circuit breakers can be used. These are so arranged that a blast of compressed air is used to extinguish arcs automatically when the contacts are opened.

Busbar coupling switches
These are usually 'off load' triple-pole air-break switches. Interlocks are normally provided to prevent the switch being operated on load. The purpose of these is that in the event of a loss of supply on one feeder cable or a fault in one of the transformers, they can be operated so that a supply may be maintained to vital equipment. A study of Figure 3.26 will show this.

The type of cables and methods of installation going out from oil-filled circuit breakers (O.C.B.) to the distribution centres within the building, and the type of cable and wiring systems going out from the distribution centre to the current-using equipment is explained in Chapter 4.

Note: The two-feeder ring main system for the incoming H.V. supplies ensured that in the event of a power failure on any one of the supplies, essential loads may be supplied by the operation of the busbar coupling switches. Figure 3.27 shows the layout of a circuit on large premises.

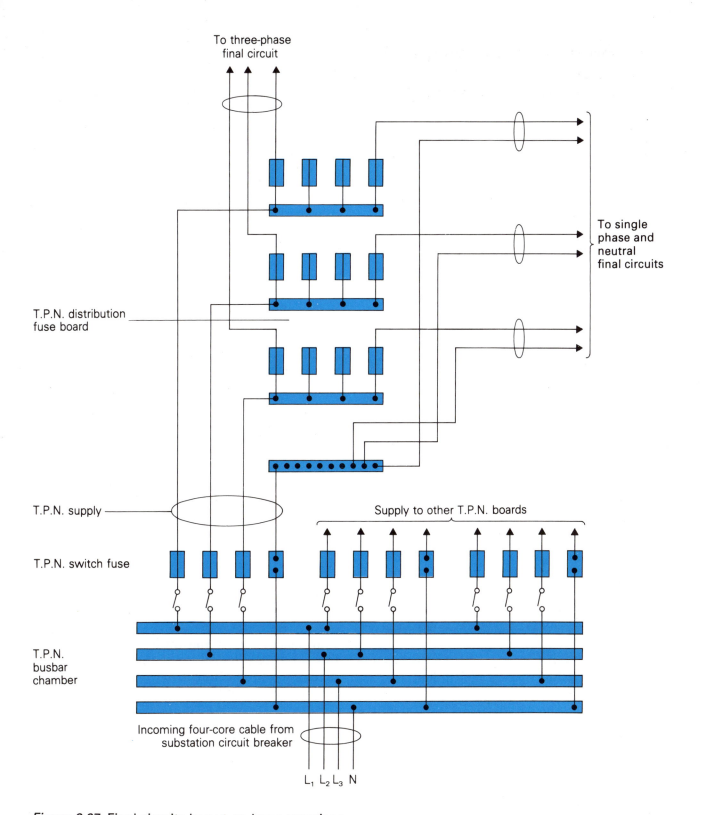

To three-phase
final circuit

To single
phase and
neutral
final circuits

T.P.N. distribution
fuse board

T.P.N. supply

Supply to other T.P.N. boards

T.P.N. switch fuse

T.P.N.
busbar
chamber

Incoming four-core cable from
substation circuit breaker

L_1 L_2 L_3 N

Figure 3.27 Final circuits layout on large premises.

Distribution on building and construction sites (temporary installation)

When a construction or building site is being considered, the supply authority will have to be notified of the following details:

1. type of supply needed for the construction work,
2. total load when the building is completed,
3. position of incoming supply, and
4. type of metering required.

The distribution equipment used during the construction work should have the following properties.

1. It must be flexible in use so that it may be moved from site to site for further contracts.
2. It must be suitable for transporting and for safe storage.
3. It must be able to withstand rough usage and be completely safe in operation.

Code of Practice BS 4363 details the features of manufacture of this equipment.

Distribution voltages

Application	Voltage
1. Heavy fixed plant, i.e. pumps, compressors	415 V three-phase (T.P.)
2. Moveable plant supplied by a trailing cable, i.e. heavy hoists and cranes	415 V three-phase (T.P.)
3. General fixed installations, i.e. site offices	240 V single-phase (S.P.N.)
4. Fixed floodlights	240 V single-phase (S.P.N.)
5. Portable hand tools	110 V three-phase (T.P.) 63 V to earth or 110 V single-phase (S.P.N.) 55 V to earth
6. Site lighting (except flood)	110 V (S.P.N.) 55 V to earth
7. Portable handlamps (general use)	110 V (S.P.N.) 55 V to earth
8. Portable handlamps (confined and damp situations)	50 or 25 V single-phase (S.P.N.)

Circuit protection

General protection must be provided on all circuits against excessive current and earth faults. The rating of the fuse and circuit breakers must allow **discrimination** in operation. Discrimination is explained in Chapter 5.

Earthing

All earthing must be in accordance with I.E.E. Regulations and, because of the lower voltage for some circuits, tests should be carried out to ensure sufficiently low earth loop impedance values for the fault current to operate the overcurrent protective devices.

Monitored earth leakage protection

This is required when flexible cables are used to supply moveable plant to ensure the continuing efficiency of the earth leakage protection. If the protective conductor in the cable becomes damaged it will not provide a sound return path for the fault current to operate the leakage device. See Figure 3.28.

Operation of Figure 3.28

Pressing the button causes a circulating current to flow through the pilot conductor and through the protective conductor. This energises the relay coil and causes it to close, thus activating the main triple-pole contactor tripping coil, causing the contactor to close and connect the load. If the earth conductor was broken, the circuit would not be complete and it would not be possible to obtain a supply to the equipment. If the earth circuit should be broken in use, again the supply would be cut off. The relay coil operates on d.c. so that the diode protects against short circuits in the cable.

Plug socket outlets and couplers

On industrial installations plugs and socket outlets of more robust construction are used to supply portable equipment using ring or radial circuits.

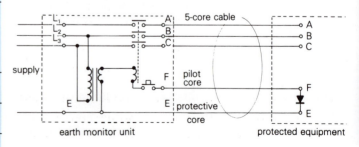

Figure 3.28 Earth monitor unit.

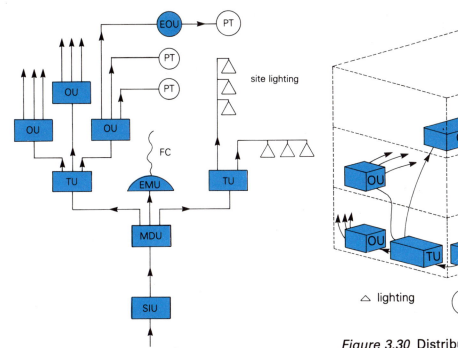

Figure 3.29 Construction site distribution.

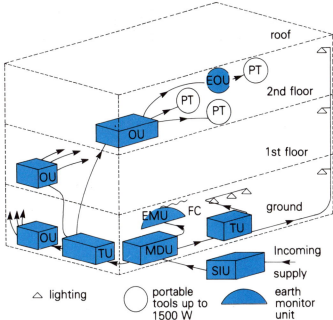

Figure 3.30 Distribution system of multi-storey construction site.

One type manufactured to BS 196 is of a 16 A rating of a two-pole with the metal body forming a scraping earth connection. When it is supplied from a centre tapped step-down transformer the plug will be fitted with fuses on both live poles. Any number of outlets can be wired on a radial or ring final subcircuit provided that the circuit protection is no greater than 32 A.

Another type manufactured to BS 4343 is available in 16, 32, 63 and 125 A ratings for use on larger equipment and three-phase supplies.

The 32, 63 and 125 A sizes must be supplied using a final subcircuit for each one.

The plugs and sockets are fitted with offset keys and keyways so that they can be inserted only into the correct voltage supplies.

Colour codings for the voltages are given in the text. BS 4363 states that all the above devices operating at 110 V are coloured YELLOW. The following colour code should also be used: 25 V – VIOLET, 50 V – WHITE, 240 V – BLUE, 415 V – RED.

Typical distribution system

Figure 3.29 shows a typical site distribution using units complying with BS 4363, while Figure 3.30 shows a typical arrangement in a multi-storey building.

The key to Figure 3.29 and 3.30 is as follows:

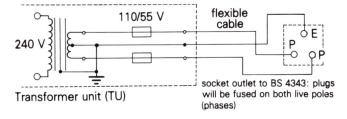

Figure 3.31 Transformer unit.

SIU   Supply incoming unit – this houses the supply authority main switchgear and meters and provides one only outgoing circuit.

SIDU   Supply incoming and distribution unit – this has facilities for several outgoing circuits at 415 V three-phase and 240 V single-phase.

MDU   Main distribution unit – contains equipment for site distribution at 415 V three-phase and 240 V single-phase.

TU   Transformer unit – providing 110 V three-phase with 63 V to earth or 110 V single-phase with 55 V to earth or both supplies. See Figure 3.31.

OU   Outlet unit – for supply and protecting subcircuits operating at 110 V, it is fed from a 32 A supply.

EOU   Extension socket outlet – for the supply and protection of subcircuits operating at 110 V single-phase. This unit is fed from a 16 A supply.

FC Flexible cable – supplying transportable equipment.
EMU Earth monitoring unit (see Figure 3.28).

■ CHECK YOUR UNDERSTANDING

● High voltages are used for power transmission from power stations in order to reduce current, and hence reduce cable sizes and costs.
● Transformers are static economical means of reducing the high transmission voltage to consumer requirements.
● Three-phase, neutral (T.P.N.) supplies are used by larger industrial and commercial consumers. Single-phase, neutral (S.P.N.) are for smaller and domestic consumers.
● The neutral conductor is connected to earth at the supply transformer to stabilise voltages and give protection against electric shock.
● Consumers' switchgear provides protection against excess current flow, electric shock and distribution to circuits.
● Socket outlets are supplied by ring or by radial circuits, lighting by 'looping in' or by three-plate ceiling rose methods of connection.
● Cable sizes for circuits are calculated by the application of rating factors for grouping, thermal insulation, diversity, ambient temperature and voltage drop.
● Power factor (pf) is the ratio of watts to volt-amperes.

$$pf = \frac{W}{V\,A}$$

● Power in a.c. circuits:

Single phase $P = VI \times pf$.
Three-phase $P = \sqrt{3}\,V_L I_L \times pf$.

● A high value of power factor reduces the current, and hence reduces cable size and costs for the supply of a given power load.
● Loads of different power factors are to be added vectorially.
● Substation construction should be fireproof, well ventilated and have provision for the escape of any oil leakage.
● Installations for a construction site should be provided with reduced voltage supplies, plugs and socket outlets to BS 4363 with colour codings for the different voltages.

1 A new cooker (stove) connected by a long twin and E multicore cable to a consumer unit became 'live' when switched on, although tests showed no faults on the cooker itself and L, C, and E were properly connected on its terminal block. Give a reason for this condition with a full explanation.

2 i) Explain the advantages of alternating current for transmission of power.
 ii) Determine the power loss in the conductors whose total resistance is 0.1 Ω when 100 kW are supplied at a voltage of (a) 240 V, (b) 33 kV.

3 A 550 V four-wire star connected balanced load takes line current of 150 A. State:
 i) the current in the neutral wire,
 ii) the current in each phase of the load,
 iii) the voltage across each phase of the load, and
 iv) show a phasor diagram of the relationship between the voltages of the supply.
 v) State the effect of a break (open circuit) in the neutral conductor.

4 A workshop is supplied from a 415/240 V four-wire a.c. supply.
 i) Explain the advantages of this over a single-phase system.
 ii) It is required to measure the power factor (pf) of a single-phase motor in the workshop.
   a) Calculate the pf if the readings on the instruments are 6 A, 240 V and 1080 W respectively.
 Note: Instrument connections are shown later.
   b) Show a connection diagram for (a).

5 i) State the reason and the economics of 'balancing' single-phase load on three-phase four-wire supply.
 ii) Three single-phase loads of 50 A each are supplied by
   a) three separate single-phase supplies,
   b) a three-phase and neutral supply.
Make circuit diagrams of these supplies and loads and mark the currents in each of the conductors in each case.

6 Explain the effects of a break (open circuit) in the live conductor of a final ring circuit on
 i) the appliances connected to the ring;
 ii) the currents in the (a) **phase** conductor, (b) **neutral** conductor, and (c) excess current device.

iii) if the break occurred close or at the point of origin of the circuit, explain any danger that this would present.

7   i) State the meaning of the connecting of electric lamps in (a) **series** and (b) **parallel**.

   ii) Give **one** application where each method could be used to advantage, giving the reasons.

  iii) Two lamps rated at 100 W, 240 V and 25 W, 240 V respectively are connected in (a) series, and (b) parallel, to a 240 V supply. Determine in each case the total current consumption and the voltage across each lamp.

8   i) Explain the reasons for the use of high voltage transmission in power distribution and methods of stepping up and stepping down the voltage at the supply and at the consumer premises.

   ii) State typical voltages at the various stages.

9   i) Define **power factor** and explain how a low value of power factor affects the current ratings of cables and switchgear required to supply a given a.c. power load.

   ii) A 240 V, 16 kW load has its power factor improved from 0.6 lag to 0.8 lag. Calculate the difference in the supply current.

10 Explain the meaning of **diversity factor** and give two examples where this is used to effect on a domestic installation.

11   i) Make a diagram of the connections showing the secondary winding of a three-phase four-wire (T.P.N.) transformer supplying three single-phase loads.

   ii) State the relationship between the line and the phase voltages.

  iii) If the three single-phase loads, all at unity pf, are 10 A, 20 A and 30 A respectively, determine the current in the neutral conductor of the three-phase four-wire supply.

12 Explain the purpose of an earth monitoring unit and describe, with the aid of a basic sketch its principle of operation. Give an example of where its use is advisable.

13 Three subcircuits of 10 kV A at 0.6 pf lag, 20 kV A at 0.8 pf lag and 15 kV A at unity pf respectively are supplied from a distribution fuse board. Determine the total kV A load input to the board.

14 The design current of a single-phase circuit is 27 A at 240 V. It is to be supplied with copper single-core PVC insulated cable installed with one other circuit in a steel conduit. If the ambient temperature is 35°C and length of run

is 30 m, determine:

   i) the correction factors to be used,

   ii) the current rating of the cable,

  iii) the minimum permitted cable size, and

  iv) the actual voltage drop in the cable if the circuit is protected by:

     a) a semi-enclosed fuse of 30 A rating,

     b) an H.B.C. fuse of 30 A rating.

15 Make a circuit diagram of a ring main supplied from the incoming 240 V single-phase mains on domestic premises. The circuit comprises eight 13 A socket outlets on the ring itself, one fixed appliance and three further socket outlets connected as spurs.

The diagram is to include all the necessary switchgear and metering in accordance with I.E.E. Regulations.

16 Calculate the minimum current rating of the main switch fuse required to protect an office building where the supply is 415 V three-phase-and-neutral, if the following loads are connected and single-phase loads are equally balanced over the phases.

240 85-W two-lamp fluorescent fittings with losses of 7 W per lamp and a power factor of 0.8 lagging.

12 ring circuits, each consisting of ten 13-A general purpose socket outlets.

21 kW of floor warming.

Three 20-kW output three-phase motors (not lift motors) 90% efficiency, power factor 0.75 lagging.

Six 12-kW cooking appliances.

Twelve 2-kW water heaters.

(C & G 'C')

17 State **two** reasons why a choke is necessary for the operation of a fluorescent discharge lamp.

18 The I.E.E. Regulations give guidance on the amount of diversity which may be allowed for various installations.

   i) Explain why such allowances are permitted.

   ii) Explain the reasons for the differences shown in allowances for:

     a) lighting in domestic premises and in offices;

     b) convection heaters in flats and hotels;

     c) stationary appliances in domestic premises and shops.

  iii) Explain why no diversity is allowed for floor warming installations.

(C & G 'C')

19   i) Draw the circuit diagram of a 16 A socket

outlet with monitored earth-leakage protection.

ii) Explain **two** advantages resulting from the use of such apparatus and give **two** examples of situations where its use would be advisable.

(C & G 'C')

20 A medium-sized factory has an incoming supply at 11 kV three-phase within a single feeder cable.

  i) Make a line diagram of the circuitry and equipment within the substation.

  ii) Show a floor plan of the layout.

  iii) State **four** safely precautions and the type of fire extinguishing system most suitable in this situation.

21 Describe a temporary installation system which could be used to provide a supply of electricity for lighting and small power during the construction of a large multi-storey office block. Your answer should detail:

  i) the type and siting of intake equipment,

  ii) the wiring system,

  iii) the voltage of apparatus, and

  iv) the type of sockets and plugs.

(C & G 'C')

22 When three-phase medium voltage portable equipment is used on a building site it is recommended that **monitored** earth-leakage protection be used to ensure the continuity of the earth conductor. Draw a suitable **monitored** earth-leakage scheme for a three-phase supply to a portable machine and explain how the system operates.

(C & G 'C')

23 i) Describe a **two feeder** main distribution system suitable for a factory premises.

  ii) State **two** advantages of this system over the single feeder distribution system.

24 60 domestic single phase and neutral consumers are supplied from a three-phase and neutral main supply with 20 consumers on each phase. State the effect on the consumers if an open circuit in

  i) one phase of the main supply, and

  ii) the neutral of the main supply when the single phase load are (a) balanced and (b) unbalanced.

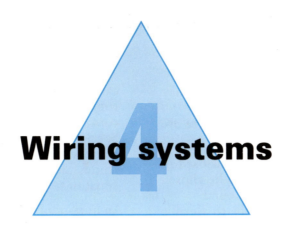

Wiring systems

Introduction

The choice of wiring system is affected by many factors such as the type of building, temperature, safety, cost, etc. The electrician needs to be able to decide upon the most suitable type of cable or wiring for a given situation.

Cables

A cable is a length of single conductor having one or several wires stranded together, or two or more such conductors, each provided with its own insulation and laid up together. These insulated conductors may or may not be further covered with an overall protective sheath to prevent mechanical damage. The insulated conductors are referred to as the **cores** of the cable.

Sometimes bare or uninsulated conductors are used for overhead installations, or they are enclosed in metal casing for rising (vertical) and lateral (horizontal) main supplies in buildings. See later notes.

> Cables consist of three essential parts:
> - the conductor to carry the current,
> - the insulation (dielectric) to provide the means to prevent the leakage of current, and
> - external overall protection against mechanical damage, chemical attack, fire or other external damaging factors to the cable.

Cable layouts and wiring systems

Because of the complexity and hazards involved in the installation of cables in the many types of building and their surroundings, there are quite a number of different types of cables and wiring systems in use. Each is designed to meet and withstand the elements it will encounter and, at the same time, fit in with the overall building construction in terms of convenience and appearance.

> It is the responsibility of the contractor, designer or sometimes the electrician himself to study carefully the building specification and decide upon the type of cables and wiring system most suitable.

Factors affecting the choice of wiring system

1. **Type of building construction** – to decide the routing, fixing and terminations.
2. **Flexibility of the system** – change of location of equipment such as in machine shops and temporary buildings.
3. **Installation conditions** – protection against mechanical damage requirements and working heights.
4. **Ambient temperatures** – to be withstood, that is, in boiler houses, and heat treatment installations.
5. **Appearance of the finished installation** (aesthetics) – can it be run on the surface or concealed?

6. **Durability** – life of the installation.
7. **Economics** – cost of the installation and money available.
8. **Safety aspect** – is it a school where there are young children, etc.?

When cables are to be drawn in or enclosed in metal conduits or trunking, they are to be chosen with the above temperatures borne in mind.

The above temperatures also apply to flexible type cables supplying heating appliances or high temperature light fittings.

> All fixed wiring systems must be suitably protected against mechanical damage, damage by heat, fire or explosion and against damp and corrosive elements which may be present on the installation.

Detailed information on the types of wiring systems and the regulations which apply to them is given in the I.E.E. Regulations.

Information on the conductor size, type of insulation, sheathing and the conditions under which the wiring system is installed, the current it is allowed to carry and the voltage drop values are given in the wiring tables of the Regulations.

Recommended maximum ambient temperatures for cable insulation

Material	Temperature (°C)
General rubber	55
PVC	65
Impregnated paper	75
M.I.C.C. with normal terminations	75
Butyl rubber	80
Silicone rubber	145
M.I.C.C. with high temperature termination (such as plastic glass)	145

The basic requirement for the installation of conductors and wiring systems are listed below.

1. All conductors and cables should be sufficient in size and power rating for the purpose for which they are to be used.
2. All live conductors should be effectively insulated or so positioned and protected as to avoid danger.
3. Every circuit should be protected against excess current and earth leakage.

4. Any metalwork associated with current-carrying conductors, or unavoidably near to live conductors should be connected to earth or c.p.c.
5. Special precautions must be taken where conductors and wiring systems are exposed to inflammable surroundings, or in wet or damp situations.

An important feature of the installation is that it fits into the building structure without causing unsightliness and too much interference or damage to the building itself.

> The various wiring operations should be carried out at the correct stage in the erection of the building to avoid unnecessary cutting, drilling and removing of the fabric of the completed building.

In most buildings, false ceilings, screeded floors and service ducts are provided to contain and conceal electrical and other services. See Figures 4.11 and 4.12.

Methods of installation of wiring systems

PVC-sheathed cables

These are cables with a PVC insulation and an overall sheath of PVC for protection against mechanical damage. The temperature range which they will withstand is 0 to 65°C. Below and above this temperature, the PVC insulation will crack and eventually fall away from the conductor.

Their main use is in domestic and similar installations, where the cables are not so liable to mechanical damage.

> In positions where PVC-sheathed cables are concealed in walls or pass through walls, they should be further protected by a channel or tube. When run under floors, they should be at a depth sufficient to prevent damage from floor fixings. At the termination, the sheath should enter the terminal housing enclosure so that no insulation is exposed to damage.

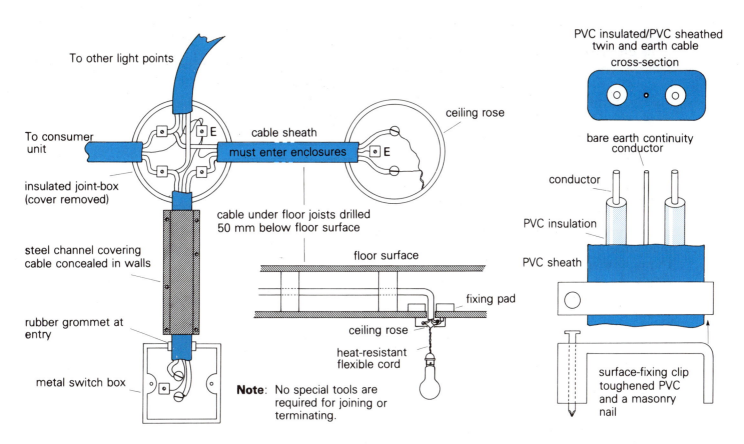

Figure 4.1 Installation of PVC sheathed cable for lighting circuits.

When installed on the surface, they are fixed in position by hardened PVC cable clips, which are fitted with a hardened nail suitable for driving into most surfaces. Distances between clips for the common sizes should be around 300 mm for horizontal runs and 350 mm for vertical runs. Any bends made in the cable should have a minimum radius as given in the I.E.E. Regulations. See Figure 4.1.

Steel conduits

> Cables provided with insulation only, cannot be run for fixed installations without further overall protection against mechanical damage.

In situations where there is likelihood of greater mechanical damage to the wiring system, such as in industrial and some commercial installations, steel conduit provides a suitable method of protection. The use of fittings such as bends, tees, through-boxes, four-way boxes, terminal boxes, etc., provides a means of joining the conduits in the various required directions.

> If the conduit system is installed correctly with inspection boxes at the correct points and distances apart, it is possible to rewire the complete installation without dismantling any part of it. For this reason, the conduits should be erected and fully completed before any cables are drawn in.

Under conditions of high ambient temperature (above 65°C), the conduit can be wired with butyl-insulated cables which will withstand temperatures of up to 80°C. For temperatures up to 145°C, silicone rubber insulated cables can be used.

Standard sizes of conduits are 20, 25, 32 and 40 mm; these are the external diameters. Above these sizes, the conduit becomes difficult to cut, bend and thread and the use of cable trunking is advisable. The conduit is annealed to allow bending and setting without fracture, but suitable formers supporting the tube walls should be used when bending to prevent distortion of the shape. The minimum radius of bends, 2.5 times the conduit diameter, is given in I.E.E. tables and also the capacities (maximum number of cables) needed to be drawn in, in order to prevent overheating of cables in conduits. We define the **space factor** as

$$\text{Space factor} = \frac{\text{area taken up by cables}}{\text{total area inside conduit}}$$

Use of terms for cable enclosures

In order to simplify the number of and various sizes of cables to meet the space factor requirements placed in enclosures such as conduits and trunking, the I.E.E. and enclosure manufacturers have introduced the 'terms' method of calculation.

Each individual size of cable together with each individual size of enclosure have been allotted a **terms number**. All the calculation involves is to divide the number of terms allotted to the enclosure by the sum total of all the cables to be enclosed.

When the two are equal in terms values, that is the maximum number of cables that can be laid or drawn in.

EXAMPLE 1

Twelve cables each having a rating of 202 terms and four of 146 terms are to be enclosed in trunking. What is the minimum rating of the trunking required?

Total cable terms = $(12 \times 202) + (4 \times 146) = 3008$
This is the minimum rating.

This figure now has to be compared with the trunking size. From Table 4G we obtain trunking dimensions of 150×50 mm. This has a term rating of 3091.

Note: In this example the above would be four three-phase and neutral circuits, with 16 mm² phase conductors and four 10 mm² neutral conductors. See Table 4A.

I.E.E. Regulations Table 4A. Cable terms for use in conduit in short straight runs

Type of conductor	Conductor cross-sectional area (mm²)	Term
Solid	1	22
	1.5	27
	2.5	39
Stranded	1.5	31
	2.5	43
	4	58
	6	88
	10	146
	16	202
	25	385

I.E.E. Regulations Table 4B. Conduit terms for use in short straight runs

Conduit diameter (mm)	Term
16	290
20	460
25	800
32	1400
38	1900
50	3500
63	5600

Note: The conductor Term remains the same when calculating the maximum number to be laid in the various trunking sizes. See Table 4G.

BESA Table 4G. Terms for trunking

Dimensions of trunking (mm × mm)		Term
Size	Gauge	
50 × 38	1.0	767
50 × 50	1.0	1037
75 × 25	1.2	738
75 × 38	1.2	1146
75 × 50	1.2	1555
75 × 75	1.2	2371
100 × 25	1.2	993
100 × 38	1.2	1542
100 × 50	1.2	2091
100 × 75	1.2	3189
100 × 100	1.4	4252
150 × 38	1.6	2999
150 × 50	1.6	3091
150 × 75	1.2	4743
150 × 100	1.2	6394
150 × 150	1.6	9697
200 × 38	1.6	3082
200 × 50	1.6	4145
200 × 75	1.6	6359
200 × 100	1.6	8572
200 × 150	1.6	13 001
200 × 200	1.6	17 429
225 × 38	1.6	3474
225 × 50	1.6	4671
225 × 75	1.6	7167
225 × 100	1.6	9662
225 × 150	1.6	14 652
225 × 200	1.6	19 643
225 × 225	1.6	22 138
300 × 38	1.6	4648
300 × 50	1.6	6251
300 × 75	1.6	9590
300 × 100	1.6	12 929
300 × 150	1.6	19 607
300 × 200	1.6	26 285
300 × 225	1.6	29 624
300 × 300	2.0	39 428

Note: Where there are a large numbers of circuits it will be more economical to have more than one trunking. All the conductors must be in the *same* overall enclosure so that magnetic flux radiation is cancelled.

Single-core PVC-insulated cables in straight runs of conduit not exceeding 3 m in length.

For each cable it is intended to use, obtain the term from Table 4A.

Add the cable terms together and compare the total with the conduit terms given in Table 4B.

The minimum conduit size is that having a term equal to or greater than the sum of the cable terms.

Erection of conduits

Modern conduits are of the screwed types (conduit threads) and are obtained in 4-m lengths with each end threaded. For jointing lengths together, a coupler is used which consists of a short length of tube with an internal conduit thread. The fittings are provided with internally threaded 'spouts' for connecting the conduits. On higher quality installations, the use of circular inspection-type boxes or fittings is preferable as it allows for easier and more convenient wiring with less danger of damage to cables when being drawn in.

> All conduit fittings and boxes should be securely fixed in position and the conduit supported along its run by 'saddles'.

Fixing saddles may be obtained in various forms:

1. a two-hole fix saddle which fastens the tube directly to the surface;
2. a single-hole fix saddle or 'spacer bar'. A single bar is fixed to the wall surface and the saddle is then fixed to the bar with two small set screws, saving time; and
3. a 'stand off' or 'distance' saddle. This provides a space between the conduit and fixing surface, used to protect the conduit against excess condensation. It also allows complete cleaning of walls in hospitals etc, where otherwise germs and dirt would accumulate between the conduit and the wall. See Figures 4.2 and 4.3.

PVC conduits

These conduits are available in similar sizes and types of fitting as the metallic conduits. They can be 'shaped' by the use of an internal bending spring and immersion in hot water.

The main advantages of PVC are its lightness and non-corrosive qualities which makes PVC conduits ideally suitable for farm, horticultural and other indoor and outdoor installations where corrosive substances are present and the temperature does not exceed around 70°C.

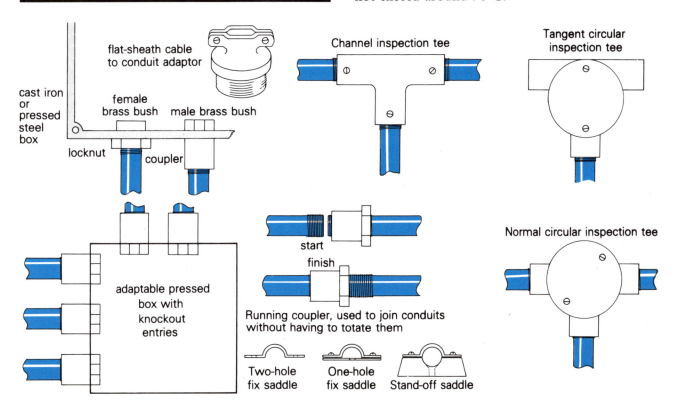

Figure 4.2 (left) Components of a conduit system.
Figure 4.3 (right) Types of fixing (saddles) for conduits.

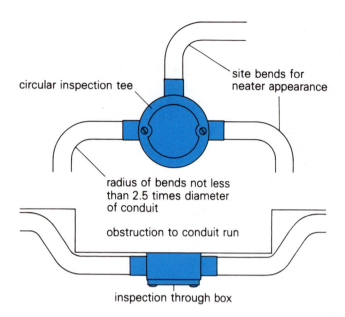

circular inspection tee

site bends for
neater appearance

radius of bends not less
than 2.5 times diameter
of conduit

obstruction to conduit run

inspection through box

Figure 4.4 Use of hand-made sets and bends in conduits.

They can be terminated into fittings and jointed by the use of adhesives or by screw threads.

The bending and the setting of all conduits for direction changes and shaping around obstacles presents a much neater appearance than the excess use of fittings (Figure 4.4). Inspection fittings should be used mainly to ease the 'drawing in' of cables, for example, after two 90° bends or equivalent sets.

> On difficult or long runs it will be necessary to use a fish wire or tape fitting with two small rollers at 90° to each other.

Mineral-insulated copper-covered (MICC) cables

These consist of solid, pliable, circular copper conductors positioned in a highly compressed magnesium oxide powder. They have a much higher working temperature than PVC or rubber-insulated cables, which makes them ideally suited for use in boiler rooms and other high temperature situations. The temperature they will withstand is only limited by the type of seal used for their terminations and these can be obtained in fibre glass for temperatures up to 150°C. The termination requires two special tools, a stripping tool and a crimping tool. The termination is sealed with a compound to exclude all moisture from entering the magnesium oxide insulation.

> The ends of the cables should never be left exposed to the atmosphere, since they will absorb moisture which will lower the cables' insulation resistance.

When a cable is cut, its ends can be sealed with a 'dab' of compound until it is to be used again. If moisture should enter, it is possible to drive it out by warming the end of the cable with heat from a blowlamp or similar device.

> After termination, an insulation test should be carried out and the value should always be infinity. Anything less will indicate a faulty seal which eventually breaks down in use.

At its termination points, the cable sheath must be firmly secured. When it enters the smaller wiring accessories, such as switches, socket outlets and ceiling boxes, the sheath is secured by a shaped clip. On the heavier industrial installations, it will terminate into a conduit entry by the use of a screwed brass gland with a conduit thread (Figures 4.6 and 4.7). Where there is risk of corrosion to the copper sheath, or when it is buried in the ground, the cable can be obtained with an overall PVC covering. PVC shrouds are also available to completely protect the termination ends. In areas where mechanical damage is likely, the cable should be further protected by a conduit or metal covering.

Cable trunking

Where large numbers of cables are to be run it is more economical to enclose them in trunking of suitable size than to install a lot of conduits, see Figure 4.8. Trunking is made from mild steel or a plastic material. The standard sizes are 50 × 50 mm, 75 × 75 mm and 100 × 100 mm. They are provided in 3-m lengths and can be bolted together by fish-plates. At all jointing points of steel trunking a copper strip is bolted across to ensure efficient earth continuity. Separate compartments can be fitted into one trunking where segregation of wiring cables is required.

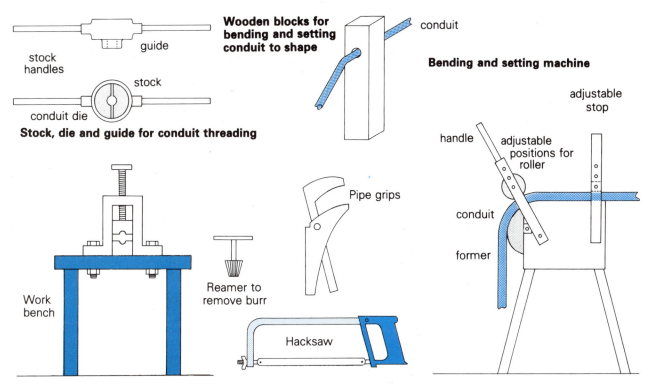

Figure 4.5 Tools for erection of a conduit system.

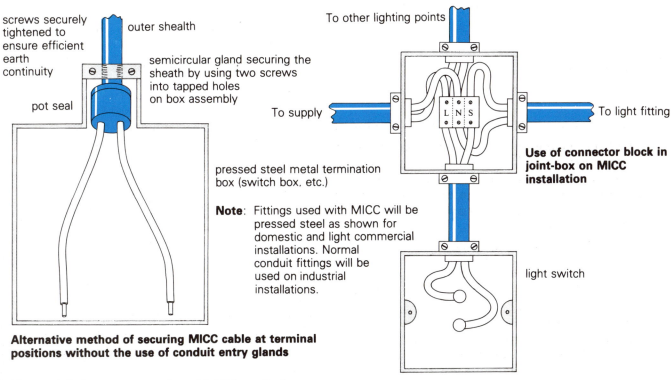

Figure 4.6 Components of an MICC installation.

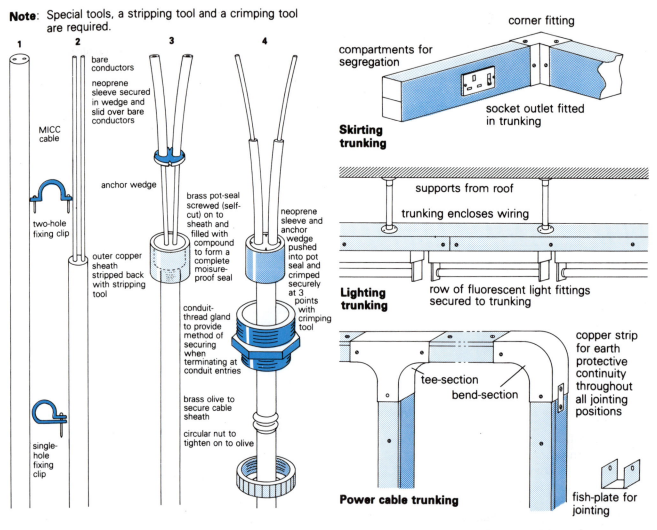

Note: Special tools, a stripping tool and a crimping tool are required.

Figure 4.7 Stages in the termination of MICC cable.

Figure 4.8 Installation of various cable trunking systems.

> Where trunking is run on its side, it should be fitted with clips to prevent the cables from falling out when the cover is removed. Vertical runs should be fitted at intervals with cable support 'pins' staggered to prevent the weight falling on one point.

I.E.E. Regulations require a space factor of 45 per cent. Both manufacturers and the I.E.E. publish tables from which the maximum number of cables of various sizes laid in the trunking may be calculated. Each size of cable is allotted a number. When the numbers corresponding to the cables used are added the total must not exceed the number allotted to the trunking, see 'terms' tables.

Fixing brackets to suit the various types of support required are usually fabricated on site.

Floor ducts and skirting trunking

This is the most effective system of providing supplies to socket outlets, telephones, electrically-operated equipment, call systems, etc., at the required position in office blocks. It is also well concealed and it can blend into the features of the building.

> With a trunking system, the cables are laid in position, while with a duct system the cables are drawn in.

Floor ducting is of wide shallow sections, laid on the concrete foundation slab in the required position and brought to the necessary number of inspection boxes.

> There must be a sufficient number of boxes to allow the duct system to be completely rewired without disturbing any part of the floor finish.

Conduits can be fitted vertically into the ducts at the position where the supplies are required for equipment and accessories which are away from the perimeter walls and partitions. The supplies for equipment and accessories to be fitted on the perimeter walls and partitions themselves can be taken from skirting trunking which joins up with the floor duct system. When the duct system is completed, it can be screeded over with a mixture of sand and cement, usually around 50 mm to 100 mm thick, on top of which the floor finish can be laid. See Figure 4.9.

> Each inspection box will be covered by a removable tile.

Overhead busbar trunking

This consists of a substantial metal trunking which contains copper bars fixed in position by insulated supports. It is a very convenient system of wiring in industrial installations where equipment and machines are frequently moved around as production requirements change. The individual supplies are connected to the busbars by 'tap-off' units which can be secured by bolts to the trunking, or by 'plug-in' type units which can be plugged into socket outlet positions provided on the trunking. See Figure 4.10.

The trunking is suspended securely from the roof supports. The supply to the machines is taken by conduits suspended from the tap-off units.

Note: The 'tap-off' unit is provided with the required fuse protection for the cables supplying the machines.

Suspended ceilings

In large buildings where aesthetics (appearance) is of importance, such as in superstores, hospitals,

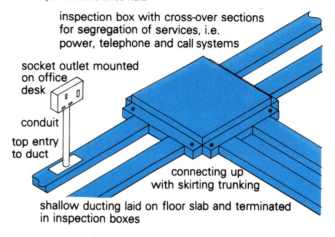

Note: Ducting will be screeded over with sand and cement mixture. Inspection boxes will have inspection covers hidden by floor tiles or removable covers. The ducting can join up with skirting trunking to supply power points around office walls.

inspection box with cross-over sections for segregation of services, i.e. power, telephone and call systems

socket outlet mounted on office desk

conduit

top entry to duct

connecting up with skirting trunking

shallow ducting laid on floor slab and terminated in inspection boxes

Figure 4.9 Under-floor duct systems.

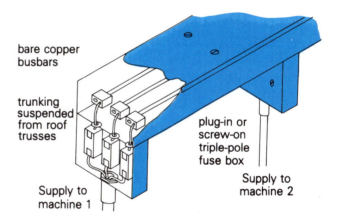

bare copper busbars

trunking suspended from roof trusses

plug-in or screw-on triple-pole fuse box

Supply to machine 1

Supply to machine 2

Figure 4.10 Overhead busbar system.

office blocks, shopping centres, electrical and other services are required to be hidden as far as is practicable. This is done by the use of a suspended ceiling hung by metal rods which are fixed to the main ceiling which is usually of concrete or steelwork. The suspended ceiling is of a lightweight grid or lattice framework in which polystyrene or similar lightweight tiles can be placed, or at intervals luminaires can be fitted so that the ceiling presents a very pleasant appearance with all the wiring, pipework, etc. hidden from public view, but easily accessible to workmen to carry out maintenance and alterations.

Note: The weight of the service pipework, conduits, etc., must be supported by the main ceiling. See Figure 4.11.

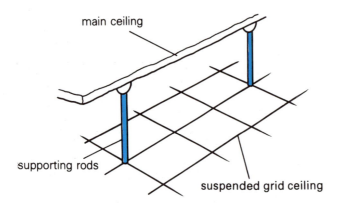

Figure 4.11 Suspended grid ceiling.

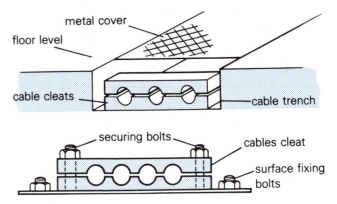

Figure 4.12 Precast cable trench. Cable cleats are spaced at intervals along trench to support cables.

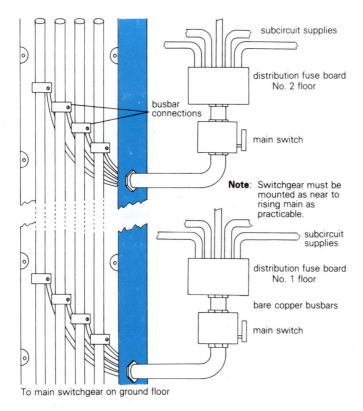

Figure 4.13 Rising main busbar trunking systems.

Cable ducts

This is another method of concealing electrical and other services, used mainly in large industrial type buildings. The services routes are marked out on the plans so that during construction, mainly of the floor, ducts are pre-cast so that at a later date the services may be installed. The cables which are normally of the larger sizes and mainly PILCSWA type are supported by cable cleats fixed either to the sides or bottom of the duct. Suitable covers are

then placed over the duct so that again this hides and protects the services and makes them easily accessible to installers and maintenance staff. See Figure 4.12.

Rising main busbar trunking

In all large buildings, supplies are run from the main switchgear at the supply intake position by submain cable to distribution boards sited in convenient positions throughout the building. From these distribution boards, the subcircuits to the lighting and power outlets are taken.

In high buildings, a rising service duct is usually positioned in the centre of the building and taken through a slot in each floor slab. At each floor, fire barriers must be provided in and around the trunking, making good any gaps.

The rising main busbar system provides a convenient method of running the main supply from the main intake switchgear on the ground floor to provide the supply at each floor level. The supply at each floor level is taken from the busbars by means of conduit, armoured cable or MICC (depending upon the wiring system) to the floor switchgear. **Note**: The distance between the rising main and the floor switchgear should be as short as practicable because of the lack of suitable excess-current protection for this cable. The subcircuits may now be taken from the floor distribution board to the lighting and power points on that floor. See Figure 4.13.

PVC-insulated PVC-sheathed steel wire armour cables

This is abbreviated to **PVC/PVC/SWA cable**.

These are cables used mainly for industrial and underground power supplies for mains and sub-

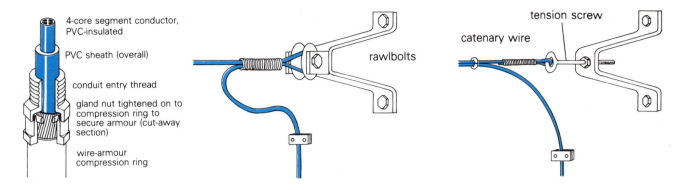

Figure 4.14 (left) PVC armoured cable gland.
Figure 4.15 (centre) Overhead suspension for cables with built-in catenary wires.
Figure 4.16 (right) Overhead suspension for separate catenary.

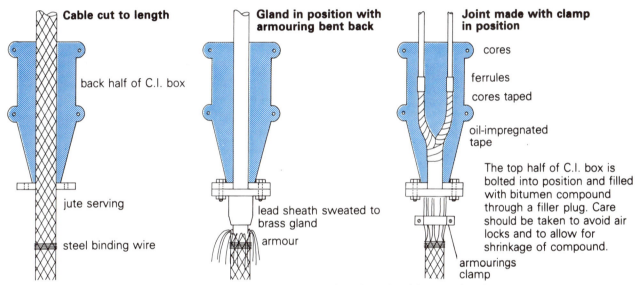

Figure 4.17 Medium voltage lead-covered and paper-insulated cable termination.

main circuits. The PVC steel wire armour is used to provide a semi-flexible protection against mechanical damage and also as the c.p.c. and is covered with an overall PVC sheath or special serving to protect it against corrosion.

For long single runs of heavier current supplies, it is more convenient than conduit or trunking, it can be shaped into position quite easily and can be fairly simply terminated. The main requirement of the termination is that the armour is secured to the brass cone gland to provide a firm mechanical anchor and efficient earth continuity. See Figure 4.14. Its temperature limits are 0 to 65°C.

These cables can also be used for overhead supplies, suspended from a steel catenary wire. See Figure 4.15 and 4.16.

Paper-insulated lead-covered steel wire armour cables

Abbreviated to **PI/LC/SWA cable**.

Impregnated paper-insulated cables have higher dielectric properties than PVC and will withstand higher temperatures than the previous cable PVC/PVC/SWA. They are used extensively for main distribution of higher voltage power supplies both underground and on the surface.

The lead sheath is to exclude moisture from the paper insulation and because of this, the jointing and termination requires a certain amount of care and skill. The lead sheath must be plumbed with plumber's solder (of a higher lead content than electrical solder) to the brass cone. Specially impregnated tapes are used to prevent the unravelling of

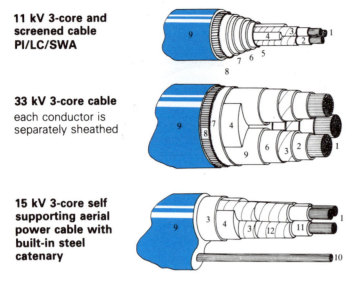

11 kV 3-core and screened cable PI/LC/SWA

33 kV 3-core cable
each conductor is separately sheathed

15 kV 3-core self supporting aerial power cable with built-in steel catenary

1   shaped stranded conductor
2   impregnated paper insulation
3   screen of metal tape
4   fillers
5   copper-woven fabric tape
6   sheath lead or lead alloy
7   bedding
8   galvanised steel wire armour
9   serving
10 steel wire catenary
11 conductor screen
12 polythene insulation

Figure 4.18 Power cables for higher voltage supplies.

3-core cable, single-wire-armoured and PVC-oversheathed

1   solid aluminium conductor
2   PVC insulation
3   taped bedding
4   galvanised steel wire armour
5   PVC oversheath

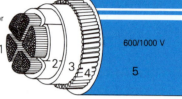

4-core cable, single-wire-armoured and PVC-oversheathed

1   shaped, stranded copper conductor
2   PVC insulation
3   extruded bedding
4   galvanised steel wire armour
5   PVC oversheath

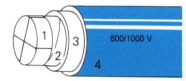

Single-core sectoral cable

The conductor consists of four sector-shaped solid aluminium conductors laid up together and bound. Extruded PVC insulation is applied over the conductor followed by a PVC oversheath. A similar armoured version is also available.

1   solid aluminium conductor
2   conductor binder
3   extruded PVC insulation
4   PVC oversheath

4-core cable, aluminium strip-armoured, PVC-oversheathed

Conductors of shaped, solid aluminium are insulated with PVC. The cores are laid up and bound with PVC tapes, followed by a single layer of aluminium strips and an overall PVC sheath.

1   solid aluminium conductor
2   PVC insulation
3   taped bedding
4   aluminium strip armour
5   PVC oversheath

Figure 4.19 Power cables for lower voltage supplies.

the paper from the conductor when the lead is stripped back. See Figure 4.17. The conductor is jointed for **through** or **tee** joints by means of shaped brass ferrules which can be soldered by the use of a blowlamp or, more commonly, by the 'pot and ladle' method to avoid waste of solder. After being suitably taped, the whole joint is housed in a suitable joint or termination box and completely filled with hot liquid bitumen compound which solidifies on cooling and forms a complete moisture-proof seal. See Figures 4.18, 4.19, 4.20 and 4.21.

Overhead wiring systems

These systems are mainly used for spans between buildings. For longer spans, intermediate supports will be required. The main requirement is that the cable must be able to withstand the strain without

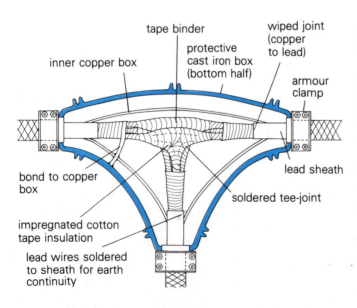

Figure 4.20 Tee-joint in three-core 11 kV paper-insulated, lead-covered, steel wire armour (PI/LC/SWA) cable.

damage or 'sagging'. Also, any insulation or sheathing must be able to withstand long exposure to the effects of direct sunshine and adverse weather conditions. There are four main systems:

1. hard-drawn copper or aluminium conductors, bare or lightly insulated, suitably supported and tensioned on porcelain insulators;
2. vulcanised rubber insulated with taped and weather-resistant compound with a built-in steel strain catenary wire, supported at both ends on insulators fixed to a tensioning bracket;
3. HSOS (house service overhead supply) cable suspended from a separate strain steel catenary wire with suitable hanging straps, or directly clipped to the catenary;
4. PVC/PVC/SWA cable suspended from a separate steel catenary with hanging straps.

Prefabricated wiring systems

With the development of industrialised building techniques, a number of prefabricated wiring systems have been devised.

> Prefabricated wiring systems are most suitable for different buildings which have similar dimensions, so the wiring and the accessories can be fitted into position in factory conditions and then quickly assembled on site.

These systems are mainly in three groups:

1. cable harness or loom systems, which can be placed in the ducts of the building;
2. pre-cut and assembled sheathed cables incorporated in the structure during factory construction;
3. hollow skirtings, door surrounds and grooves purpose-built to contain the wiring. They may be pre-wired before delivery to site.

Earthed concentric wiring systems (TN-C)

In this system, metal-sheathed cables (such as mineral-insulated copper-sheathed) are employed, and the sheath is used as a return conductor. The I.E.E. Regulations permit the use of such a system if:

1. it is supplied by a transformer or convertor in such a manner that there is no metallic connection with a public supply, or

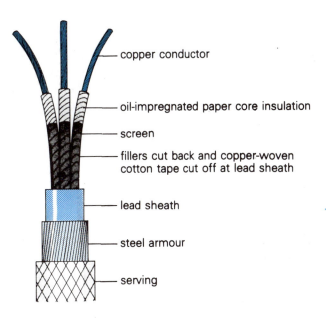

Figure 4.21 Section of a PI/LC/SWA and screened cable.

- copper conductor
- oil-impregnated paper core insulation
- screen
- fillers cut back and copper-woven cotton tape cut off at lead sheath
- lead sheath
- steel armour
- serving

2. it is connected to an a.c. public supply system on which multiple earthing of the neutral (PME) has been authorised by the Ministry of Power, or
3. the supply is obtained from a private generating plant.

See Regulations.

The system has several advantages. Since the sheath acts as a conductor, a single-core cable replaces the conventional two-core cable for single-phase (S.P.N.) systems and a three-core cable replaces the four-core cable for three-phase and neutral (T.P.N.) systems. This leads to a considerable saving in the diameter of the outside cable and of conductor material. Also, the sheath is always of greater area than the separate insulated conductor.

> The external conductor must be earthed and on d.c. installations it should, where possible, be negative to the internal conductor. No fuse, non-linked switch or circuit breaker must be inserted in the earthed external conductor.

Earthing the conductor is most important because the external conductor serves as both neutral conductor and circuit protective conductor. (See Chapter 5.)

At termination points, that is, socket outlets and switches, a special plate or conducting device must be provided for ensuring the continuity of the conductor. This system is at present used mainly in large multi-occupier buildings, such as large blocks of flats, multi-story commercial buildings, etc. These, in many instances, have their own supply transformer, so that no other installation would be liable to potential danger.

Where the system uses MICC cable, one method of ensuring the continuity of the external conductor is by using tail pots. See Figure 4.22.

Termination and jointing of aluminium conductors

Because of the increasing price of copper, it has become necessary to use aluminium for the conductor material in electric cables. The greater saving is of course on the use of heavy conductors, that is, busbar systems and heavy current cables.

The main problem encountered with the installation of these cables and conductors is in the jointing and termination. Several techniques have been adopted for these processes and the following is a summary of them.

Soldering techniques

1. Solder pot and ladle with the basting method, Figure 4.23, using an aluminium solder which consists of 53 per cent lead/45 per cent tin with 2 per cent as mentioned zinc. The soldering temperature should not exceed 350°C to prevent charring of the flux. The joint or termination can be wiped to shape with a mole skin cloth as in normal methods. Solidification will begin to occur at around 200°C. Insulation must be protected during this operation and the pot must be far enough away to prevent excessive heat increase.
2. Another soldering method is to use friction solder of a 70 per cent tin/30 per cent zinc composition which does not require flux. The aluminium can be tinned by heating and then rubbing the solder, after which it can be joined to copper or brass in the normal manner.
3. Solid aluminium conductors can be terminated into suitable lugs (cable sockets) by the indent compression method using hand pressure for the smaller sizes and a hydraulic press for the larger conductors. Indent jointing needs a lower compression force than a full surface pressure method and it also pierces the 'skin' of the conductor, which gives a better contact.

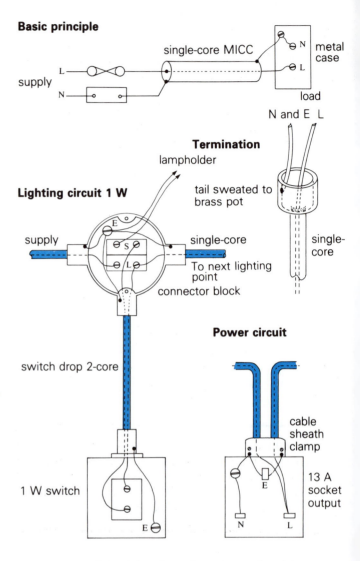

Figure 4.22 Principle of earth concentric wiring.

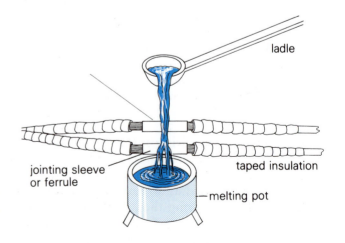

Figure 4.23 Basting methods of soldering cable joints.

Corrosion

Care must be taken to avoid bi-metallic corrosion in damp situations where aluminium is bolted to copper or brass. Tinning of the copper or brass will help to reduce this. Also application of a grease-based compound such as 'Densal' between the current-carrying surfaces will help to exclude moisture.

I.E.E. Regulations for wiring systems

The Regulations provide details of the following requirements for wiring systems.

Types of cable for fixed wiring systems	Segregation of circuits
Overhead lines	Bonding and segregation
Flexible cables	Identification of conductors
Insulation and sheathing	Identification of pipes
Protection against corrosion	Terminations
Voltage ratings	Joints in fixed cable
Voltage drop	Joints in flexible cords
Protection against mechanical damage	Installation of bare conductors
Protection against direct sunlight	Installation of bare collector wires
Cables in lift shafts	Metal sheathed and armoured cables
Temperatures	Space factor
Cable supports	Metal conduit system
Protection against heat	Wiring between buildings
Busbar terminations	Heating wire and cables
Fire precautions	

Bells and bell circuits

The electric bell converts the magnetic effect of an electric current into sound. It therefore enables audible warnings or signals to be transmitted as currents over long distances by the running of electric conductor cables. See Figure 4.24.

For most bell circuits, the use of lower voltages is employed, which necessitates the installation of a bell transformer. See Figure 4.25. Bells can be operated from manually-operated push-buttons, or automatic switching from alarm devices, such as door or window devices for burglar-alarm systems, or detection devices for fire outbreaks.

Figure 4.24 A single stroke/trembler bell.

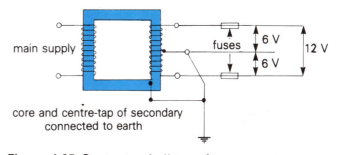

Figure 4.25 Centre tap bell transformer.

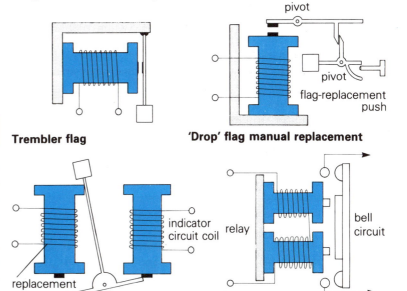

Figure 4.26 Indicators and relays used in bell circuits.

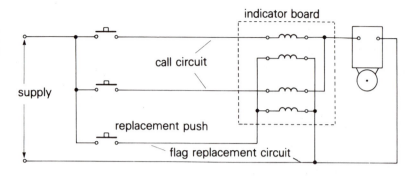

Figure 4.27 Circuitry of an electrical replacement indicator and bell.

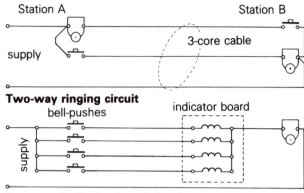

Two-way ringing circuit

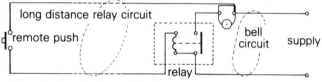

Four-way indicator board circuit

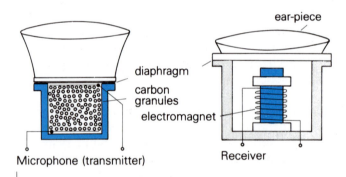

Use of relay for long circuits

Figure 4.28 Use of relay for lengthy circuit, four-way indicator circuit and two-way ringing circuit.

On a call system when one bell is used to give an audible alarm from a number of positions, such as a call system in hotels, or a fire-alarm system covering a number of different sections, a visual indicator board will be required to display the location of the call. See Figures 4.26 and 4.27.

For very long circuit runs, the use of a relay which operates on a very much smaller value of current will be required to reduce the voltage drop in the circuit. See Figure 4.28.

Telephones and telephone circuits

This is a means of transmitting speech over long distances by the use of electric conductors.

The telephone consists basically of two devices: the transmitter and the receiver, known as the hand-set. The simple type of transmitter employs the use of a thin diaphragm and carbon granules. See Figure 4.29. When the sound waves from the voice impinge on the diaphragm, movement is set up which causes varying amounts of pressure on the carbon granules. Their overall resistance will vary in sympathy with these pressures, which means that as the sounds change they will be converted into resistance changes. These resistance changes will cause current changes when a voltage is applied.

The receiver basically consists of two coils of wire mounted on an iron core with a diaphragm just above the poles of the iron core. When the current in the coil varies, the magnetic force on the diaphragm will cause it to move. This movement sets up movements of the air thus converting the electric charges into sound waves.

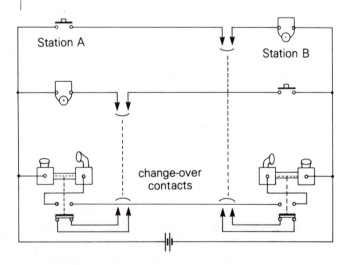

Figure 4.29 Telephone transmitter and receiver.

Figure 4.30 Two-way speaking and ringing circuit.

More modern forms of telephone employ the use of crystal-type microphones and receivers. The use of relays and switches enables the same conductors between the hand-sets to be used for both ringing and speech circuits. See Figure 4.30.

Note: When the hand-sets are lifted the change-over contacts disconnect the ringing circuit and connect the speaking circuit.

Wiring of temporary installations

It is often necessary for a temporary electrical supply to be installed on a construction site for the running of lighting, portable power tools and electrically operated plant (for example, tower cranes).

Although an installation may be temporary, the wiring must in all ways comply with the requirements laid down in I.E.E. Regulations for permanent installations, and all cables must be of regulation types.

The fact that the installation is temporary must not be used as an excuse for poor workmanship or a lack of safety precautions.

As in a permanent installation, a temporary installation must be provided with a main switch, be adequately fused and switched, and have full protection against earth leakage currents. Although cables need not be permanently secured, they must be protected against possible mechanical damage.

The name of the person responsible for the installation must be displayed as near as possible to the main switch, and an inspection should be carried out every three months or at shorter intervals as considered necessary.

Use of reduced voltage supplies

Where possible 110 V supplies should be used from double-wound transformers, with the secondary winding centre-tapped to earth. This should be quite feasible for providing power for lighting circuits and portable electric tools.

With certain electrically-operated plant it may not be possible to use a reduced voltage, and in this case monitored earth circuits should be used. This system ensured that the equipment is completely disconnected from the supply in the event of a break in the earth circuit.

To summarise, the important points to remember about a temporary installation are:
- that the installation is correctly wired and fused,
- that it is protected against mechanical damage and moisture,
- that adequate earth protection is provided, and
- that it is inspected at least every three months.

Temporary installations are dealt with more fully in Chapter 8.

CHECK YOUR UNDERSTANDING

- The essential parts of a cable are conductor, insulation and protection against mechanical damage.
- Conduits and trunking of either steel or PVC with use of inspection fittings are commonly used for cable protection.
- A space factor
$$\frac{\text{c.s.a. of cables}}{\text{c.s.a. of enclosure}}$$
is used to calculate the number of cables contained by using 'terms' numbers from I.E.E. tables.
- For large premises and underground distribution SWA or tape is used for protection.
- MICC is designed for high temperature installations with special sealing termination glands.
- Floor ducts and skirting trunking systems are most suitable for offices and buildings where multi-outlets at floor or desk level are needed.
- Overhead busbars in trunking are used to supply machines from tap-off boxes in workshops. This keeps the floor area clear.
- Rising main busbars will tap off points at each floor level and are suited to multi-storey installations.
- Overhead supplies are fitted with a supporting catenary, either separate or contained within the cable itself.
- Prefabricated 'harness' wiring systems are beneficial where a large number of identical units are to be wired.
- Suspended ceilings are used to 'hide' overhead services in buildings where a neat appearance is required.
- Call services with bells or other sounders with

pushes and indicator boards to locate call position are fitted in hospitals, hotels, etc.

● Relays are used on long circuits to reduce current and voltage drop. The conductors only carry the small coil current necessary to operate the contacts for heavier current sounder-circuit.

REVISION EXERCISES AND QUESTIONS

1 i) Explain why it is necessary to seal some types of cable terminations against the ingress of moisture.
   ii) Name **two** types of cable which require this, giving the reasons.
   iii) State how the seal is obtained in each of the named types of cable.

2 i) Give three examples of where cord or cable grips are used and state the purpose of these.
   ii) It is suggested that when an extension lead wound on a cable drum is used to carry heavy current, it should be unwound. Give reasons for this.

3 i) State reasons why PVC cables are unsuitable for use in extremes of high and low temperature.
   ii) Why are cables of similar conductor size but different type of insulation given different current ratings in the I.E.E. tables?
   iii) If a twin core cable has 4 mV per ampere per metre and is 50 m long, what is the resistance of one core?

4 i) Explain the meaning of 'earthed concentric wiring'.
   ii) State **one** advantage of this system.
   iii) Under what conditions may this system be used?

5 The following three final circuits are to be drawn into a conduit
   1. a three-phase and neutral whose phases are 16 mm² and the neutral 10 mm²,
   2. a single-phase of 6 mm²,
   3. a single-phase of 4 mm².
   i) a) Using Tables 4A and 4B calculate the minimum size of conduit required.
       b) State the reason for the reduction of the neutral size in circuit 1.
   ii) If a trunking system had been used for enclosure of the cables, from Table 4G calculate the minimum size required.

6 On conduit systems why is it important that
   i) a) the conduit is erected before the cables are drawn in?

       b) all the conductors of the same circuit are drawn into the same conduit?
   ii) a) Explain the use of a 'fish' wire or tape.
       b) Give two reasons why the 'bending' or 'setting' of conduit is preferable to the use of fittings.
       c) State the minimum radius of a bend in a conduit system.

7 i) List all the factors that determine the choice of a wiring system.
   ii) What type of wiring system would you recommend for a
       a) petrol station,
       b) office block,
       c) farm settlement,
       d) distribution in factory, and
       e) engineering workshop.

8 A house is to be wired for lighting and power with PVC sheathed cable. Quote the relevant I.E.E. Regulations regarding the joints, mechanical protection and proximity to other services, such as gas and water pipes.

9 Describe the trunking system of installing cables in buildings and give examples where its use is preferable to a steel conduit installation.

10 Describe, with the aid of sketches, how to install a rising main consisting of bare copper conductors on porcelain insulators. State the advantages of this type of installation.

11 Draw the circuit diagram and explain the action of an electric bell made up of a trembler bell, continuous action relay with a reset and a push. The circuit is served by a double-wound transformer.

12 Six adjoining hospital rooms are each provided with a bell push with which to call the nurse. The circuit includes the six pushes, one bell, a battery and a six-way indicator board.
   Draw the circuit diagram and explain the importance of the indicator board.

13 An overhead busbar trunking system is often used for supplying machines in an engineering workshop through 'plug-in' boxes.
   i) State **two** advantages of this system compared with conduit.
   ii) With the aid of a sketch, describe a tapping-off box showing how a connection is made to the busbars.
   iii) State the requirements of the I.E.E. with regard to temperature changes.

14 The earth concentric system of wiring is to be used in a new office block.
   i) Explain what is meant by the term 'earthed concentric wiring'.

ii) State **one** advantage of this method of wiring.

iii) State **two** systems of supply to which it is restricted.

iv) State **one** type of cable which is ideally suitable.

v) Make a sketch of one lighting point controlled by a one-way switch showing the method of termination.

15 A six-storey block of flats is to be fed from a 415 V three-phase four-wire rising main system.

i) Make a diagram showing how one floor would be supplied from the rising main.

ii) Show the sequence of the switchgear at the 'take-off' point at the floor level.

iii) Show the switchgear at the 'in-take' point in one flat.

iv) State the precautions to be taken to prevent spread of fire through the rising main.

v) Explain how the complete installation load could be 'balanced' over the incoming supply.

16 Write down the basic points of the I.E.E. Regulations concerning a temporary electrical installation with reference to the following:

i) types of cables to be used;

ii) fixings, protection against mechanical damage and moisture;

iii) protection against overcurrent and earth leakage;

iv) inspection and testing;

v) provision of reduced voltage supplies.

17 Describe the precautions which should be taken in order to minimise the risk of fire in **each** of the following:

i) vertical rising-main busbars in a specially formed duct in building structure,

ii) oil filled transformers in a factory substation,

iii) lighting a spray painting room,

iv) petrol pumps of a filling station.

(C & G 'C')

18 Describe the causes of corrosion and the methods of minimising corrosion when installing each of the following:

i) mineral-insulated, metal-sheathed cables installed outdoors;

ii) sheet steel switchgear;

iii) iron pipework.   (C & G 'C')

19 Describe with the aid of sketches how to carry out the following:

i) a joint between two multi-core, PVC-insulated, PVC-sheathed, armoured underground cables;

ii) termination of a mineral-insulated, metal-sheathed three-core cable at the terminal box of a furnace.

(C & G 'C')

20 Explain, with the aid of sketches, where necessary, methods of overcoming problems likely to be encountered when installing screwed conduit wiring systems in each of the following particular situations:

i) conduits in cast *in situ* concrete floors 125 mm thick;

ii) conduits to be fixed above a suspending ceiling, but the latter must not take the weight of the conduit;

iii) conduits laid in a long concrete flat roof in which provision is made for expansion of the roof due to temperature changes.

(C & G 'C')

21 i) Describe, using sketches, the construction of the following types of cables, using sketches to illustrate:

a) PVC insulated, split concentric for use on single-phase distribution;

b) paper insulated, three-core cable with lead sheath and steel wire armour.

ii) Describe how you would terminate **one** of the above cables into an isolator.

iii) What precautions should be taken against corrosion when using steel wire armoured cables?

(C & G 'C')

Earthing, excess current protection and testing

Introduction

Earthing is the connecting of one point of the supply transformer and the metallic parts of an installation which are exposed to touch, to the general mass of earth.

This is to prevent the potential of live conductors rising above the declared value, and to cut off the supply automatically when any appreciable leakage current flows as the result of an insulation fault. This, in turn, prevents the danger of electric shock from exposed metal which may be live, and the danger of fire caused by overheating from leakage current flow.

All public supplies over 30 V a.c. or 50 V d.c. must be earthed in accordance with I.E.E. and Electricity Supply Regulations.

The earthing system begins at the consumer's supply transformer by connecting the star-point of the three-phase secondary winding to earth and this connection also forms the **neutral conductor** of the consumer's supply. When all the exposed metalwork on the installation is connected back to this main earth point, an electrical circuit is formed.

The presence of a voltage or potential due to a leakage must cause sufficient current to flow in this earth conductor to operate the excess current protection device and cut off the supply.

Earthing arrangements and protection conductors

Definitions of terms

Earth Conductive mass of earth whose potential is taken at zero.

Earth electrode The conductor in contact with the general mass of earth by a spike, tapes, etc. See Figure 5.12.

Earth electrode resistance The resistance of the earth electrode to the general mass of earth.

Main earth terminal The terminal, usually placed at the consumer's intake position for connection of consumer's c.p.c.s, bonding conductors and the earthing lead.

Earth lead Conductor which connects the main earth terminal to the earth electrode.

Circuit protective conductor (c.p.c.) This connects all exposed parts of metallic electrical equipment and extraneous metalwork on the installation together and back to the main earth terminal.

Extraneous metalwork Exposed metalwork which needs to be earthed which is not part of the electrical equipment, for example, metal sinks, cisterns, baths, etc. They are connected to the c.p.c. by conductors known as bonding.

Types of c.p.c.s

1. PVC insulated single core cables coloured green/yellow stripe.
2. PVC sheathed cable carrying a bare conductor which must be sleeved with green/yellow cover where it leaves the cable.
3. Copper strip on heavy current circuits and bonding.

4. Metal conduit: this will need supplementing on special installations.
5. Metal ducting and trunking: again may need supplementing.
6. MIMS cable sheath.
7. Lead covered and wire armouring of cables.

Figure 5.1 shows the layout of the switchgear, metering and earthing protection together with conductor sizes at the intake position of the consumer's premises for a 100 A single-phase and neutral supply for three different methods of earthing.

The SCO (**supply cut out**) is installed by the authority and is their property. It contains a 100 A HBC type which is sealed against misuse.

The **meter** is also their property and again is sealed.

The MET (**main earth terminal**) is usually fitted by the authority who also connect the earthing and bonding conductors to it. From then on the equipment is the responsibility of the consumer including the RCD (**residual current device**).

> Note carefully the arrangement of the earth protection for three different types of supply.

The earthing circuit

This is made up of three basic parts: circuit protective conductor, earth conductor and earth electrode.

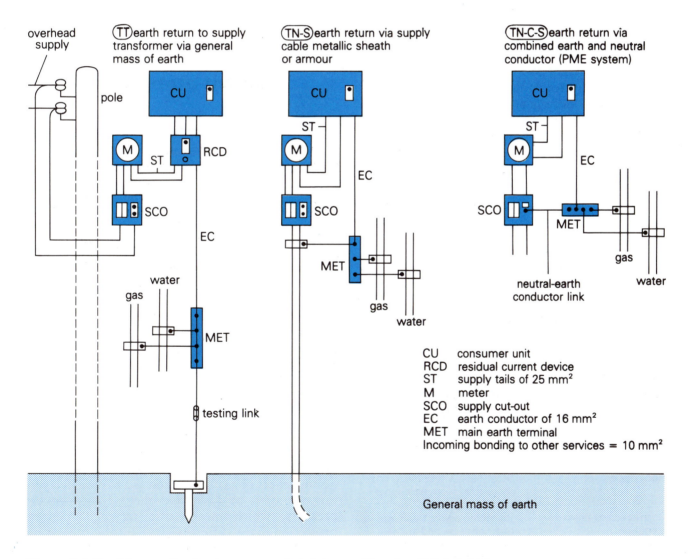

Figure 5.1 Earthing methods at consumer's intake position for 100 A S.P.N. supply.

Circuit protective conductor (c.p.c.)

This is the conductor which joins up all the metal-work which is to be earthed. It may be the metallic sheath of the cable, the metallic enclosure of the cables, conduit or trunking, or, in the case of all insulated cables, a separate conductor run specifically for that purpose.

Earth conductor or lead

The c.p.c. is finally brought back to the consumer's earth terminal and the earthing lead connects this terminal to the earth electrode.

Earth electrode

This is the electrode which makes the final connection to the general mass of earth.

It may be a copper rod, tape or plate, or a constructed lattice-type metal material, depending upon the nature of the subsoil (Figure 5.2). All, however, are buried in the ground, leaving a protected earth connection just below the surface, suitably labelled and protected by inspection covers. The limitations of this type of electrode are stated later. See Figure 5.12.

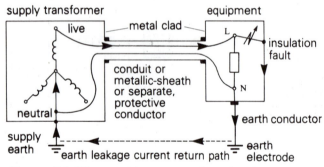

Figure 5.2 The earthing protection circuit.

I.E.E. requirements of earthing conductors

Type	Size and other requirements
Copper	Must comply with I.E.E. Regulations. Maximum size 70 mm.
ELCB	2.5 mm² insulated.
Non-copper	Must have a resistance not more than required copper lead.
Connection to earth electrode.	Protected against damage and corrosion and suitably labelled. Solidly soldered or clamps to BSS.

I.E.E. requirements of circuit protective conductors

Type of circuit protective conductor	Size and other requirements
Contained within the overall cable sheath.	In accordance with British Standards and cable manufacturers.
Within a flexible cable or cord.	Not smaller than the largest conductor contained therein.
Separate copper conductor.	See I.E.E. Regs. Insulated green with yellow tracer.
Metal conduits, ducts or trunking.	Resistance not more than twice the largest conductor therein. Joints must be electrically sound and protected against corrosion. Alternatively, a separate conductor can be used.

Circuit protection

Excessive current flow in a circuit is caused by breakdown of insulation either between live parts and earth, or between live parts connected to different phases of the supply. The former is usually referred to as an **earth fault**, while the latter is called a **short-circuit fault**.

On consumer installations, the two types of protection used against these faults are:

1. **fuses**;
2. **circuit breakers**.

Fuses operate on the basis of the heating effect (I^2R) of the excess current which melts the fuse element.

Circuit breakers are of two types – magnetic or thermal – both of which set up mechanical forces which cause movement and operate the switch on excess current flow. Because of the time lag in the heating effect of a current, there is a natural delay in the operation of fuses and thermal-type circuit breakers, which means that varying types of protection have different time-current operating characteristics. See Figure 5.3 for their basic construction.

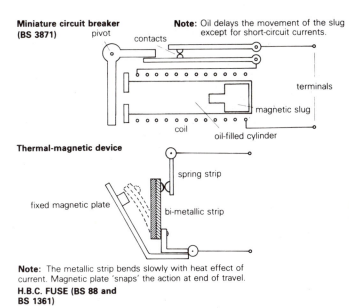

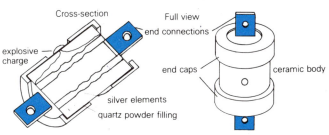

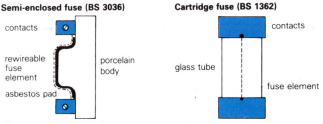

Figure 5.3 Circuit protection devices.

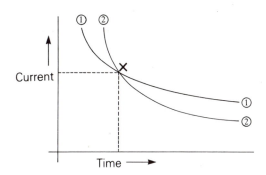

Figure 5.4 Relationship between two different types of excess current devices.

2. high breaking capacity (H.B.C.) fuses (BS 88 and BS 1361),
3. circuit breakers (BS 3871) miniature and moulded case types.

Discrimination

If the different time–current operating characteristics of the various excess current devices are mixed on the same installation, it is possible that the higher current-rated devices could operate before the lower rated ones. This would result in main distribution circuits being cut off while the local circuit fuse failed to operate.

> The differences in operating times and currents of excess current devices results in a lack of discrimination in overall operation, which is referred to simply as discrimination.

Terminology

Fuse rating is the current the fuse will carry without undue deterioration.
Fusing current is the current at which the fuse will suddenly melt.
Fusing factor is the ratio between fuse rating and fusing current

$$= \frac{\text{fusing current}}{\text{fusing rating}}$$

Circuit breaker setting is the current setting above which the breaker will operate and open the circuit.

The protection devices mentioned can be divided into three categories:

1. semi-enclosed or rewireable fuses (BS 3036) and cartridge fuses used in plugs (BS 1362),

Proper discrimination on circuit protection can be obtained by reference to the inverse time/current characteristics of the various protection devices. A study of these will show the current and time at which they will operate.

The graph in Figure 5.4 shows the inverse time/current characteristics of two different types of excess current devices. Device No. 1 has a higher current rating than No. 2, but if the fault current is higher than at point X, No. 1 device would operate before No. 2. Because this would be in a main circuit board it would result in power being cut off to healthy circuits and equipment. For correct discrimination, these curves must not cross. Similar excess current devices made by the same manufacturer will provide correct discrimination.

The appendices in the I.E.E. Regulations show

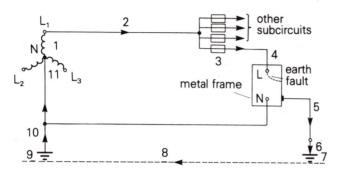

1 supply transformer winding
2 supply phase conductor
3 consumer's protection device
4 consumer's phase conductor
5 consumer's protective conductor
6 consumer's earthing conductor
7 consumer's earth electrode
8 return earth fault conductor
   (cable) sheath or general mass
   of the earth
9 supply earth electrode
10 supply earthing conductor
11 supply transformer star point

Figure 5.5 Total earth-loop path.

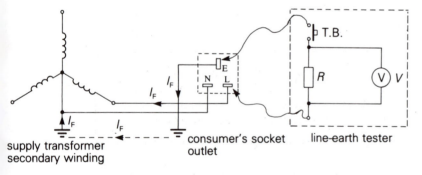

Figure 5.6 Line earth-loop impedance test.

figures of the characteristics of the various types of protective devices. A study of these will enable the student to compare them and to note that the operation of a rewireable fuse (BS 3036) is not as close to its rating as an H.B.C. (BS 88) or BS 1361 fuse or a circuit breaker (BS 3871).

> The main purpose of the circuit protective device is to protect the cable against excessive current flow which would lead to its overheating and damage to its insulation with fire and shock risks.

Thus the I.E.E. Regulations state that, in general, the current at which the device will operate and hence cut off the current flow must not exceed 1.45 times the current rating of the smallest cable it protects.

The operating current of a rewireable fuse (BS 3036) is almost twice its rating and because of this, a multiplying factor of 0.725 of the cable rating must be applied to the fuse protection.

EXAMPLE 1

A certain cable having a rating of 30 A is to be protected by a rewireable fuse BS 3036. Determine its fuse rating.

$$\text{Fuse rating} = \text{cable rating multiplied by } 0.725$$
$$= 30 \times 0.725 = 21.7 \text{ A}$$

The nearest standard fuse wire size is 20 A.

Where H.B.C. (BS 88) and BS 1361 fuses or circuit breakers BS 3871 are used, the above factor need not be applied since their operating current is much closer to their rating and is well within the 1.45 factor.

Earth-loop impedance (ELZ)

The total length of the protective circuit is known as the **earth-loop** and its total opposition to the current flow when a fault occurs is called its **earth-loop impedance**. See Figure 5.5.

Earth-loop impedance value

On a completed installation where the supply is connected, this value can be measured by a test carried out on the consumer's installation. It is known as the line-earth impedance test, shown in Figure 5.6. The tester contains a fixed resistor R, a voltmeter V and a test button T.B. When the button is pressed, a current of around 20 A is circulated in the earth-loop and the voltmeter measures the voltage drop across the resistor.

$$Z_s = \frac{V}{I} \ (\Omega)$$

The voltmeter scale is calibrated in ohmic values so that Z_s is read directly in ohms or fractions thereof.

Earth fault currents

To prevent fire and shock dangers it must be ensured that when a fault occurs the current value will be large enough to operate the circuit protective device within the stated regulation time, 0.4 s for socket outlet circuits and 5 s for fixed apparatus circuits.

$$\text{Now } I_F = \frac{V_P}{Z_s} \text{ where } \begin{aligned} I_F &= \text{fault current (A),} \\ V_P &= \text{phase voltage (V),} \\ Z_s &= \text{loop impedance } (\Omega). \end{aligned}$$

EXAMPLE 2

If an installation supplied at 240 V develops a direct earth fault and the earth-loop impedance is 1.8 Ω, calculate the fault current.

$$I_F = \frac{V_P}{Z_s} = \frac{240}{1.8} = 133 \text{ A}$$

Incomplete installations

When the mains supply is not connected to an installation, it is obviously not possible to measure the total earth-loop impedance value. In these cases it is only possible to measure the value of the consumer's protective circuit conductor path, namely items 3, 4, 5 and 6 on the total earth-loop path diagram (see Figure 5.5). This value is added to items 7, 8, 9 and 10 to obtain the total loop value.

$$Z_s = Z_E + \text{consumer's protective circuit } (\Omega)$$

where Z_s = total loop,

Z_E = external or supply loop value.

Protective conductor size

Where it is not possible to measure the value of Z_s for the reasons mentioned or, say, in the design stage of an installation, I.E.E. Regulations 413–5 show tables of Z_s values which must be used in the calculation of fault currents for specific types of excess current devices. This is for guidance in determining the size for the type of protective conductor to be used.

Table 5A shows that for circuit cables up to 16 mm², the protective conductor should be the same size as the live conductors. Note that this rules out the use of combined twin and earth cables now in common use where the protective conductor is smaller than the live conductors. However, Regulations do give an alternative method of calculation of protective conductor size which is

$$S = \frac{\sqrt{I^2 t}}{k}$$

where S = protective conductor size (mm²),
I = fault current (A),
t = operation time of the protective device (s),

which is obtained from the inverse time/current characteristics in the Appendix 3 of the I.E.E. Regulations;

k = temperature factor permitted for the type of cable used.

EXAMPLE 3

A copper twin and earth PVC-insulated cable protected by a 30 A (BS 3036) fuse supplies a domestic circuit at 240 V. Calculate the minimum size of the protective conductor permitted.

Regulation tables shows that for this type of protection the maximum earth loop impedance (Z_s) is 1.1 Ω. Therefore, the fault current

$$I_F = \frac{V_P}{Z_s} = \frac{240}{1.1} = 218 \text{ A, say } 200 \text{ A}$$

From I.E.E. Appendix 3 curves, time (t) of protection device = 0.5 s (approx) and the temperature factor (k) for this type of cable = 115.

$$\text{Protective conductor size } S = \sqrt{\frac{(200)^2 \times 0.5}{115}}$$

$$= 1.23 \text{ mm}^2$$

The nearest standard size (above) to this = 1.5 mm². On reference to the characteristics of an H.B.C. type fuse or a circuit breaker of 30 A rating, the loop impedance Z_s may be increased. This would result in a lower permitted value for the fault current and hence a reduction in permitted protective conductor size. Students are advised to make these changes and calculate the new protective conductor sizes.

Note: For fixed apparatus circuits, the excess current device operating time is up to a maximum of 5 s. For socket-outlet circuits it is 0.4 s.

Measurement of consumer's loop

The method is shown in Figure 5.7. The resistance of the protective conductor and the phase are inversely proportional to their respective areas. Therefore if the ohmmeter reading is multiplied by the neutral area and then divided by the sum of the

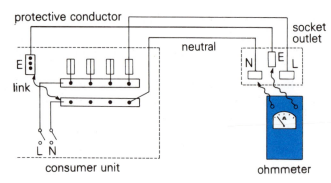

Figure 5.7 Test of consumer's protective loop.

protective conductor and the neutral areas, the result will be the resistance of the protective conductor only.

EXAMPLE 4

A consumer's earth-loop resistance using a 2.5 mm twin cable with a 1 mm combined protective conductor is 0.8 Ω. Determine the protective conductor resistance only.

Protective conductor resistance

$$= \frac{\text{ohmmeter value (52)} \times 2.5 \text{ (mm)}}{(1 + 2.5) \text{ (mm)}}$$

$$= \frac{0.8 \times 2.5}{1 + 2.5} \ \Omega$$

$$= \ 0.56 \ \Omega$$

> To assist in calculating the resistances, lengths and sizes of consumers' protective conductors, the I.E.E. show values of the resistance in ohms per metre (Ω/m) for conductor sizes.

I.E.E. resistance values include the phase plus the protective conductor resistance, which constitutes the consumer's earth-loop.

EXAMPLE 5

A consumer's earth-loop circuit consists of a 10 mm² phase conductor and a 4 mm² protective conductor each 20 m long. Calculate the value of the resistance of:
i) protective conductor;
ii) earth loop.

From I.E.E. Table 6A a 10 mm² phase conductor plus a 4 mm² protective conductor has a resistance of 6.44 mΩ per metre.

i) Resistance of earth loop

$= \text{m}\Omega/\text{m} \times l(\text{m})$

$= 6.44 \times 20 \text{ m}\Omega$
$= 128.8 \text{ m}\Omega$
$= 0.1288 \ \Omega$

ii) Resistance of c.p.c. $= \dfrac{\text{total loop} \times 10 \text{ m}}{10 + 4 \text{ m}}$

$= \dfrac{0.1288 \times 10}{14} = 0.092 \ \Omega$

Calculation of earth fault currents by the use of I.E.E. tables

> The basic calculation of fault currents is to divide the voltage by the resistance of the circuit conductors up to the point where the fault occurs.

At one time the resistance was calculated from the use of the resistivity formula ($\rho \ l/a$) (see Chapter 2).

The I.E.E. now publish tables which show the milliohms per metre (mΩ/m) resistance for the different types and sizes of cables. They also include a multiplying factor for the various types of cable insulation. These can then be used to calculate the value of $R_1 + R_2$ for the consumer circuits.

On smaller installations where the electrical appliances or machines etc. are supplied by final circuits directly from the incoming supply point, the consumer's loop impedance will simply be $R_1 + R_2$ of that circuit where R_1 = live conductor resistance R_2 = c.p.c. resistance.

With larger installations where the loads are supplied from distribution boards which in turn are supplied from the main switchgear at the incoming supply point, the consumer's earth loop will consist of two circuits, connected in series. See Figure 5.8.

> The total loop impedance will therefore be the addition of the two.

The value of Z_E (external earth circuit of supply authority) is stated. For purposes of calculation

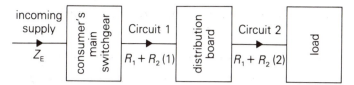

Figure 5.8 Consumer distribution circuits in series.

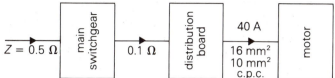

Figure 5.9 Diagram of Example 5.

sometimes the value of $R_1 + R_2$ on consumers' circuits is also given, however where it is not, it must be calculated by use of the I.E.E. tables.

EXAMPLE 6

A 415 V three-phase motor takes a full load current of 40 A. It is supplied from a distribution board which is 40 m away by a multi-core cable with 16 mm² copper conductor and a 10 mm² c.p.s. The cable is PVC insulated without armour.

The distribution board is supplied from the main intake switchgear by a cable whose loop values $R_1 + R_2 = 0.1\ \Omega$. The external loop value is given at 0.5 Ω. See Figure 5.9.

Using the I.E.E. Tables, 6A and B calculate:

i) volts drop between distribution board and the motor;
ii) prospective earth fault current (I_f) at the motor terminals connection.

i) From I.E.E. Table 7 mV/A/m for cable = 2.4

$$\text{Volts drop along cable} = \frac{2.4 \times 40 \times 40\ \text{V}}{1000}$$
$$= 3.84\ \text{V}$$

From Table 6
A copper conductor multi-core cable of 16 mm² with a 10 mm² c.p.c. has a resistance of 2.98 mΩ/m, and for PVC a multiplier of 1.38.

$$\text{Cable loop } R_1 + R_2 = \frac{2.98 \times 1.38 \times 40}{1000} = 0.164\ \Omega$$

Total earth loop impedance Z_s

$$= Z_E + (R_1 + R_2) + \text{cable } (R_1 + R_2)$$
$$= 0.5 + 0.1 + 0.164 = 0.764\ \Omega$$

ii) Earth fault current $I_f = \dfrac{V}{Z_s} = \dfrac{240}{0.764} = 314\ \text{A}$

The disconnection times for values of fault currents can be determined from the inverse time/current characteristics of appropriate protection device.

I.E.E. Regulations Table 6A. Value of resistance/metre for copper and aluminium conductors and of $R_1 + R_2$ per metre at 20°C in milliohms/metre

Cross-sectional area		Resistance/metre or $R_1 + R_2$/metre	
Phase conductor	Protective conductor	Plain copper	Aluminium
1	–	18.10	
1	1	36.20	
1.5	–	12.10	
1.5	1	30.20	
1.5	1.5	24.20	
2.5	–	7.41	
2.5	1	25.51	
2.5	1.5	19.51	
2.5	2.5	14.82	
4	–	4.61	
4	1.5	16.71	
4	2.5	12.02	
4	4	9.22	
6	–	3.08	
6	2.5	10.49	
6	4	7.69	
6	6	6.16	
10	–	1.83	
10	4	6.44	
10	6	4.91	
10	10	3.66	
16	–	1.15	1.91
16	6	4.23	–
16	10	2.98	–
16	16	2.30	3.82
25	–	0.727	1.2
25	10	2.557	–
25	16	1.877	–
25	25	1.454	2.4
35	–	0.524	0.868
35	16	1.674	2.778
35	25	1.251	2.068
35	35	1.048	1.736

I.E.E. Regulations Table 6B. Multipliers to be applied to Table 6A

Insulation material		85°C		90°C thermosetting
		PVC	Rubber	
Multiplier	54B	1.30	1.42	1.48
	54C	1.38	1.53	1.60

It is to be noted that the closer the fault is to the incoming supply the lower is the consumer's loop impedance and hence the higher the fault current.

The multipliers given in Table 5B are based on the simplified formula given in BS 6360 for both copper and aluminium conductors namely that the resistance–temperature coefficient is 0.004 Ω per °C at 20°C.

54B applies where the protective conductor is not incorporated or bunched with cables, or for bare protective conductors in contact with cable covering.

54C applies where the protective conductor is a core in a cable or is bunched with cables.

Earth leakage circuit breakers (ELCB)

When the maximum value of earth-loop impedance for over-current protection devices cannot be obtained, then the use of an ELCB is required.

Generally, in order to operate a load current protection device directly when earth leakage occurs, it is necessary to have a metallic path back to the neutral (star) point earth on the supply transformer via the metallic protection of the cable or the neutral conductor (PME). In these installations, the supply authority provides the consumer with an earth terminal which is connected via the metallic cable sheath right back to the transformer. On installations where this is not provided, such as those in rural areas supplied by overhead lines, it is uneconomic to provide a sufficiently low impe-

dance path by the use of the earth electrodes mentioned previously.

As a general rule it can be stated that when the consumer has to provide his own earth electrode, the use of an ELCB will be required.

From tests on earth electrodes described later, it is found that in average subsoil, the earth electrode resistance of a single rod driven into the ground to a depth of 2 m is around 60 Ω, which is much in excess of the required value for current protection device operation.

Operation of fault voltage-operated ELCB

Figure 5.10 shows the circuit diagram of a fault voltage-operated ELCB. When a leakage occurs between a live conductor and the earth circuit on the consumer installation, the earth terminal will rise in potential. This potential or voltage causes a current to flow in the coil of the ELCB, and the magnetic field set up causes the contacts to open and cut off the supply. A test button is provided to check the ELCB operation. When pressed, it disconnects the consumer's earth and pushes a small current through the coil causing its operation if it is in order. The resistance R is to limit the coil current to a safe value on testing. This type is now rarely used.

The test button is only a check on the ELCB operation, not the installation.

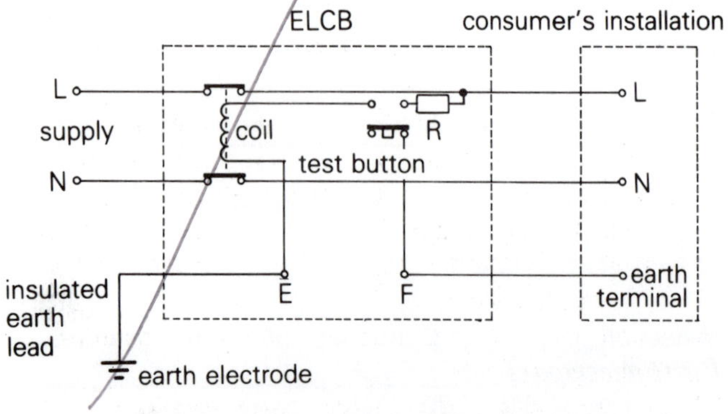

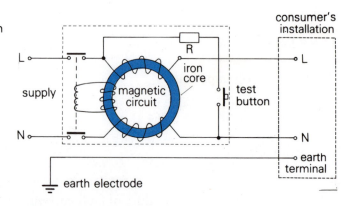

Figure 5.10 Fault voltage operated earth leakage circuit breaker.

Figure 5.11 Residual current operated earth leakage circuit breaker.

Figure 5.11 shows the circuit diagram of a residual current device (RCD). With no earth leakage current, the currents in each of the two L and N coils on the magnetic circuit iron former will be equal and since they are in opposite directions (180° apart), the magnetic fluxes will cancel each other so that no voltage will be induced in the operating coil.

> When an earth leakage current occurs from the live conductor, this leakage current does not return through the neutral conductor, so that an 'out-of-balance' situation in the L and N coils in the magnetic circuit arises. This results in a magnetic flux being set up in the iron core which induces a voltage in the operating coil, causing the contacts to open and cut off the supply.

Comparisons of fault voltage and residual current ELCB

Although the voltage type ELCB is cheaper and more sensitive than the current type, its disadvantage is that it is liable to nuisance tripping by small current leakages on appliances which are subject to such leakages such as cooker hot plates and immersion heaters. They can also be 'tripped' by faulty adjacent installations where unknowingly the areas of earth resistance around the various earth electrodes overlap.

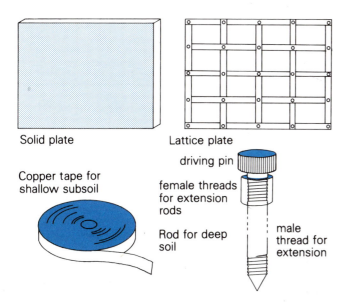

Figure 5.12 Types of earth electrodes for various subsoils.

The RCD is less sensitive than the voltage ELCB and therefore is not liable to nuisance tripping. The I.E.E. Regulations state that the maximum voltage to earth when a fault occurs should not exceed 50 V.

Precautions

The earth electrodes must be situated outside the resistance area of any other electrode so that no parallel paths to earth are formed, thus restricting the current in the operating coils. The earthing conductor from the voltage type to the earth electrode must be insulated to prevent accidental shorting out of the operating coil.

> Flexible conduits may not be used solely as a c.p.c. Gas, water and pipework of other services are not permitted for use as protective conductors but must be bonded where necessary to comply with Regulations on equipotential bonding.

Note: Bonding is necessary where the appliance and equipment are close to metalwork or other services such as in bathrooms, kitchens and toilets. I.E.E. Regulations state special protective measures are required in bath and shower-rooms. Bonding is to prevent differences of potential existing between metals which are so close to each other that a person's body could be in contact with the two at the same time, thereby causing severe shock. It is referred to as **equipotential bonding**.

> To assist in equipotential bonding gas, water pipes and the consumer's earth terminal are bonded together at the incoming supply on the consumer's installation.

Note: The bonds are made on the consumer's side of the stop taps and meters unless it has been ascertained that the incoming pipes are all metallic.

All joints and connections in earthing conductors must be made by means of soldering or recognised mechanical clamps.

Earth electrodes

Earth electrodes must satisfy tests laid down in Appendices of the I.E.E. Regulations. Gas and water pipes must not be used as earth electrodes.

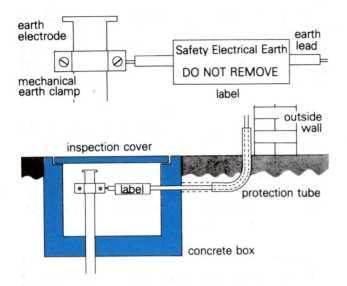

Figure 5.13 Protection of earth lead and electrode.

I.E.E. Regulations give the requirements concerning earth electrodes. See Figures 5.12 and 5.13.

Protective multiple earthing PME (TN-C-S)

Protective multiple earthing is a system of protection which has been introduced by the supply authorities. In this system, the consumer's earth terminal is connected to the supply authority's neutral conductor at the incoming terminals.

It takes the form of a copper link connected only by the supply authority. The supply neutral conductor now forms a low impedance return path for the earth leakage currents back to the transformer. It removes the need for ELCB and earth electrodes where no supply earth terminal is provided. One danger associated with this system is that if the neutral conductor becomes open circuit it is possible for the metalwork on the consumer's side of the break to become live. To reduce this risk, the supply neutral is earthed at intervals along its run back to the transformer. The installation must display a notice at its income supply – 'THIS INSTALLATION IS PME'.

Testing of installations

All new installations and alterations to existing installations must be inspected and tested in accordance with Appendix 14 of the I.E.E. Regulations. This now calls for visual inspections of thirteen items before testing.

The 16th Edition of the I.E.E. Regulations recommend that the tests should be carried out in the following sequence.

1. Before supply is connected test:
   A) continuity of c.p.c.s,
   B) continuity of ring circuits,
   C) polarity,
   D) insulation resistance,
   E) earth electrode resistance (where applicable).
2. With supply connected:
   A) recheck polarity (with test lamp),
   B) test earth fault loop impedance (using L–E tester),
   C) test operation of the RCD when fitted.

Note: When testing 2 (C) the installation is disconnected from the RCD and a current equal to the tripping current (usually 30 mA) is applied between the phase conductor and the c.p.c. on the load side terminals which should cause tripping in less than 200 ms.

Note: It is essential to ensure that all voltage sensitive devices which are normally fitted in electronic equipment should not be subjected to the 500 V insulation test voltage.

Polarity test

This is to ensure that all fuses, single-pole switches and centre connections of screw lampholders are connected in the live conductor only. It should be noted that under the Regulations, every outlet termination of the fixed wiring must have an earth terminal provided, which is connected to the circuit protective conductor right back to the consumer unit. The use of this terminal in polarity testing can eliminate the use of long test leads. It simply entails the connecting of a temporary link between the earth terminal and the connection which should be connected to the live conductor. All tests can now be carried out from the consumer unit.

Figure 5.14 illustrates the polarity test for switches and screw lampholders.

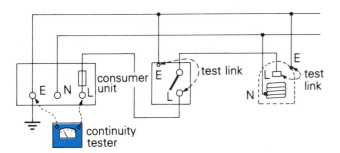

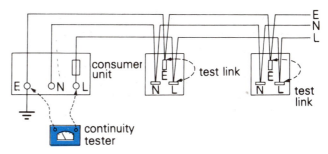

Figure 5.14 Polarity tests for switches and screw lampholders.

Figure 5.15 Polarity tests for socket outlets.

Note: After testing the switch, the link is removed and the switch closed before testing the lampholder.

Figure 5.15 illustrates the polarity test for socket outlets.

This method of polarity testing is used where the mains supply is not available. On installations where there is a supply, an approved type of test lamp may be connected between the positions where the links are shown and the lamp should light if the polarity is correct.

To avoid long test leads the method for this test is similar to the polarity test. With **supply off** the links can be connected in turn between the remote ends of the outlet points as shown using the live conductor as the return path.

Note: For accuracy, the resistance of the return live conductor must be deducted from the reading. The live conductor resistance can be obtained by connecting the test link between L and N taking the reading and dividing it by 2.

Earth-loop impedance test

In order to measure the maximum impedance values permitted to enable the protection device to operate, the test illustrated in Figure 5.6 is required. The values are given in Regulation 413–5 table.

The method shown is known as the **line-earth**

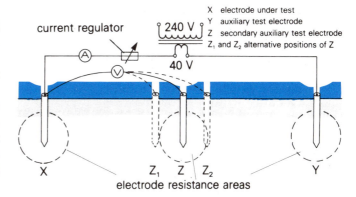

Figure 5.16 Earth electrode test.

test and is the one most commonly used for all installations. The arrow-heads show the path of the loop current under test.

Earth electrode test

When it is necessary to install an earth electrode, it is advisable to test for its effectiveness. This is known as its **earth electrode resistance test**. The I.E.E. Regulations give a description and circuit diagram of this test. See Figure 5.16. With a steady a.c. current flowing between X and Y, the electrode resistance of X =

$$R = \frac{V}{I}\Omega$$

Measurement of circuit protective conductor resistance

Test current	Test voltage	Maximum value (Ω)
1. A.c. installation: around 1.5 times the rating of the subcircuit under test up to a maximum of 25 A.	Up to 40 a.c. at supply frequency.	All values must be low enough when added to the supply protective conductor circuit (Z_E) to satisfy I.E.E. Reg. 413–5. Or, alternatively, by calculation to cause operation of protective device in regulation time limit.
2. With lower current values than (1) such as a continuity test or megger on the continuity range.		
3. D.c. installation: use of direct current from battery or megger on continuity range.		

The test should be repeated for positions Z_1 and Z_2 to check the first result. If the three results are the same then this is the true value for X, since the resistance areas of the electrode do not overlap. **Note:** The resistance area is that area within which it is possible to measure the resistance. Outside this area, the conductivity of the general mass of earth is so good its resistance is difficult to measure.

Insulation resistance test

Cable insulation resistance is inverse to conductor resistance. The insulation can be considered as parallel paths of resistors, so that the longer the cable the greater the number of resistors in parallel. See Figure 5.17.

From the parallel resistance formula, total resistance R_T

$$\frac{1}{R_T} = \frac{1}{r_1} + \frac{1}{r_2} + \frac{1}{r_3} + \cdots$$

therefore the total resistance will decrease as the cable length increases.

Hence when insulation tests are carried out on a large number of cables at any one time, a low ohmic value will be obtained which can be mistaken for a fault or undue leakage. For this reason the regulations advise the splitting up of circuits and testing separately.

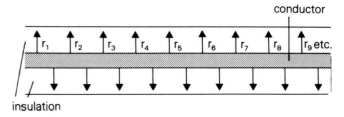

Figure 5.17 Earth electrode resistance test.

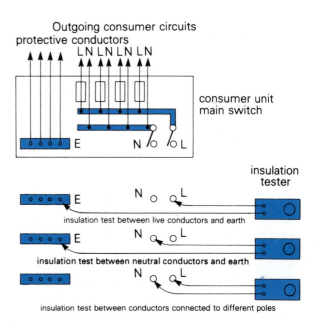

Figure 5.18 Insulation tests at consumer's switchgear.

I.E.E. requirements

Method of test	Minimum values (MΩ)
Insulation to earth test with all fuses in place, switches closes, i.e. all conductor insulation under test.	0.5
Insulation between any two poles or different phase conductors with all lamps removed and all switches closed.	0.5
Insulation of fixed apparatus that cannot be disconnected for test E8.	0.5

EXAMPLE 7

A certain cable has an insulation resistance of 150 MΩ per metre length, calculate the insulation value of 50 metre length of this cable.

$$\text{Insulation } R = \frac{\text{resistance per m}}{\text{length (m)}} = \frac{150 \text{ M}\Omega}{50}$$
$$= 3 \text{ M}\Omega$$

These are tests of the insulation between the conductors themselves and between the conductors and earth.

The insulation test '**megger**' must provide a d.c. test voltage of not less than twice the normal supply voltage but need not exceed 500 V for circuits up to 650 V.

On a large installation, the insulation value will be lower because of the number of insulation resistance values in parallel.

On such installations, the installation circuits should be subdivided and each subcircuit tested separately. Figure 5.18 illustrates these tests.

Test for ring circuit continuity

Study of a ring circuit will show that each conductor starts at the supply terminal and returns to that terminal, that is, it is continuous throughout. For this test it is only necessary to disconnect the same conductor, that is, L, N or E at any point where they are joined in a socket or at the consumer unit and separate the two ends.

A continuity test between these ends should show the continuous paths resulting in a very low ohmic reading.

Rupturing capacity

On heavy current supplies fed with large cables and situated near to the transformers and generators, the current flow in the event of a short circuit or earth fault will be very large indeed. It is therefore essential that this current is interrupted as quickly and as safely as possible.

The flow of fault energy before interruption is known as **let through energy** and its value is I^2Rt joules or watt-seconds. Because of the high value of energy released when the fault occurs, the switchgear must contain this without damage to itself or the surrounding area – it must contain the explosion and arcing within itself.

The term **rupturing capacity** is used for switchgear which states the maximum short circuit kV A it will interrupt with safety. It is therefore necessary to calculate this value when installing switchgear for heavy current supplies.

Calculation of short circuit kV A

Generators, transformers and feeder cables have impedance values which are expressed as percentages. On a.c. circuits, the resistances are very small compared with the reactances, so for practical purposes, the impedance may be taken to be the reactance.

Meaning of percentage value

A reactance value of say 5 per cent means that 5 per cent of the rated voltage would cause full load current to circulate in the winding of a generator or a transformer, or if that voltage is applied between the ends of the cable conductors. Since alternators and transformers are rated in kV A values, so percentage reactances are expressed in terms of percentage kV A of the full load kV A. Similarly, for convenience, feeder cables are also expressed in terms of the percentage kV A they carry at full load.

Generators and transformers in series

In a single radial circuit which comprises generator, transformer and feeder cables, all in series and all rated at the same full load kV A, the total percentage reactance of the circuits is obtained simply by adding all the percentages together.

EXAMPLE 8

A three-phase HV generator supplies a transformer which in turn supplies a busbar chamber. If the generator, transformer and feeder cables connected as shown in Figure 5.19, are rated at 1000 kV A and have percentage reactances as shown, calculate the short-circuit kV A.

Total percentage reactance = 4 + 5 + 5 + 6 = 20%
This means that 20%, or 1/5 of the full voltage would cause full load kV A or current to flow in the system.
Therefore, if the full supply voltage is maintained then:

$$\frac{100\%}{20\%} = 5 \text{ times the full load value.}$$

So that short-circuit kV A = $1000 \times \dfrac{100\%}{20\%} = 5000$

If the voltage on the secondary side of the transformer is 415 V, calculate the short-circuit current on this side.

A three-phase system kV A $= \dfrac{\sqrt{3}\ V_L I_L}{1000}$

$$I_L = \frac{kV\ A \times 1000}{\sqrt{3}\ V_L}$$

Therefore, at short-circuit condition

$$I_L = \frac{5000 \times 1000}{1.732 \times 415} = 6956 \text{ A}$$

Where equipment and cables in a common system have differing values of rated kV A, it is usual to

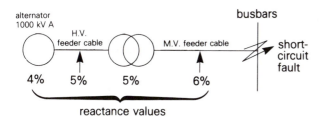

Figure 5.19 Series addition of percentage reactances, Example 8.

adjust these to a common base kV A value. If, for example, a length of cable had a full load rating of 5000 kV A and only 2500 kV A was being transmitted, then the current would be halved and only half of the voltage drop rating at full load would occur. This means that if the percentage reactance at 5000 kV A was 8 per cent, then at 2500 kV A base, it would be 4 per cent. This also applies to generators and transformers.

EXAMPLE 9

A transformer has a rating of 10 000 kV A with a reactance of 4 per cent, a generator has a rating of 5000 kV A and a reactance of 5 per cent and the interconnecting cables have a rating of 5000 kV A at a reactance of 2 per cent. The transformer supplying the busbars is 11 kV/415 V three-phase. Calculate

i) the short-circuit kV A
ii) the short-circuit current when a fault occurs on the busbars.

i) Take a common base of 5000 kV A. The transformer reactance is now

$$4\% \times \frac{5000}{10\ 000} = 2\%$$

The generator and cables remain the same.
The total reactance now = 2 + 5 + 2 = 9%

$$\text{Total kV A at short-circuit} = 5000 \times \frac{100\%}{9} = 55.55$$

ii) $\text{Short-circuit current} = \dfrac{55\ 550 \times 1000}{1.732 \times 415} = 77\ 290\ \text{A}$

Generators and transformers in parallel

The equivalent resistance is calculated in the same way as for resistors in parallel:

$$\frac{1}{\%\times\text{total}} = \frac{1}{\%X_1} + \frac{1}{\%X_2} + \cdots$$

EXAMPLE 10

Two three-phase 3.3 kV generators rated at 1000 and 1500 kV A respectively have reactances of 8 per cent and 10 per cent respectively. They are connected in parallel to supply a set of common

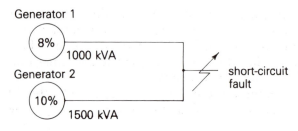

Figure 5.20 Parallel addition of percentage reactances, Example 9.

busbars. Calculate the short-circuit kV A and current when a fault occurs on the busbars. See Figure 5.20.

Using 2500 kV A based:

$$\text{No. 1 generator } \%X = 8 \times \frac{2500}{1000} = 20$$

$$\text{No. 2 generator } \%X = 10 \times \frac{2500}{1500} = 16.7$$

Total percentage reactance

$$\frac{1}{\%X_T} = \frac{1}{20} + \frac{1}{16.7}$$

$$\%X = 9.1$$

$$\text{Short-circuit kV A} = 2500 \times \frac{100}{9.1} = 27\ 472$$

$$\text{Short circuit current} = \frac{27\ 473}{\sqrt{3} \times 3.3} = 4806.6\ \text{A}$$

■ CHECK YOUR UNDERSTANDING

● The consumer's earthing circuit consists of the c.p.c., earthing conductor and the earth electrode.
● The type of earth electrode will depend upon the nature of the soil. Soft soil use long rods, shallow soil use plates or lattice frameworks.
Connection to electrode must be protected and labelled. Its resistance is measured by the three spike method.
● A PME system uses the neutral conductor of the supply system as the earth fault return conductor back to the supply transformer.

- Earth fault current

$$I_p = \frac{V_p}{Z_s} \quad p = \text{phase values}$$

- Size of c.p.c. $= \sqrt{\dfrac{I^2 t}{k}}$

$$k = \text{temperature factor}$$

- A residual current device operates on 'out of balance' current between the circuit conductors when an earth fault occurs.
- Discrimination is the term used for the difference in operating time against fault current for the various excess current devices.
- I.E.E. tables state the resistance of cables in $m\Omega$/m length in order to calculate the value of fault current at a given position on the circuit.
- The value of insulation resistance of a cable is inverse to its conductor resistance.
- Rupturing capacity of switchgear is the maximum kV A it will safely interrupt in the event of a short circuit on the system.

Short circuit kV A

$$= \frac{\text{rated kV A value of equipment} \times 100\%}{\% \text{ reactance value}}$$

- Let through energy is that between the fault time and the operating time of the excess current device to interrupt the current $= I^2 R t$ joules.

REVISION EXERCISES AND QUESTIONS

1　i) Under what circumstances do the I.E.E. Regulations require the bonding of electrical apparatus to the metalwork of other services?
　ii) State **two** examples where bonding is necessary, giving reasons.

2　i) Explain why it is essential for a final circuit to have a low earth loop impedance.
　ii) An earth fault occurs on a circuit where the loop impedance exceeds that quoted in Table 41 A2 of the I.E.E. Regulations.
　　a) State the danger that exists.
　　b) Explain a method of reducing the danger in (a).

3　A rod earth electrode is driven into the ground on a farm.
　i) Describe with the aid of a diagram how to test its resistance.
　ii) If the resistance is above that required how could it be reduced?
　iii) What danger may result if the electrode is exposed to touch in this situation and how can it be overcome?

4　An agricultural installation which has BS 1363 socket outlet provision is to be connected to a TT system.
　i) With the aid of a fully labelled diagram, show the sequence of control and protection equipment.
　ii) Describe how any slight earth leakage current causes the supply to be 'cut off' from the installation.
　iii) Explain the meaning of earth electrode resistance.
　iv) State the recommended disconnection time for the installation.

5　i) Explain what is meant by PME (TN-C-S)
　ii) Draw a labelled diagram showing the arrangement at the consumer's intake position.
　iii) State **one** advantage of this to **each** of:
　　a) supply authority, and
　　b) the consumer.

6　An earth loop impedance test on a 240 V installation protected by a 30 A rewireable fuse gives a reading of 6 Ω. On investigation a conduit joint is found to have a resistance of 4 Ω.
　i) If a short circuit fault between the phase (live) conductor and the conduit occurred, calculate
　　a) the leakage current,
　　b) the power developed at the joint, and
　　c) the voltage across the joint.
　ii) What would be the effect of the fault in (i) on (a) operation of the fuse, and (b) safety?

7　An agricultural installation including S/Os is to be connected to a TT system.
　i) Using a labelled diagram show the sequence of controls and protective system.
　ii) Explain fully how the installation is earthed.
　iii) State **four** precautions to be taken with the final connection to earth.
　iv) If the ground soil is shallow, state a suitable type of earth electrode.

8　i) With the aid of a diagram explain how a voltmeter, ammeter and battery can be connected at one end of a two-core cable to measure the total resistance of the conductors.

   ii) The total conductor resistance of a 50 m length of twin cable is 1 Ω, calculate
      a) the millivolts per ampere per metre drop, and
      b) the maximum length of run when carrying 18 A so that the voltage drop does not exceed 4 per cent of the 240 V supply.

   iii) If the insulation resistance is 4000 MΩ per m length, calculate the total insulation resistance.

9   i) Explain what is meant by inverse time/current characteristic.
   ii) Name three types of excess protection devices and state the BS number for each.
   iii) State the permitted time for the operation of a circuit supplying (a) socket outlets and (b) fixed appliances. Give reasons for the difference.
   iv) Using the alternative formula method, calculate the size of the c.p.c. where $I = 200$ A, $t = 0.42$ s and $k = 115$.

10 i) Define the following terms:
      a) earth conductor, (b) circuit protective conductor, (c) earth-loop impedance (d) earth electrode and (e) equipotential bonding.
   ii) What is meant by earth electrode resistance area?

11 i) Draw a labelled diagram of the complete earth-loop path when a consumer's installation fed from a substation develops an earth fault. The installation is earthed by a driven rod-type electrode.
   ii) Describe a method to determine the resistance of the earth electrode only.

12 An installation consists of a four-way consumer unit, one way of which feeds two lighting points with screw-type lampholders, each lamp being controlled by a one-way switch. It is connected to a 240 V single-phase supply.
   i) Draw the circuit diagram for this.
   ii) With the aid of the diagram, describe how the following tests should be carried out on the installation:
      a) insulation tests between conductors and earth and between the conductors themselves and (b) polarity.
   iii) State the nature of the insulation test voltage and minimum resistance values.

13 A consumer's 13 A socket outlet is wired in steel conduit. When an earth-loop impedance test is carried out on the socket its value is 10 Ω but it is found that a faulty joint in the conduit run has a resistance of 8 Ω.
   i) If the supply is 240 V and the circuit is protected by a 30 A fuse state (a) the value of the current had an earth fault occurred; (b) the power (heat) generated at the faulty joint, and (c) the dangers presented by this situation.
   ii) When the joint is made sound its resistance is reduced to zero. State the new values for (a) and (b) above.
   iii) Give reasons why the dangers are removed in (ii).

14 i) What is meant by **protective multiple earthing** (PME)?
   ii) Make a labelled sketch showing the arrangement at the consumer's intake supply position when PME is used.
   iii) State **two** advantages of PME to **each** of the following: (a) supply authority and (b) consumer.
   iv) Explain the likely dangers in the use of PME and the methods used to reduce these.

15 i) State the reasons for the use of **earth leakage circuit breakers** (ELCB).
   ii) Explain briefly the principle of operation of (a) fault voltage ELCB and (b) residual current ELCB.
   iii) What is the purpose of the test button?

16 i) Show the earth-loop path on a consumer's installation only and how its value may be measured before connection to the mains supply.
   ii) If its value is measured at 0.5 Ω and the value of the mains supply external loop is given as 0.75 Ω, calculate the value of the prospective earth fault current if the supply is 240 V.

17 Give reasons why the type of circuit protective device used affects the sizes of:
   i) live conductors,
   ii) protective conductors when the same load current is being supplied.

18 i) Explain what is meant by the term 'prospective short circuit fault rating' as applied to a consumer's installation.
   ii) A consumer's medium voltage switchboard is fed by three 2000 kV A 11 kV/415 V transformers connected in parallel, each transformer having a 4 per cent reactance. The interconnection between each transformer and its associated medium voltage circuit breaker consists of cables having a 2 per

cent reactance at 1000 kV A. Ignoring the effect of the supplies up to the 11 kV transformers, find the maximum short circuit MV A and the current which will flow in the event of a short circuit fault on the busbars of the medium voltage switchgear.

(C & G 'C')

19 Where the prospective fault current of a circuit is known or can be calculated from inverse time/current tables, write down the formula which enables the size of the protective conductor to be determined, stating the other factors involved.

20 A certain load which takes a current of 24 A is protected by a 25 A m.c.b. Calculate the c.p.c. (with PVC insulation) size, given that the disconnection time is to be 4 s and the temperature factor for the PVC = 143. From the inverse time/current characteristic for this type of m.c.b. the fault current is to be 175 A.

Lighting, heating and cooling systems

Introduction

Light is radiation of electromagnetic waves in a narrow frequency band between 4×10^{14} and 7×10^{14} hertz. The eye is sensitive to these frequencies. Light is radiated by many sources: from the Sun; from bodies whose temperatures are raised to a very high value as in the case of a filament lamp, and also when a current is passed through a gas to cause a discharge of energy in the light frequency waveband as in discharge lamps.

A flow of light (luminous) flux is measured in **lumens**. The amount of luminous flux falling on a given surface area is measured in **lumens per square metre**, known as the lux (abbr. lx).

> In company with other forms of energy which is radiated in all directions, the intensity of light falls off as the **inverse square** of the **distance** it has travelled. It is also decreased by the angle at which it falls on the surface.

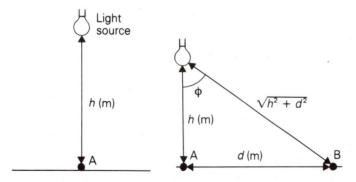

Figure 6.1 Inverse square law.
Figure 6.2 Cosine law.

The laws of illumination for calculation purposes are based on the above two facts.

Illumination

Laws of illumination

The unit of **luminous intensity** from a light source is the **candela** (symbol I) (abbr. cd).
The unit of **luminous flux** is the lumen (symbol Φ (abbr. lm).
The unit of **illumination** at a point on a surface is the lumen per m² known as the **lux** (symbol **E**) (abbr. lx)

Inverse square law
The illumination on a surface will fall off as the inverse square of the distance from the light source.

$$\text{Illumination at A} = \frac{I}{h^2} \frac{\text{(lux)}}{\text{(m)}}$$

This assumes the point A is **directly** below the light source. See Figure 6.1

Cosine Law
When the surface to be illuminated is not directly beneath the light source then the angle of the light rays to the light comes into the calculation. See Figure 6.2.
Illumination at point B,

$$E = \frac{I}{(\text{distance})^2} \times \cos \phi$$

$$= \frac{I}{h^2 \times d^2} \times \frac{h}{\sqrt{(h^2 + d^2)}}$$

EXAMPLE 1

If a light source of intensity of 450 cd is 3 m directly above a point on a horizontal bench, calculate

i) the illumination on that point;
ii) the illumination on a second point on the bench which is 4 m from the first point. See Figure 6.3.

Illumination on 1st point $= \dfrac{450}{3^2} = 50 \text{ lux}$

Illumination on 2nd point $= \dfrac{450}{(3^2 + 4^2)} \times \dfrac{3}{\sqrt{(3^2 + 4^2)}}$

$= \dfrac{18 \times 3}{5} = 10.8 \text{ lux}$

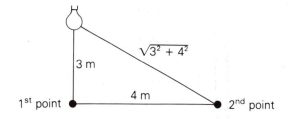

Figure 6.3 Cosine example.

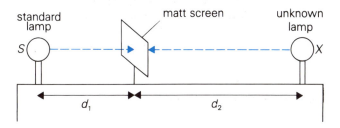

Figure 6.4 Photo bench.

Photo bench

This is used to determine the output candela of an unknown lamp using a known standard lamp. See Figure 6.4. At balance when the illumination (lux) is equal on both sides of the matt screen

$$X = \frac{s \times (d_2)^2}{(d_1)^2} \text{ candela}$$

Illumination meter

This consists of a selenium photocell connected to a very sensitive microammeter. When light rays fall on the cell it causes electrons to be released, so that a small current is supplied to the microammeter.

The value of the current is proportional to the amount of light received, so the instrument scale can be calibrated directly in lux. See Figure 6.5.

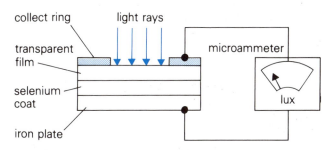

Figure 6.5 Illumination meter.

Because they operate at unity pf, the operating current consumption in amperes is equal to

$$\frac{\text{watts rating}}{\text{voltage}}$$

but it is important to note that the filament resistance is much lower when cold so that the initial switch-on current is much higher, see Chapter 2. Light output is measured in **lumens**.

Filament lamps are cheaper than the discharge types of lamp, but their efficiency

$$\frac{\text{(light output in lumens per watt)}}{\text{power input}}$$

is much lower and they have a shorter life than discharge lamps.

Because filament lamps operate at very high temperatures, I.E.E. Regulations state that they must be placed or guarded so as to prevent the ignition of inflammable materials. Normal filament lamps are designed to operate in a vertical (cap uppermost) position.

Lighting systems

Filament lamps

Filament lamps consist of a tungsten filament wire suspended by metal supports and enclosed in an inert gas-filled envelope. When connected to a supply, the current raises the filament temperature to around 3000°C so that light is emitted. Filament lamps can be obtained in standard sizes with bayonet-type connection caps up to 150 W. Above this power rating, they can be obtained with Edison-screw (ES) connection caps up to 200 W or with Goliath Edison-screw connection caps (GES) up to 1500 W.

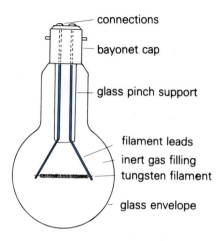

Figure 6.6 Filament lamp.

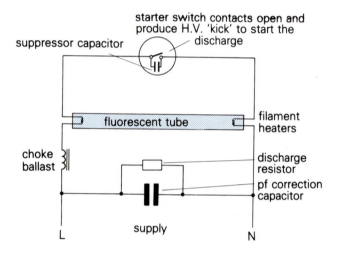

Figure 6.7 Fluorescent lamp with an inductance and starter switch.

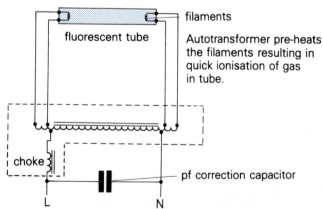

Note: The autotransformer and choke are normally contained in one unit known as an instant-start ballast unit.

Figure 6.8 Fluorescent lamp with an autotransformer and no starter switch.

When suspended on a flex, such as a ceiling pendant, insulation of the flex must be of the heat-resistant type.

The Regulations also state the maximum weight of the lighting fittings which can be supported by a given size of conductor flex. See Figure 6.6.

On domestic installations, which are main users of filament lamps, the I.E.E. Regulations state that each lamp is given a minimum rating of 100 W so that on a 240 V supply, where the consumer's lighting circuits are protected by a 5 A fuse, the maximum number of lighting points would be twelve on each subcircuit. The cable size would be 1 mm² or 1.5 mm², dependent upon the length of the circuit run to limit volts drop. See Chapter 3 for information on voltage drop and rating factors.

Discharge lamps

Fluorescent lamps

Fluorescent lamps consist of a tubular discharge lamp, internally coated with a powder which fluoresces under the action of the discharge, producing a shadowless white or coloured light, dependent upon the type of powder used and the type of gas.

The lamp sizes range from about 60 cm in length, rated at 20 W up to 2.6 m in length rated at 125 W. The calculation of **metricated** current demand is discussed later. Control gear, referred to as **ballast**, is necessary with all discharge lamps, not only to produce the high voltage to start the discharge but to keep the discharge and the lamp current at a steady value once it is in operation. It is partly this gear which accounts for the higher cost of the installation.

There is a choice of starting and control equipment.

1. An inductance (known as the choke) and a starter switch can be used. See Figure 6.7.
2. An auto-transformer can be used without a starter switch. See Figure 6.8.
3. A resistance ballast which may be a filament lamp and a starter switch can be used. This is a cheaper method but because of the power consumption (I^2R) of the resistance, the running

costs are higher. In this circuit, the resistance takes the place of the choke.

Fluorescent tubes which operate from low d.c. supplies such as car batteries can be obtained using an **inverted thyristor** power pack providing high frequency a.c. outputs. For large installations, tubes may be mounted end to end on trunking supported from the roof supports. The trunking contains the necessary ballast equipment and wiring.

High pressure mercury-vapour discharge lamps (HPMV)

The construction of these lamps is shown in Figure 6.9.

> The light of a HPMV lamp is produced by the discharge of current in a mercury-vapour gas which causes radiation of light waves. The initial discharge is caused by an auxiliary electrode mounted very close to the main electrode.

There is a delay of around four minutes between the initial discharge and full light output, while the gas pressure increases. If the lamp is switched off and on again, there will be a delay while the gas pressure falls and the initial discharge can com-

mence again. The high-pressure mercury-vapour lamp circuit is shown in Figure 6.10.

Sodium-vapour discharge lamps

The construction of these is shown in Figure 6.11. They are mainly used for external lighting installations and emit a yellowish coloured light. On some types, it is possible to replace the outside vacuum jacket. Sodium is highly flammable. Care must be taken if the lamp is broken.

Note: Unless they are of the **universal** type, sodium-vapour discharge lamps must be horizontally mounted.

The main advantage of discharge lamps is their high efficiency. In general, they give four times as much light per watt as filament lamps. They also have longer life. The disadvantages are the higher initial costs and power losses in the control (ballast) equipment. Figure 6.12 shows a sodium vapour lamp circuit.

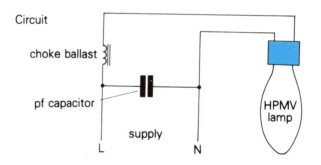

Figure 6.10 High-pressure mercury-vapour circuit.

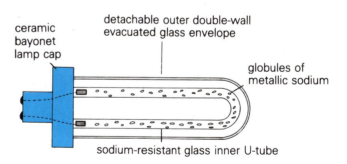

Figure 6.11 Sodium-vapour lamp construction.

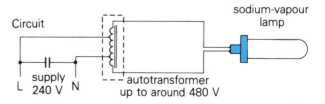

Figure 6.12 Sodium-vapour lamp circuit.

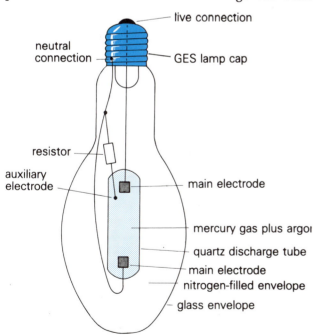

Figure 6.9 High-pressure mercury-vapour (HPMV) lamp construction.

Installation of discharge lamps

> Because discharge lamps and their associated control gear have a low pf (which is corrected somewhat by the use of capacitors in the circuit) and also because of harmonic currents which are not included in the power rating of the lamp, it is necessary to uprate the cable and switch loadings.

If exact values of current in the circuit are not known, a factor of 1.8 is used to multiply the power rating of the lamp for cable sizes, and a factor of two for the switch rating (unless the switch is designed to operate on an inductive circuit).

For example, for circuit loading a 125 W discharge-type lamp operating on a 240 V supply the current value calculation would be:

$$\frac{125}{240} \times 1.8 = 0.94 \text{ A}$$

and for switching loading:

$$\frac{125}{240} \times 2 = 1.04 \text{ A}$$

Because of the heat radiation from the ballast unit, discharge lamps must be ventilated and mounted on non-flammable material. In most cases, they are suitably mounted and contained with the lighting fittings themselves. Where they are separately mounted, they should be as close to the associated lamp as practicable, although in some installations, such as chemical works, care should be taken to prevent the atmosphere from damaging the choke insulation. This can be done by providing suitable protection or by mounting the lamps in a cleaner atmosphere. Again, because of momentarily high voltages, all live parts must be suitably screened against accidental contact.

Stroboscopic effect

When the discharge takes place in the gaseous envelope, there is a movement of ions and electrons which reverses when the polarity of the supply changes, that is, twice every cycle of the supply voltage. On a 50 Hz supply, this means 100 times every second.

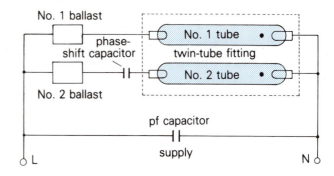

Figure 6.13 Use of twin-tube fitting with a phase-shift capacitor.

> When the reversal of ion and electron movement coincides with the speed of a revolving machine, the machine appears to be stationery, which presents an obvious danger.

The following methods are adopted to reduce this effect:

1. where a T.P.N. supply is available, adjacent lamps are connected to different phases of the supply;
2. the use of a twin-tube fitting where one tube has a capacitor connected in series with it to produce a phase shift of the current in that tube. See Figure 6.13.

Basic design of a lighting installation

An even value of illumination may be obtained over a given surface area by arranging suitable spacing of the light fittings. The illumination (amount of light) on a surface in terms of the light which falls on a unit area is termed lux (E) which is lumens per metre^2 (lm/m^2).

Factors to be considered

1. **Utilisation** Some of the light output (lumens) from the light fitting is absorbed by the lighting fitting itself and also by the wall and the ceiling surfaces and hence there is a reduction in the amount of useful light.
2. **Maintenance** Lack of maintenance causes a further reduction of useful light which is caused by an accumulation of dirt on reflecting surfaces and the ageing of the lamps.

Total lumens required from the light fittings for a given installation

$$\frac{\text{lux value required (lm/m}^2) \times \text{area of working surface (m}^2)}{\text{utilisation factor} \times \text{maintenance factor}}$$

EXAMPLE 2

A room 40 m by 15 m is to be lit by fluorescent fittings rated at 65 W each which have an efficiency of 70 lumens per watt. The illumination value is to be 180 lx. If the utilization is 0.5 and the maintenance factor is 0.8

i) determine the number of fittings required;
ii) on a sheet of graph (squared) paper draw the room plan to scale and a suitable spacing for the fittings.

i) Total lumens required $= \dfrac{180 \times 40 \times 15}{0.5 \times 0.8} = 270\,000$

Light output of each fitting
$= 70 \times 65 = 4500$ lumens

Hence number of fittings required

$= \dfrac{270\,000}{4500} = 60$

ii) Room length:width ratio = 40:15 = 2.67:1

By inspection, nearest lamps spacing ratio for 60 fittings is 12:5 = 2.4:1. This would mean 5 rows with 12 fittings in each row.

It is not normally practicable to have an exactly even spacing of light fittings, it must be adjusted to fit in as closely as possible with the room dimensions and the number of lighting fitting required. In some installations one or two more fittings may have to be used to achieve this.

High-voltage signs

These are glass tubes moulded into shapes such as letters and again gas-filled, so that when a sufficiently high voltage is applied to electrodes at each end of the tube, a discharge takes place and lights the tube. Because these are normally mounted on the outside of buildings and high voltages are present, the I.E.E. Regulations lay down special requirements for their installation which, for most, includes the provision of a fireman's switch.

The maximum voltage to earth allowed for high voltage signs is 5000 V, although the use of centre-tapped transformers enables a voltage of 10 000 V to be applied to the sign.

The voltage needed to ionise the gas is dependent upon the length and the diameter of the tube. In a large sign, the letters or small groups of letters are supplied from separate transformers.
Note: If the transformer is over 500 W rating, it must have circuit breaker protection.

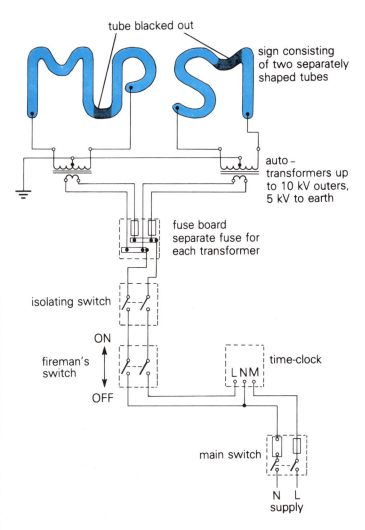

Figure 6.14 High voltage display sign circuit.

Figure 6.14 shows the wiring of a high-voltage display sign. I.E.E. Regulations deal more fully with the requirements of these signs.

Tungsten–halogen lamps

These are lamps in which a tungsten filament is contained within a quartz envelope filled with halogen gas. It enables the filament temperature to be raised to very high values and, together with a suitable reflector, gives a beam of light of very high density.

Tungsten–halogen lamps are used mainly for floodlight installations, such as sports grounds, railway sidings and public buildings, etc. Since any dirt on the surface of the lamp itself or on the reflecting surface will cause absorption of heat, it is essential that these are very carefully handled on installation. Terminal contacts are at each end of the tube. The lamps need no ballast equipment and are connected directly to the mains supply. They are obtainable in sizes from 250 W up to 1500 W. See Figure 6.15.

Because of the high current loading of industrial lamps, they will be limited to very few on a subcircuit. For the largest sizes, the number will be limited to one per circuit.

I.E.E. Regulations concerning industrial and commercial lighting circuits

The ratings of the lamps used are in the order of 300, 500 and 1000 W. Therefore the number of lamps on a circuit must be limited. In general the lighting circuits are rated at 15 A, which means that on a 240 V supply six 500 W or three 1000 W will be supplied.

The cable and switch size would be calculated in the normal way using the rating factors for ambient temperature, trunking, etc, and for discharge lamps the 1.8 and 2 as mentioned; voltage drop not to exceed 4 per cent. Where the cables are subject to the heat radiated from these high power lamps, that is they are within or close to fittings, they must be shrouded with high temperature sleeves or heat resistant cable used.

▲ Control gear must be mounted on non-combustible material usually placed away from the luminaires or industrial installation where corrosive or dirty conditions are present.

On installations where three-phase and neutral supplies are used for lighting, luminaires connected to different phases must be at least 2 m apart or marked that 415 V is present.

On high voltage discharge lighting the cable carrying the high voltage must be metal sheathed or armoured and the appropriate 'Danger' notice be displayed.

Where MIMS cables are used on inductive circuits, the terminations should be fitted with 'flash over' points called **surge arrestors**. See Chapter 2 on flux changes.

Heating systems

Specific heat capacity

Specific heat capacity is the amount of heat energy in joules (watt-seconds) required to raise the temperature of a given substance of mass 1 kilogramme by 1°C.

$$\text{Heat (J)} = \text{mass of substance (kg)} \times \text{specific heat capacity} \times \text{temperature rise (°C)}$$

The value for specific heats of substances are published in heating tables.

EXAMPLE 3

10 litres of water is to be raised from a temperature of 20°C to boiling point (100°C), calculate the amount of electrical energy in kW h required, given that 1 litre of water has a mass of 1 kg. The specific heat of water is 4200.

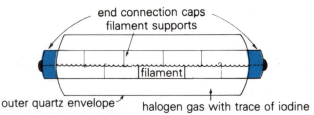

Note: The lamp fitting is designed to dissipate the high temperature from small dimensions and must be well ventilated.

Figure 6.15 Tungsten-halogen lamp.

Heat energy required $J = 10 \times 4200 \times 80$
$$= 336 \times 10^4$$

Note: $1 \text{ kW h} = 3.6 \times 10^6$ joules

$$\text{kW h required} = \frac{336 \times 10^4}{3.6 \times 10^6} = 0.933$$

If the tank is fitted with a 3 kW immersion heater on a 240 V supply and because of the heat loss from the tank which contains the water its efficiency is 80 per cent. Calculate

i) time taken,
ii) heater current,
iii) cost of the energy if the tariff is 6p/unit.

Because of the efficiency the input will be

$$\frac{0.933}{0.8} = 1.167 \text{ kW h}$$

i) Time taken $= \dfrac{\text{kW h}}{\text{kW}} = \dfrac{1.167}{3} = 0.39 \text{ h}$

ii) $I = \dfrac{3000 \text{ W}}{240 \text{ V}} = 12.5 \text{ A}$

iii) Cost $= 1.167 \times 6 \text{ p} = 7 \text{ p}$

Room or space heating calculations are a little more involved and needs reference to tables of insulation, values of building fabrics for heat transmission. They are also affected by opening of doors (air changes) and draughts. Calculations also require reference to density of air (kg per m³) of volume and its specific heat value.

However, given these values, the formula remains the same.
Heat energy required in kW h

$$= \frac{\text{density of air (kg per m}^3) \times \text{volume of room (m}^3) \times \text{specific heat} \times {}^\circ\text{C rise}}{3.6 \times 10^6}$$

Air heaters

These can be divided into two types.

1. Indirect or storage heaters are operated on the cheaper 'off-peak' supplies (see Chapter 9). They can be of the type which have their own thermal storage, known as **storage radiators**, or of the type which uses the thermal storage properties of the building itself, such as underfloor heaters.

2. Direct heaters use electricity at the standard rate

and have the advantage of flexibility of performance and immediate response.

The two systems may be used independently or may be combined to meet the heating requirements of the particular building.

Indirect/storage systems

> Indirect/storage systems are charged during the 'off-peak' cheap-rate period and retain the heat and release it at a later stage when the supply is 'off'.

This is done by means of heating units filled with material which absorbs the heat and are so enclosed that heat release is gradual throughout the 24 hours. There are fan-assisted types, which can give a 'boost' of heat when required. The basic types are as follows.

Storage radiators
These consist of heating elements mainly of nickel-chrome wire embedded in a storage core, usually of refractory bricks. The elements are then surrounded by a layer of fibre glass material and encased in a metal container with removable covers. The heat input can be controlled by a **bimetallic thermostat** which consists basically of a bimetallic strip which bends and breaks the input current at a predetermined temperature. The length of time required to cause the break is adjusted by a manual control which alters the difference in distance between the fixed and moving contacts. There is also a safety heat fuse fitted which consists of a heat-fusible element, so that if an excessive temperature is reached because of failure of the thermostat control, this element will melt and disconnect the supply.

The rating of these is around 3 kW each, so that on a 240 V supply, the current will be 12.5 A. Each heater is wired back to the 'off-peak' consumer unit on its own radial subcircuit of 15 A rating. The cable size will normally be 2.5 mm² terminated at the heater end with a single-pole switch unit, from which the short, heat-resistant flexible cable will connect into the heater terminals. See Figure 6.16.

> Because of excessive weight, storage radiators are assembled on site.

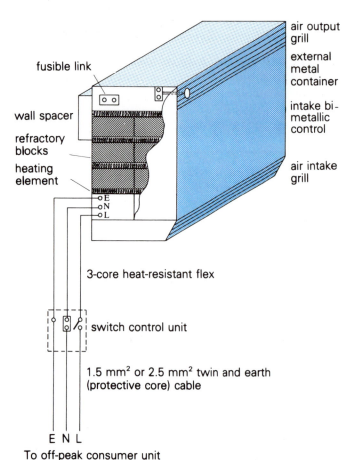

fusible link

wall spacer

refractory blocks

heating element

air output grill

external metal container

intake bi-metallic control

air intake grill

E
N
L

3-core heat-resistant flex

switch control unit

1.5 mm² or 2.5 mm² twin and earth (protective core) cable

E N L

To off-peak consumer unit

Figure 6.16 Cross-sectional view of storage heater.

Centrally-sited warm air unit

This is a development of storage radiators. The warm air from the unit is blown by a fan into ducts or pipework which lead to the rooms which require heating. A room thermostat keeps the air temperature at the desired level by operating the fan. For a normal-sized domestic dwelling, the power rating of a warm air unit is around 15 kW so that the current will be around 60 A and will require its own double-pole switch fuse of suitable rating connected through the time clock at the intake consumer terminals.

The supply to the fan circuit will be taken from the normal-rate tariff consumer unit since this works in conjunction with the room thermostat and is required at any period over the 24 hours.

Underfloor warming

With this system, the heating element usually consists of a resistance wire insulated by a refractory material and enclosed in an overall metallic sheath, similar to the construction of mineral-insulated cable or it may have butyl or silicon rubber insulation, giving it greater flexibility. The heating cable is shaped around circular formers and arranged in parallel lines on top of the floor concrete slab, leaving the termination available for connection to the supply. It is then covered with a sand–cement mixture screed of about 65 mm thickness, on top of which is placed the floor finish tiles, etc.

Direct systems

These take the form of radiant fires, convectors, panels, tubular heaters, fan heaters and combined heat–light units. These appliances may be portable, supplied by flexible cords from socket outlets through a fused plug from a radial or ring power supply circuit, or they may be of a fixed type, in which case they are treated as stationary appliances and supplied from a fused spur unit. This may be switched or unswitched and again, connected to a radial or ring-type power circuit.

Radiant fires

These range from 750 W to 3 kW and consist of a heating element wound in various shapes on a refractory former. The heat is radiated and reflected in the desired direction by a polished reflector.

Panel heaters

These can be fixed on a wall or suspended from ceilings. The enclosed panels are about 30 cm × 60 cm.

Tubular heaters

These are similar to panel heaters but are tubular-shaped for wall mounting. They are available in sizes from 60 cm up to 1.8 m in length, rated at 60 W to 80 W per 30 cm loading.

Oil-filled radiators

These give out heat by radiation and convection. The radiator consists of an immersion heater enclosed in a pressed steel case filled with a high grade oil.

▲ Because the three types of heaters: panel heaters, tubular heaters, and oil-filled radiators are placed in positions where they are liable to be touched, the power loadings must be such that the surface temperature does not burn the skin on contact, that is, no higher than 80°C.

Water heating systems

For water heating systems, the heating medium is placed directly in the water itself so that maximum transference of heat to the water is achieved.

Note: This is distinct from water heating for cooking or food processing, where the water is contained in a separate vessel from the heating element.

There are two types of heaters used in hot water systems:

1. **immersion heaters** which consist of an element embedded in an insulating refractory material and enclosed in a metal tube which is screwed directly into the water tank;
2. **electrode heaters** which use the water as the heating element. Metal electrodes connected to the supply are positioned in the water, so that the passage of current between them through the water raises its temperature. Since the conductivity of water can vary with hardness, it may be necessary in some areas to treat the water to be heated to achieve the safe power loading.

Convector heaters

These consist of a low temperature heating element inside a metal cabinet. Cool air enters the lower inlet and the heated air at around 85°C is expelled by convection through the top outlet into the room.

Fan heaters

These operate on the convector principle but use a fan to circulate the warm air. They are available in all sizes, from the domestic range up to the industrial sizes, from 750 W up to around 21 kW. It is possible to arrange the thermostat switching on fan heaters to switch on only the fan in warm weather in order to cool the building.

Infra-red heaters

These consist of a nickel-chrome element in a silica glass tube with terminals at each end. The glass tube is backed by a polished reflector. These are intended for local heating in large areas such as workshops, market halls and exhibition sites where no interference with floor space is desired. They are frequently hung from roof area supports. They can be obtained in short lengths for wall mounting in bathrooms, or in circular shapes combined with the lighting fitting.

▲ Because of the potential danger from live electrodes immersed in water, special requirements for the type of switchgear and earth leakage protection necessary are laid down in the I.E.E. Regulations.

Ceiling heating

Where floor space is restricted and ceilings are comparatively low, ceiling heating panels at low surface temperatures can be fitted to match the existing ceiling finish.

Immersion heaters

For domestic purposes, these are made in the 3 kW rating size and positioned in the hot-water tank. The temperature-control device, the **thermostat**, is contained within the heater itself and is either a rod-type, which is placed in a separate tube, or a contact-type, placed in the connection terminal box of the heater. Because of convection currents, usually only the water above the thermostat reaches the temperature control setting, so that the positioning of the immersion heater is very important.

At this stage, it may be possible to examine the construction of the types of heaters described. Also, students are advised to study the basic principles of the transmission and effect of heat waves, and to understand the meaning of conduction, convection and radiation.

If all the water in the hot-water tank is to be heated, the immersion heater must be mounted horizontally at the bottom. If only a small quantity of hot water is required, the heater must be positioned vertically from the top.

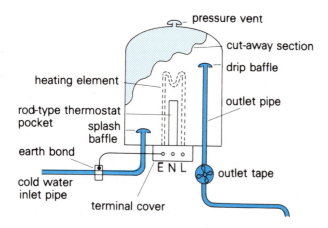

Figure 6.17 Free outlet water heater.

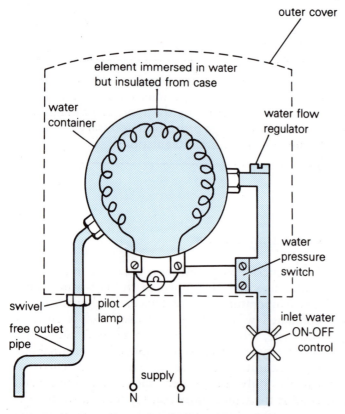

Figure 6.18 Instantaneous water heater.

If positioned at the top, the length of the heater would affect the amount of water heated. The standard lengths are from 40 cm up to 90 cm.

It is possible to take advantage of the 'off-peak' tariff charges because of the thermal storage capacity of water but in this case a large volume of water must be heated and suitable **thermal-lagging jackets** must cover the tank, particularly the topmost portion.

Because of the continuous current flow of around 12.5 A for the 3 kW size, it is recommended that immersion heaters are supplied from a separate subcircuit from the consumer unit. The fixed wiring should be terminated in a single-pole switch unit and a suitable heat-resistant flexible cord passed into the terminal box of the heater.

Free-outlet storage heaters

These heaters are suitable where hot water is required at a local point, such as over a wash basin or a sink. The cold water is fed from a **header tank** as shown in Figure 6.17 and the hot water inlet is controlled by a tap. The tank is fitted with its own 3 kW immersion heater and thermostat.

Instantaneous water heaters

These heaters do not depend on water storage but are activated by water pressure. When the tap is turned on, the pressure operates the electricity supply switch, at the same time the water is split up into droplets which flow over the heating element. See Figure 6.18. Instantaneous heaters are also suitable for use in local positions where hot water is required.

▲ Since instantaneous water heaters involve no hot water storage, they are economical to use, but because the water is in contact with the live element and the heaters are connected to metalwork, they require special earthing and bonding. See I.E.E. Regulations.

Electrode boilers

For heating water loads over about 50 kW and for steam-raising purposes, the electrode flow boiler is used.

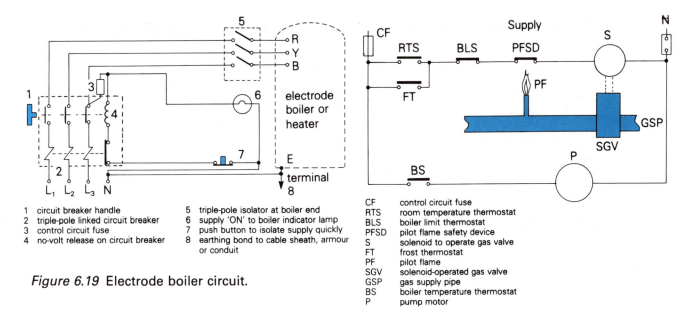

1 circuit breaker handle
2 triple-pole linked circuit breaker
3 control circuit fuse
4 no-volt release on circuit breaker
5 triple-pole isolator at boiler end
6 supply 'ON' to boiler indicator lamp
7 push button to isolate supply quickly
8 earthing bond to cable sheath, armour or conduit

Figure 6.19 Electrode boiler circuit.

CF	control circuit fuse
RTS	room temperature thermostat
BLS	boiler limit thermostat
PFSD	pilot flame safety device
S	solenoid to operate gas valve
FT	frost thermostat
PF	pilot flame
SGV	solenoid-operated gas valve
GSP	gas supply pipe
BS	boiler temperature thermostat
P	pump motor

Figure 6.21 Control of central heating with gas fuel.

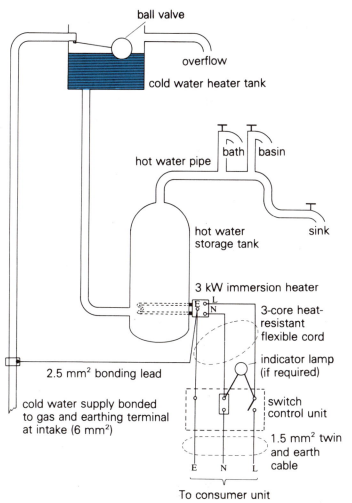

Figure 6.20 Domestic water heating system with immersion heater.

A thermostat fitted into the storage tank is used to control the boiler temperature. A second boiler thermostat is provided as a safety measure against excess temperature together with a safety valve to prevent a possible explosion.

The control of the power loading is by means of insulating shields which can be raised or lowered by hand over the electrodes themselves. Because of the high current demand, these are usually designed for operation on three-phase four-wire T.P.N. supplies at 415 V, or in larger installations at 11 kV. See Figure 6.19. The N conductor must be at least half the c.s.a. of the phase conductors. Figure 6.20 shows a domestic hot water installation fitted with an immersion heater.

Figure 6.21 shows a basic circuit diagram of the automatic temperature and protection control required in a domestic gas-fired central heating installation.

Automatic temperature control devices

These are obtainable in various forms to meet the requirements of a particular situation, but all operate on the principle of the expansion of a gas (air), liquid or solid with increase in temperature. The

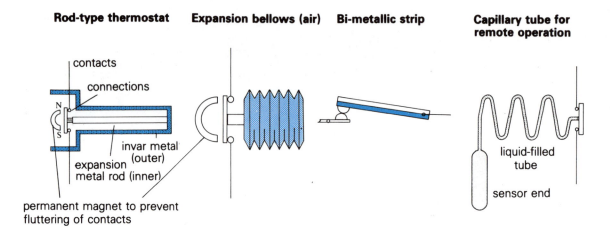

Figure 6.22 Types of heat control devices.

movement will cause the opening or closing of the circuit contacts or, in some cases, the tilting of a mercury-type switch.

Thermostats

These have been mentioned on numerous occasions in the preceding description of heating systems.

See Figure 6.22 for basic types of thermostat construction.

> When heavy current circuits are controlled, the use of a contactor is required so that the thermostat and the control circuit wiring contacts have to carry the contactor coil current only.

Bimetallic control
To reduce the time delay between the temperature change and the operation of the **bimetallic strip** which can cause large fluctuation in temperature, a small heater in the form of a resistor is fitted close to the bimetallic strip.

The heater is connected in the circuit as shown Figure 6.23 and it can cause the temperature at that point to rise and fall more rapidly than the outside (room) temperature and so helps maintain a more uniform value.

Thermocouple
A junction of two dissimilar metals which, when heated, generates small electric currents proportional to the temperature rise. They are used for

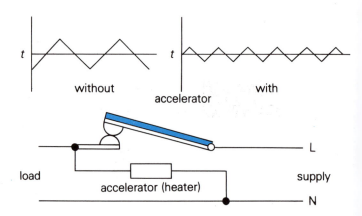

Figure 6.23 Accelerated bimetallic control.

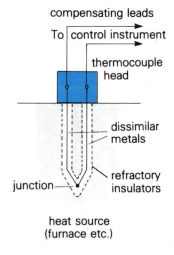

Figure 6.24 Thermocouple.

high temperature control industries which use furnaces for heat treatment. Thermo-couples are also used as pilot light failure detection devices on gas or oil-fired heating installations. See Figure 6.24.

Domestic heating appliance controls

Simmerstat
Where the heating elements of ovens, hot plates and wash boilers are connected as one circuit, the simmerstat control is used to regulate the temperature. It operates by regulating the current flow in ON–OFF steps, thereby controlling the amount of energy and hence the amount of heat being generated.

When the contacts are closed, some current flows in the heating element of the bimetallic strip which, after a time, causes it to bend and open the supply to the appliance. At the same time, it disconnects the bimetallic strip supply, so that it begins to cool and eventually returns to its ON position and current again flows. This cycle of events is repeated. The duration of ON/OFF periods is controlled by the setting of the variable resistance. On some types, the control setting simply varies the distance which the bimetallic strip has to move. See Figure 6.25.

Three heat switch
This is used where the heating elements of the appliance are divided into two circuits.

For a low level of heat, the two are connected in series across the supply. For a medium level, one element only is connected to the supply. For a high (maximum) level of heat, the two are connected in parallel across the supply.

Study Figure 6.26 and calculate the power input to the appliance in each of the three positions, if the elements are each rated at 1 kW. (Answer: 0.5, 1, 2 kW.)

Refrigeration

The objective of refrigeration is to maintain an area or object in a continuously cooled condition. This can be achieved by the use of a freezing mixture or, as detailed here, by the rapid evaporation of a volatile gas.

The basic components used in the vapour-compression method of refrigeration are:

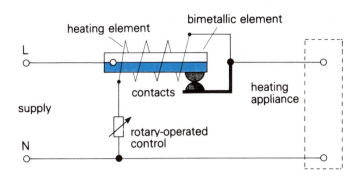

Figure 6.25 Simmerstat.

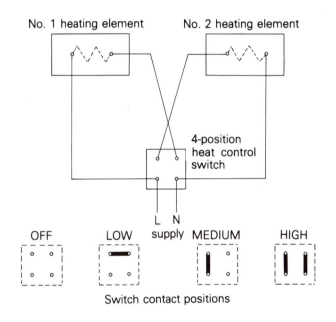

Figure 6.26 Three-heat switch control.

1. a **compressor** driven by an electric motor;
2. a set of **condenser tubes** which are either air or water-cooled, dependent upon the capacity of the refrigerator;
3. a **receiver tank** which stores the liquid refrigerant;
4. an **expansion valve** or flow control which regulates the flow to the evaporator tubes;
5. the **evaporator tubes** which are in contact with the air to be cooled and reduce the air temperature by the evaporation of the liquid.

Principles of refrigeration

The hydrocarbon **refrigerant** (Freon) gas is pressurised by the motor-driven compressor so that it evaporates and leaves the compressor as a high pressure, high temperature gas. The refrigerant gas flows to the condensers where it condenses on contact with the condenser tube walls, giving out heat, and the liquid refrigerant flows to the receiver tank for storage. The liquid tube carries the liquid refrigerant from this tank, still at high pressure, to the expansion valve which regulates its flow to the evaporator tubes and maintains the pressure difference between the condenser and the evaporator. Heat is removed from the air passing over the cold evaporator tubes, causing the air to fall in temperature. During this time, the liquid refrigerant evaporates or 'boils off' and returns as a gas at low pressure back to the suction side of the compressor and the cycle is repeated. See Figure 6.27.

Types of refrigeration

Domestic refrigerators
These are small cabinet units for food storage; the whole system is hermetically sealed. The evaporator tube compartment is at the top, inside the cabinet, the condenser air-cooled tubes are mounted on the back of the cabinet, the compressor and motor are mounted underneath the cabinet. Power rating is generally around 150 W.

Commercial freezers
These are made in large cabinet sizes for food storage or display and range from 250 W up to 10 kW power rating. The units are normally self-contained

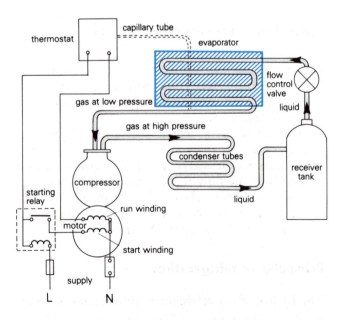

Figure 6.27 Principles of refrigeration.

cabinets, although where ventilation of the condenser tubes is restricted, water-cooled condensers must be used.

Industrial refrigerators
For manufacturing processes where the units are much larger, the motor is mounted away from the compressor using 'Vee' type belt drives. Water-cooled condensers are also used and in the larger plant, recycling of the cooling water is achieved by the use of external cooling towers.

Air-conditioning systems

Air-conditioning is the process of extracting the warm and dirty atmosphere from enclosed areas such as rooms, offices, factories, hospitals, etc., cooling and cleaning it, and returning it to these areas. It combines the use of air filters, normally water washed, with a refrigeration plant.

Packaged units

Factory-assembled air-conditioning package units can be obtained for installation in buildings. The usual arrangement is for the condensing units and the motor compressor to be mounted separately. The evaporator coils are mounted in the air-handling section of the air-conditioning unit.

The electric installation will require the installation of the compressor motor, pump and fan motors together with automatic temperature and humidity controls which must be located in selected positions in the building.

The humidity control contains an element whose electrical conductivity changes with the amount of moisture in the atmosphere. When the air is too dry (lack of moisture) the humidity sensor will trigger the water pump in the air-conditioning unit to spray jets of water into the air before the air returns to the room. This means that the air that is returned to the area will be cool, clean and of the desired humidity.

■ CHECK YOUR UNDERSTANDING

● Luminous units
Luminous intensity (I) is the candela (cd).
Luminous flux (Φ) is the lumen (lm).
Illumination on a surface (E) is the lux (lumens/m²)

● Laws:

Inverse square law $E = \dfrac{I}{h^2}$ (lux)

Cosine law $E = \dfrac{I}{d^2} \times \cos ø$ (lux)

● Total lumens required

$$= \dfrac{\text{lux value} \times \text{surface area (m}^2)}{(\text{utilisation} \times \text{maintenance) factors}}$$

● A photo bench is used to compare the output from an unknown lamp with a standard.
● A selenium photocell is used for lux measurement.
● The tungsten filament lamp uses the heat effect of current.
● Fluorescent and discharge lamps (HPMV and sodium) use the chemical effect. Ballast is needed to stabilise the current. Phase-shift devices combat unwanted stroboscopic effects.
● Neon signs use gaseous glass tubes bent to shape and supplied with high voltages from transformers.
● Heat

Joules required = kg × specific heat of substance × °C temperature rise.

● Water heater types: immersion, pressure, non-pressure, instantaneous, electrode boiler.
● Space heater types: storage (off-peak) radiators, under floor elements, wall panels, tubular, oil filled radiators, convectors, heated air fans.
● Heat controls: thermostats, simmerstats, three heat switches, thermocouples.
● Refrigeration components: compressor, condenser tubes (outside), evaporator tubes (inside), receiver tank, flow control valve.

REVISION EXERCISES AND QUESTIONS

1 A 2000 cd luminaire is suspended 2 m above the centre of a circular table 2 m in diameter. Calculate the illumination at
  i) the centre and
  ii) the edge of the table.
  iii) State what is meant by efficacy of a luminaire.
2 i) Some thermostats for temperature control are rated at 20 A a.c. or 0.1 A d.c. State reasons for this.
  ii) Explain with the aid of diagrams how the movement (action) of the contacts are 'speeded' up, giving the reason.

iii) There is a time lag (delay) between the actual temperature under control and the action of a thermostat. Again with the aid of a diagram show how this delay can be reduced.
3 A test using the following instruments and switch connected in circuit was carried out on a 400 W HPMV lamp with a power input of 440 W. With the lamp at full brilliance and S open, A_1 reads 3.5 A. With S closed A_2 reads 1.6 A. Draw a phasor diagram to scale and find the current on A when S is closed.

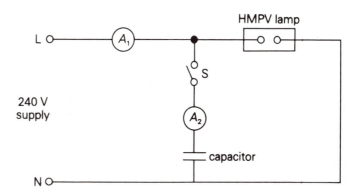

4 A number of 400 HPMV lamps are used for a car park
  i) What are (a) the advantages of these lamps, and (b) the disadvantages?
  ii) Why is the input power to each greater than 400 W?
  iii) Describe briefly the principle of operation of an instrument which is used to measure the illumination on the car park. State the units marked on the scale of the instrument.
5 i) What is meant by the term 'stroboscopic effect'?
  ii) In what way can this be dangerous?
  iii) With the aid of a labelled diagram, explain how fluorescent lamps may be connected to minimise the stroboscopic effect when connected to a single-phase supply.
6 Illustrate with diagrams the equipment necessary to supply a storage heater from the incoming supply.
7 Explain with the aid of diagrams, why the power on each switch position of a three-heat control switch varies. State ratios of the power in each position.
8 With the aid of sketches, explain the differences between the pressure-type water heater and the free outlet type.

9 Describe the requirements of the I.E.E. Regulations covering the following:
   i) capacitors,
   ii) fireman's emergency switches,
   iii) lampholders in a bathroom,
   iv) portable appliances, and
   v) discharge lamp loadings on a subcircuit.

10 List the essential component parts in the vapour-compression type refrigerator and explain briefly the function of each in the refrigeration cycle.

11 A gas-fired central heating system is to be installed in domestic premises. Make a diagram of the electrical control circuit for this installation and label all items of equipment.

12 i) Make a full diagram of a sodium-vapour lamp circuit fed from a 240 V 50 Hz single-phase supply.
   ii) If the light output is 5500 lumens, the total power input is 68 W and ballast loss is 13 W, calculate the efficiency of the lamp.
   iii) The current is 0.35 A, but if the capacitor is disconnected the current increases to 1 A. Explain the reason for this and calculate the value of the power factor in each case.
   iv) Why must care be taken if a lamp is broken?

13 i) Make a sketch of the internal components of a high-pressure mercury lamp.
   ii) What is the purpose of the auxiliary electrode?
   iii) If the lamp is switched off, why does it take three to four minutes to restart?

14 An office measuring 17.3 m by 17.3 m is to be provided with an illumination of 200 lux using 80 W fluorescent tubes having an efficiency of 40 lumens per watt. If the utilisation factor is 0.65 and the maintenance is 0.8:

i) a) determine the number of tubes required, (b) make a plan of the office and show the spacing of the tubes,
ii) a) What is the total assumed current demand of the installation for selection of cable size is the supply is 240 V? (b) What is the cost of lighting the office for eight hours if the cost of electricity is 4.5 pence per kW h?

15 i) Draw a labelled sectional sketch of a block storage heater.
   ii) Describe how this type of heater should be connected to the incoming supply when an off-peak tariff is employed.

16 A controlled output block storage heater is to be installed on a timber boarded floor in domestic premises.
   i) Detail the precautions to be observed in respect of siting the heater.
   ii) Describe the method of connecting the heater to permanent wiring.

17 A neon sign is to be installed on the fascia of a shop front. Explain, with the aid of sketches and diagrams the method of installation.

(C & G 'C')

18 Draw the circuit diagram of a three-phase electrode boiler fed via a remote circuit breaker from a three-phase and neutral medium voltage supply. Mark on each part of the diagram the relevant I.E.E. Regulation.

(C & G 'C')

19 In a test on a photometric bench, a lamp was placed 50 cm from the photometer head, while the standard lamp of 60 cd was 35 cm from the photometer head when balance was obtained. Determine the luminous intensity of the lamp under test.

The basic operation of electrical machines

Introduction

Electrical machines can be used to convert electrical energy into mechanical energy (**motors**) or to convert mechanical energy into electrical energy (**generators**).

Direct current machines

See Chapter 2 for basic theory.

> A d.c. machine can be used either as a motor or as a generator, that is, when the shaft is driven by a prime mover it will generate a voltage at the terminals or if a d.c. supply (voltage) is connected to the machine terminals the shaft will rotate.

Remember the voltage is generated in the revolving conductors (**armature**), the yoke or **stator** provides the flux for the generation.

When the machine is used as a motor the generated e.m.f. is referred to as the **back e.m.f.** because it opposes the supply voltage. The current taken by the machine when running as a motor

$$I = \frac{V - E}{R_a} \text{ (A)}$$

where V = supply volts,
E = back e.m.f.,
R_a = resistance of the armature.

It can be seen from this that in standstill position, that is, where the armature is not revolving, the current would be limited only by the R_a because there is no generated (back) e.m.f.

For this reason an external resistance is connected in the armature circuit at starting and gradually reduced as the speed increases and the back e.m.f. (*E*) builds up. It is known as a **face-plate starter** which also incorporates the excess current and no-volt protection devices. See Appendix A.

EXAMPLE 1

A d.c. shunt motor has resistance of 0.5 Ω at standstill. It is to be connected to a 120 V supply. Calculate

i) the value of the resistance of a faceplate starter to limit the starting current to 40 A,
ii) the value of the supply current when the motor has reached full speed and the back e.m.f. is 110 V if the start resistance is short-circuited.

i) Total circuit resistance R_T to limit current to 40 A

$$R_T = \frac{V}{I} = \frac{120}{40} = 3 \ \Omega$$

Starter resistance $= R_T -$ motor resistance
$\qquad\qquad\qquad\quad = (3 - 0.5) = 2.5 \ \Omega$

If the starter resistance is short-circuited then the total resistance is now only the motor resistance, which is 0.5 Ω.

ii) New current at full speed

$$I = \frac{\text{supply } V - \text{back e.m.f.}}{\text{motor } R}$$

$$= \frac{120 - 110 \text{ (V)}}{0.5 \ \Omega} = 20 \text{ A}$$

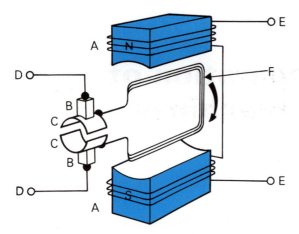

A field coils wound on yoke (stator)

B carbon brushes in contact with segments on commutator

C commutator segments connect to armature coil. There would be two segments for each coil.

D armature terminals

E field coil connections

F armature coil wound on laminated iron core. In practice there will be a number of these to produce a smoother voltage.

Figure 7.1 Basic operation of a d.c. machine.

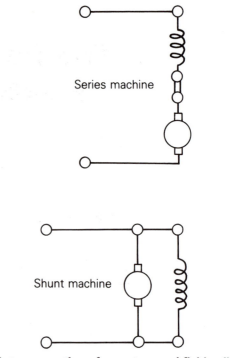

Interconnection of armature and field coils

Armature reaction

From Figure 7.1 it can be seen that the armature coils are connected to the commutator and the supply to the coils is either fed (when a motor) or collected (when a generator) by carbon brushes in contact with the segment of the commutator.

> It is arranged that the brushes or brushgear are placed in a position where they short-circuit the adjacent segments when there is zero e.m.f. being generated in the coils connected to those segments. This position is known as the neutral axis.

When the armature coils are carrying a current there is a magnetic field set around them and this interacts with the main field set up by the yoke field coils and causes a shift in the neutral axis.

The degree of the shift will depend upon the value of the armature current. To compensate for this shift, additional poles are placed on the yoke between the main poles and are connected in series with the armature winding. They are referred to as **compensating** or **interpoles**.

Types of d.c. machines

These are known by the method in which the armature and the field winding are interconnected and this governs the machine characteristics.

> There are three types of d.c. machines:
> - **shunt** – where the field windings are connected in parallel with the armature winding,
> - **series** – where the two above windings are connected in series,
> - **compound** – which is a combination of shunt and series.

Machine characteristics

Generators

Shunt
The voltage generated will fall off slightly as the current increases due to *IR* drop in the armature. The field flux will remain constant.

Series
The voltage will rise as current increases because of the increased flux due to the field winding.

Compound
It can be arranged that the slight fall off in voltage on load by the shunt generator can be offset by the increase of voltage due to the series winding. This means it will produce a constant voltage at all values of current up to full load.

> The output voltage of a generator can be regulated by varying the strength of the field current. This is done by connecting a variable resistance known as a **voltage regulator** in the field winding circuit.

See Appendix A.

Motors

Shunt
These run at fairly constant speed because the field flux is constant at all loads.

Series
As the mechanical load increases and the motor takes more current, the yoke flux will increase and cause a speed reduction with an increase of torque. It makes the motor suitable for traction work, it behaves as a gear box. If the load is completely removed, however, the armature will reach very high speeds and could cause damage.

Compound
These windings can be arranged so that by assisting or opposing each other the speed will remain constant or fall or rise as the load varies.

> The speed of the d.c. motors can be varied by connecting a variable resistor in the field circuit known as a **speed regulator**.

See Appendix A.

A summary of shunt and series motors and generator performance is illustrated in Figure 7.2. It can be seen that the d.c. series motor is ideal for lifting and traction work. It acts as a gear change. The d.c. series generator has little use in practice but the series winding is used on the compound generator to offset the fall in voltage by the shunt winding only.

Alternating current motors

These are mainly of the induction type, the voltage and hence the current flow and the fluxes in the rotor are induced from the stator windings.

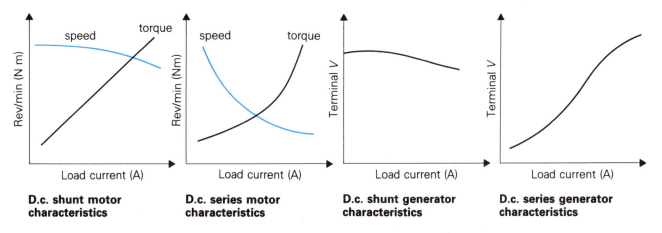

D.c. shunt motor characteristics   **D.c. series motor characteristics**   **D.c. shunt generator characteristics**   **D.c. series generator characteristics**

Figure 7.2 Characteristics of d.c. machines.

Single-phase motors

A single-phase a.c. supply to a single winding does not 'set up' a turning action on the rotor, it requires two fluxes which have a **phase displacement**.

> To provide the phase displacement a second winding called a **start winding** is placed on the stator core. This winding is either connected in series with a capacitor so that the current leads by 90° or it is a highly inductive winding where the current lags by 90°.

Whichever method is used, a phase shift of almost 90° is sufficient to create a starting torque on the rotor.

When the rotor is up to speed this winding may be switched out of the circuit. See Appendix A.

Reversal of rotation can be obtained by reversing either the start winding connection or the run winding connections.

These motors are used in the smaller sizes where a three-phase supply is not available, mostly in domestic equipment.

Single-phase universal motors

> The field and armature winding are connected in series so that fluxes in both change direction every half cycle of the supply so that the motor will continue to run in one direction. They are fitted with a commutator and brushes similar to a d.c. series motor.

Reversal of rotation is obtained by reversing either armature or field winding connections. These motors are used largely on domestic appliances and portable tools.

Three-phase a.c. motors

A three-phase supply will produce a rotating magnetic field in the stator so there is no need for a start winding. These motors do take a heavy current when starting so that in some cases for the larger sizes they do need a starting device to limit the current. This reduces the voltage to the stator until the motor gathers speed.

On wound rotor slip-ring motors, a resistance is connected in the rotor circuit on starting in order to reduce the stator current. Induction motors run at a fairly constant speed at all loads up to full load, only falling off slightly with increase in load.

> The speed at which the magnetic flux in the stator revolves is known as the synchronous speed. It is governed by the number of pairs of poles on the stator and the frequency of supply.

$$\text{Synchronous speed} = \frac{f}{p} \text{ revs per s (r.p.s.)}$$

where f = frequency of supply in hertz,
p = number of pairs of poles.

Rotor slip

The actual speed of the rotor is a little less than the synchronous speed, this difference is referred to as the **slip**, it will vary from around 1 per cent on no load to 5 per cent on full load.

$$\text{Slip} = \frac{\text{synchronous speed} - \text{rotor speed} \times 100\%}{\text{synchronous speed}}$$

The greater the slip, the greater is the motor states current.

Figure 7.3 shows the characteristics of an induction motor. The motor has a low initial start torque with a high start current. The start torque may be increased by the use of a double-cage rotor or the use of a wound rotor with external resistors con-

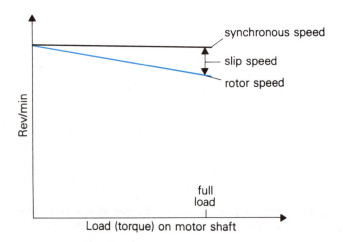

Figure 7.3 A.c. induction motor characteristics.

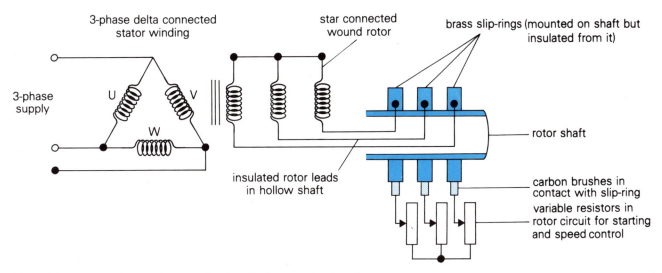

Figure 7.4 Three-phase wound rotor induction motor.

nected in the rotor circuit, that is, a slip-ring motor.
Note: D.c. motors with field current regulators can achieve a finer control of speed which is suitable for many processes in industry.

EXAMPLE 2

A three-phase a.c. motor is fitted with two pairs of poles. It is connected to a supply having a frequency of 50 Hz. Calculate

i) synchronous speed,
ii) rotor speed if slip is 4 per cent.

i) Synchronous speed $= \dfrac{50}{2} = 25$ r.p.s.

$$= 1500 \text{ r.p.m.}$$

ii) Rotor speed $= 1500 - (4\% \times 1500)$
$$= 1440 \text{ r.p.m.}$$

See diagrams of motors and starters in Appendix A.

Figure 7.4 shows a diagram of a three-phase wound rotor induction motor. Figure 7.5 shows diagrams to illustrate the basic operation of a three-phase a.c. **squirrel cage** induction motor.

On all three-phase inductive equipment the total magnetic flux produced in the core in the sum total of all the phase ampere-turns (A.T.).

It is therefore essential that the windings are correctly phased to ensure the three fluxes are

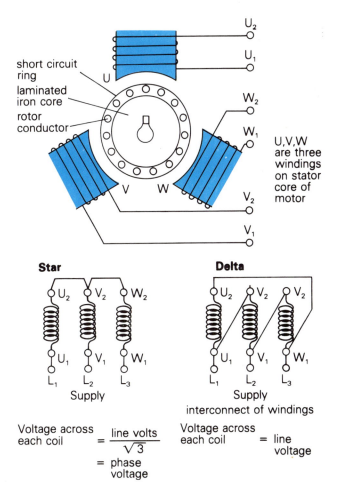

Figure 7.5 Basic operation of three-phase a.c. squirrel cage induction motor.

acting in the correct direction. This means that the start and the finish ends of the windings must be correctly identified before star or delta interconnections are made.

When connected in star the same three ends must be connected together to form the star point and the other same three ends connected in turn to the three-phase supply.

When connected in delta the finish of one winding is connected to the start of the next winding and so on. The three joining points are then connected to the three-phase supply.

For this reason the winding ends are identified by numbers 1 and 2, such as $U_1 U_2$, $V_1 V_2$, $W_1 W_2$.

If one winding should be reversed in relation to the other two, the fluxes would cancel and the equipment would take a very heavy current from the supply with possible burn out of the windings.

> In the reversal of a three-phase motor it is the two supply conductors which are changed over **not** the motor windings.

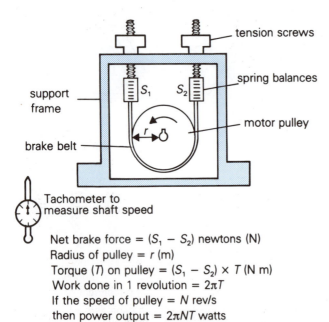

Net brake force = $(S_1 - S_2)$ newtons (N)
Radius of pulley = r (m)
Torque (T) on pulley = $(S_1 - S_2) \times T$ (N m)
Work done in 1 revolution = $2\pi T$
If the speed of pulley = N rev/s
then power output = $2\pi NT$ watts

Note: The electrical input power can be measured on a wattmeter. Motor efficiency = P_{out}/P_{in}.

Figure 7.6 Brake test to measure power output of motor.

Conversion of electrical power to mechanical power

Electric motors convert electrical power to mechanical power.
Power is rate of doing work.
The unit of power is the **watt**.
For mechanical conversion
watt = newton-metre per second = N m/s.

Note: 1 newton = $\dfrac{1}{9.81}$ kg

or 1 kg = 9.81 N.
The mechanical power output produced at the shaft of a motor can be measured by the brake test as described in Figure 7.6.

$$P = 2\pi NT \text{ (W)}.$$

Note: The addition of the 2π to the above formula is to convert the radius of the brake pulley to its circumference.

EXAMPLE 3

A motor is driving a pump which raises 1500 litres of water to a height of 40 metres every minute. Calculate the power output of the motor if 1 litre of water weighs 1 kg.

Weight of water = 1500×9.81 (N)

$$P \text{ (N m/s)} = 1500 \times 9.81 \times 40 \times \frac{1}{60} \text{ (W)}$$
$$= 9810 \text{ W} = 9.81 \text{ kW}$$

If the efficiency of the pump is 85 per cent and that of the motor 90 per cent, calculate the power input to the power.

$$P = \frac{9.81}{0.85 = 0.9} = 12.8 \text{ kW}$$

Regulations concerning motor circuits

The **current rating** is the full load current of the motor (not the starting) for calculation of cable sizes.

On domestic installations the motors are contained within the appliance they power and are governed by the regulations applying to that appliance.

On industrial installation, where power ratings are much higher, in nearly all cases a separate circuit is required for each motor. Like all circuits where the rating is over 15 A, a separate circuit is required. Each motor over 0.37 kW must be provided with a suitable **isolator** which is easily located and suitably labelled. If there is a remote control it is to have a lock-off position.

The motor must be protected against excess current so that in the event of overload or faults the supply will be automatically cut off.

The motor must also have protection against restarting if the supply is interrupted and then restored, this is referred to as **no-volt protection**.

Where there are groups of smaller motors, for example in a small workshop etc., they may be protected by one device for no-volt protection. In this case it may be necessary to install a series of 'Stop buttons' at clearly labelled positions around the workshop, so that in the event of danger the whole of the machines can be readily stopped. See Chapter 3.

Motors and control gear are illustrated in Appendix A; motor characteristic are shown in Appendix B.

CHECK YOUR UNDERSTANDING

● D.c. machines have rotating armature coils and stationary field coils, the machine can be used either as a generator or as a motor.

Motor current $I = \dfrac{V - E}{R_a}$

V = terminal voltage, E = generated or back e.m.f., R_a = armature resistance.

● Generator voltage $V = E - I_a R_a$.

● Field windings are connected either in series or in parallel (shunt) with the armature, or in a combination of the two (compound). The way they are connected determines the characteristics of the machine.

● Interpoles are used to offset the flux distortion set up by armature reaction.

● Control of motor speed and the generator voltage is obtained by variable resistors in the field coils circuit.

● A.c. induction motors induce the current in the rotor windings.

Single-phase induction motors need a phase 'split-ting' device to create a starting torque.

Three-phase supplies produce a rotating field in the stator.

● Cage type rotors have a low start torque.

Three-phase wound rotors with slip rings have a higher start torque and a means of speed control.

● Rotor speed = synchronous speed − slip

Synchronous speed = $\dfrac{f}{P}$ rev/s (r.p.s.)

● Power conversion

watt = newton-metre per second (N m/s).

● Brake test is used to measure shaft power of motor:

$P = 2\pi \, NT$ watts

REVISION EXERCISES AND QUESTIONS

1 Describe briefly the following parts of a d.c. machine:
  i) a) armature, (b) commutator and (c) field system.
  ii) Draw a circuit diagram for (a) a d.c. series motor, (b) a shunt motor and (c) a compound motor.

2 Explain the dangers concerning d.c. motors of:
  i) switching directly to the full supply voltage,
  ii) the field coils of a shunt motor becoming open circuit,
  iii) removing the load completely from a series motor.

3 i) What is meant by interpoles or compensating poles on a d.c. machine?
  i) Explain their function and show in which part of the circuit they are connected.

4 A three-phase 415 V a.c. motor develops an output power of 20 kW when running at a speed of 900 r.p.m. Calculate
  i) the driving torque,
  ii) the line current taken if the motor is 90 per cent and the pf is 0.8.

5 The terminations of a three-phase cage motor and the terminals of a three-phase supply are shown

L_1 L_2 L_3

SUPPLY

U_1○ V_1○ W_1○

U_2○ V_2○ W_2○

i) Redraw the above and show how the motor would be in star.
ii) Repeat to show how they would be connected in delta.
iii) If the supply is 415 V, state the voltage across one winding of the motor.

6 What materials are used for the following parts on machines?
  i) Commutator segments
  ii) Slip rings
  iii) Brushes
  iv) Armature core
  v) Rotor conductors on a cage motor

7 i) Show with the aid of diagrams the method of reversing the direction of the following induction motors: (a) single-phase split phase, (b) three-phase.
  ii) State two methods of starting three-phase cage type induction motors.
  iii) Explain what is meant by the slip of an a.c. motor.

8 The initial start current of a 300 V 2 kW motor is limited to twice the full load armature current by connecting a resistor (R) in series with the armature as shown. When the armature current falls to one-fifth of the full load value R is shorted out by means of a relay contactor.
The efficiency of the motor is 85 per cent, the armature resistance is 2 Ω and the field resistance is 400 Ω.
Calculate
  i) initial start current,
  ii) value of R,
  iii) the back e.m.f. when the armature current

has fallen to one fifth of full load armature current,
  iv) the armature current immediately after R is shorted.

9 A test on a three-phase electric motor is to be carried out to determine its pf and efficiency at certain values of loadings.
  i) List the items of test equipment required and their function.
  ii) State the formula and explain the units to calculate (a) power output, (b) power, (c) efficiency, (d) power factor.
  iii) Show the connections for the power input instrument.

10 When checking the current using a 'clip-on' ammeter on the conductor supplying an a.c. motor, why is it necessary
  i) to allow the motor to run up to speed before testing?
  ii) to test each conductor separately?
  iii) Explain the method of extending the current range of the instrument. Show a basic diagram.

11 i) Explain why it is essential that on a three-phase motor winding the start and finish ends of each winding are correctly interconnected.
  ii) Make a diagram of the six ends of the three windings connected to the three-phase supply in (a) star, (b) delta.
  iii) If the line current taken by a three-phase is 40 A, determine the current in each of the three windings when they are connected in (a) star, (b) delta.

Installation and maintenance of machines

Introduction

For safe and efficient working, electrical machines must be firmly mounted and correctly installed and connected to the supply. They may also need to be enclosed for protection against ambient conditions. If d.c. is required a **rectifier** will be needed to convert a.c. to d.c.

All electrical machines should be inspected and tested regularly, both in operation (supply on) and when standing (supply off).

Installation and mounting of machines

There are three factors which need to be considered:

1. **mounting** or fixing the motor in position,
2. **coupling** the motor to the load it has to drive,
3. **connecting** the motor to the electrical supply.

Mounting

This will depend upon the nature of the surface, which must support and hold the motor in a firm position. If the floor is a thick layer of concrete, the motor may be directly bolted to it, or the concrete may be built up to a sufficient thickness with extra concrete. The motor-feet fixings in this case may be of **rawlbolts** or **ragbolts**.

If the motor is to be mounted on a wooden-boarded floor, the weight must be spread over several joists. The boards may also require strengthening with extra wooden or steel joists at right angles to the existing joists.

Coupling

When the motor is on the same horizontal level as the driven machine and is to run at the same speed, a direct type of coupling may be used. Flexible couplings are often used to take up any slight misalignment between the two shafts and rubber bushes are used to reduce vibration. When the motor is sited some distance from the machine, or the two are to run at slightly different speeds, the transmission will be of the belt or chain type of drive. With these, the use of slide rails is required to tension the belt or chain correctly. The slide rail is bolted to the floor foundation and the motor is, in turn, bolted to it. See Figures 8.1, 8.2 and 8.3. Alignment of the transmission is shown in Figure 8.3.

Connecting

See later, 'connection to supply'.

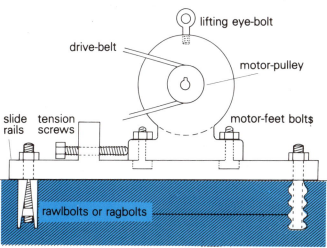

concrete bed depths up to 10 kW = 10 cm
10–25 kW = 20 cm
25–40 kW = 30 cm
40–80 kW = 45 cm

Figure 8.1 Mounting of machines.

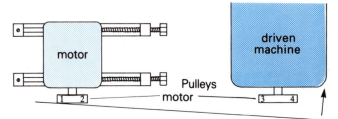

Note: String line or straight edge held fixed at point 1 and moved towards point 4. Machines should be aligned to just touch all four points at the same time.

Figure 8.2 Alignment of belt or chain drives.

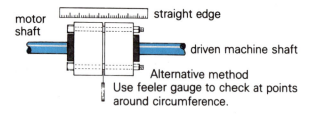

Figure 8.3 Coupling alignment.

Gear transmission

When the motor and machine have to be mounted close to each other and a relatively large speed difference is required, a gear type of drive will be required. For large reduction drives, a **multi-gear train** or **gear-box** will be required.

Note: With belt drives, the speeds of motor and machine pulleys are inversely proportional to their diameters; that is, the larger the diameter, the lower the speed. With chain and gear drives, the speeds of the toothed wheels are inversely proportional to the number of teeth. The small-toothed wheels are referred to as **pinions**, the larger ones as **spur-wheels**.

On driven machines requiring a high starting torque, it is necessary for the motor to start off-load and then take up the drive as it gathers speed. This is achieved by the use of specially designed couplings.

Fluid-coupling

The two halves of the coupling have specially shaped blades which are not connected to each other, that is, the motor and the machine are not coupled in the stationary position. These blades are enclosed in oil and as the motor shaft begins to revolve, the half-coupling on the motor shaft scoops the oil and flings it against the driven machine half-coupling, causing it to start rotating slowly. After a while, they will both run at full speed.

Note: Fluid-coupling can also be used to reduce the high starting current of motors as an alternative to the more expensive types of electrical starter connected in the motor supply circuit.

Eddy current coupling

This is a type of variable coupling between the motor and the machine which uses electromagnetic force. When a d.c. supply is connected to the winding in the coupling, the motor and driven machine become magnetically connected so that the motor takes up the drive.

Motor speeds

A.c. induction motors run at standard speeds dependent upon the number of poles on the stator windings and the speed of the stator magnetic fields. This is known as the **synchronous speed**. Its value is given by

$$n = 60f/p$$

where n = speed (rev/min),
  p = number of pairs of poles on the stator winding,
  f = frequency of the supply.

On load, the rotor (shaft) speed will fall slightly. This is known as **rotor slip** and is expressed as a percentage of the synchronous speed. It will vary from around 1 per cent on no load to 5 per cent on full load. See Chapter 7.

> The lower the number of poles, the higher the speed. Also, for a given output power rating, the higher the speed the smaller, and hence cheaper, will be the motor.

It may therefore be preferable to use a high-speed motor with a mechanical reduction drive to the machine, since, if the driven machine is not in the standard speed range of the a.c. motor, a change in speed will be required anyway.

Motor efficiency is the $\dfrac{\text{output power}}{\text{input power}} \times 100\%$.

Standard speeds of induction motors with five per cent SLIP on load

2-POLE = 3000 rev/min − SLIP
     = 2850 rev/min approx.
4-POLE = 1500 rev/min − SLIP
     = 1425 rev/min approx.
6-POLE = 750 rev/min − SLIP
     = 712 rev/min approx.

> Below this speed, the motor becomes large and expensive for a given rating and it is preferable to reduce the speed by mechanical methods.

The output power of a motor may be measured by means of a 'brake' test on the rotor shaft, the input power by a wattmeter. A motor rating is stated in terms of its shaft power in kW. See Chapter 7.

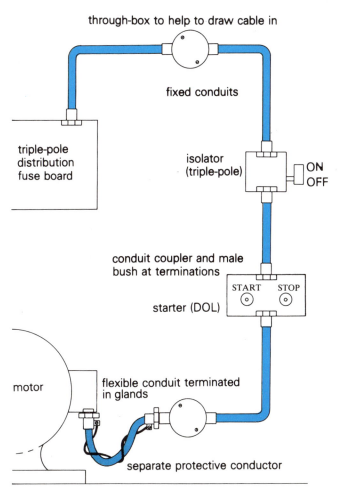

Figure 8.4 Motor final circuit equipment layout.

through-box to help to draw cable in

fixed conduits

triple-pole distribution fuse board

isolator (triple-pole)

ON
OFF

conduit coupler and male bush at terminations

START STOP

starter (DOL)

motor

flexible conduit terminated in glands

separate protective conductor

Connection to supply

The system of wiring from the supply to the motor will depend upon the site conditions (see Chapter 4), but a flexible connection to the terminal box is necessary to allow for movement of the motor for alignment and belt-tensioning, where applicable. It also allows for any vibration which would otherwise cause work hardening of fixed conduit, trunking, etc., and lead to possible loss of the earthing circuit.

On a conduit system, a conduit through-box would be fitted between the fixed conduit and the flexible conduit to the motor. See Figure 8.4.

> Note the separate protective conductor on the flexible conduit.

Where MICC cables are used, a loop is made near the terminal box.

Safe use and protection of motors – I.E.E. regulations

> ▲ Every motor must be provided with the means to stop and start, the stop device to be within easy reach of the operator.

Provision must be made to prevent unexpected restart after stopping, owing to drop in voltage, or failure of supply, both are dangerous. One device could serve a group of motors, that is, if several small motors are fed from a distribution board, then a no-volt coil-release fitted in the supply to that board would be sufficient. See Figure 8.5.

> When the control equipment is sited some distance away from the motor, additional equipment may be required near the motor or the facility provided to lock off the supply.

Every motor rated over 0.37 kW must have means of protection against excess current. Cables supplying the motor shall be rated at the full load current taken.

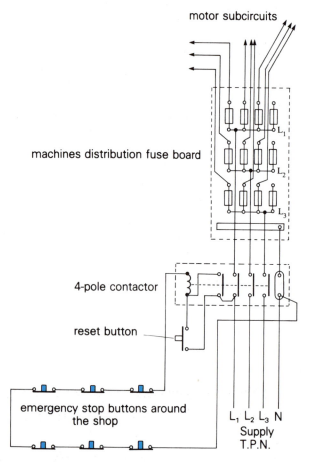

motor subcircuits

machines distribution fuse board

4-pole contactor

reset button

emergency stop buttons around the shop

L₁ L₂ L₃ N
Supply
T.P.N.

Note: Means of compliance with I.E.E. Regulations for a group of small motors in a machine shop.

Figure 8.5 Machine shop installation.

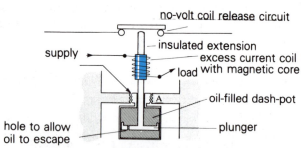

no-volt coil release circuit

supply

insulated extension
excess current coil
load with magnetic core

oil-filled dash-pot

plunger

hole to allow oil to escape

Note: When excess current flows, its movement is delayed by the suction of oil on the plunger in the dash-pot. The delay time can be varied by different sized escape holes in the plunger. This is mainly used on motor switchgear to prevent tripping operation during the start period.

Figure 8.6 Time delay of excess current protection device.

Note: For frequent stop-starting, the cables may have to be heavier because of heavier starting currents.

> Where the starter provides excess current protection for the motor, the circuit fuses in the distribution board may be up to twice the cable rating to accommodate the heavy starting current.

Note: The motor excess current device operation is purposely delayed for this reason. This is normally provided by an oil dash-pot on magnetic types. See Figure 8.6.

Slip-ring rotor cables must be suitable for starting currents. Refer to the motor nameplate for details.

Generally, all three-phase motor installations require a separate subcircuit from the distribution fuse board, and suitable protection against excess current (**overloads**) and unexpected restart (no volt release). Isolation should be provided by the motor control gear.

Note: All terminals on three-phase supplies must be enclosed in earthed metal or in all-insulated enclosures.

Selection of motor and control gear

When motors for machine drives are to be installed, the following factors need to be considered:
- power output required from the motor,
- operating speed of the motor and the speed characteristics,
- speed control,
- methods of starting,
- starting torque,
- type of frame enclosure,
- nature of atmosphere and temperature in which it is to operate,
- nature of electrical power supply, that is, single-, three-phase or d.c.

Motor application

For domestic purposes only a single-phase a.c. supply is normally available. The single-phase supply does not produce a rotating magnetic field, so that, with the exception of the universal motor, a form of starting device is required. See Chapter 7 and Appendix A.

For commercial and industrial usage there is a choice of supply to suit the input requirements of the motor. The most common supply for motors is the three-phase system, which produces a true rotating magnetic field in the stator of the motor, so that there is a steady and continuous torque set up on the rotor, which produces a smooth rotation.

> A three-phase, squirrel-cage, rotor-type motor is the cheapest, most economical and trouble-free motor that can be employed for a given power output, providing its characteristics suit the application.

Where a wide range of speed control and higher starting torques are required, other types, although more expensive, will have to be installed.

In some cases where a fine control of speed over a wide range is necessary at a steady torque, a d.c. motor will be most suitable. This also entails the extra cost of installing the rectifying equipment to convert the incoming a.c. mains supply to d.c. See Figure 8.7 for the motor installation final circuit wiring.

See starting and speed control diagrams and electric motor data sheet (Appendices A and B).

> The starting current of a motor is around five or six times the full load value. This means that the larger motors need special starter equipment which will depend upon the nature of the supply and type of motor.

Machine checks

Various instruments are required to perform checks on machines and associated equipment, either when the supply is on and they are in operation, or when the supply is off and the machines are

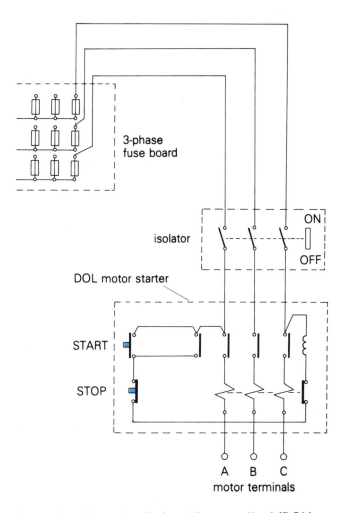

Figure 8.7 Motor intallation 'direct on line' (DOL) circuit.

standing. Instruments required will include an insulation tester, continuity tester, ductor tester, feeler gauge, spring balance, and straight edges and string lines.

Instruments required for supply-off checks

Insulation tester

This is also referred to as a **megger**. This is an instrument which produces a d.c. output of 500 V which is sufficient test voltage for machines operating on supplies up to 650 V. Tests can be applied to check the insulation values between connections, terminals and windings connected to different poles, or between these and the exposed metalwork of the equipment. Circuit diagrams, or electrical knowledge of the plant is required to ensure that there are no connections which would lead to false values being obtained. If, for example, the insulation between the three-phase windings of a machine was being tested, the **star** or **delta** connection points would have to be broken to separate them. See Figures 8.8 and 8.9.

> The minimum insulation value should be around 1 MΩ, although if the machine is damp, it may need drying out to obtain this figure.

Continuity tester

This is a meter used to check the actual ohmic values of the windings of a machine, or resistance values of starting or speed control equipment. Again, detailed knowledge is required to ensure that there are no parallel paths when the equipment is fully connected which would lead to false low values being obtained, or if any alternative circuit is connected across (in parallel) with an open circuit winding.

Ductor tester

This is a device for the measure of very low resistance values which are not practical to read on the continuity tester, that is, small fractions of an ohm, may be 0.01 Ω or so. The tester circulates a heavy current and measures the millivolt (mV) drop across the resistance path. If a ductor is not available, this form of test can be carried out using a heavy current supply, such as a car battery and

connecting an ammeter in series, with a voltmeter across in parallel with the resistance path to be measured.

$$R = \frac{V}{I}\ \Omega$$

For example, if, on such a test, the current in the circuit is 60 A and the millivoltmeter reads 30 mV the resistance would be 0.0005 Ω, a very difficult value to read directly on an ohmmeter.

This instrument is used for the measurement of heavy-current armature windings of d.c. machines, the copper bars in the rotor of a squirrel-cage motor, or the joints and terminations on busbar and heavy-current cable installations.

Feeler gauges

These are sets of long, parallel blades ranging in thickness from 0.0254 mm, up to around 0.762 mm. They are used for checking air gaps between the rotor and stator core of rotating machines, to give an indication of the amount of wear in the bearings. If the bearings are not worn, the readings will be the same all round the circumference. If they are worn, the gap at the top will be higher than that at the bottom. If the difference is large, new bearings will be required to prevent 'fouling' between the cores on rotation.
Note: On machines which are almost enclosed, inspection covers at 90° are positioned on the 'end covers' of the motor frame to enable the air gap to be checked.

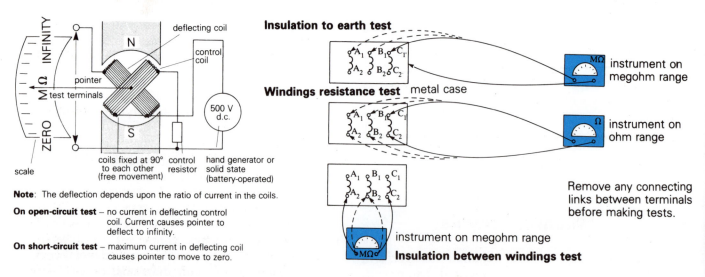

Figure 8.8 (left) Insulation 'megger' tester.
Figure 8.9 (right) Insulation and resistance tests on a three-phase winding.

Spring balance

This is used to check the tension on contacts and on brush gear of machines and equipment. The brush is hooked to the balance, gently pulled away from the slip ring or commutator and the tension value read on the scale. It can then be compared with the manufacturer's instructions.

Straight edges and string lines

These are used to check horizontal and lateral alignments.

Instruments required for supply-on checks

Voltmeter

This is a meter designed to measure voltages at the supply and at different points on the switchgear and the machines. These can be compared with the manufacturer's data or against the readings of similar machines etc.

> The presence of voltage with a voltmeter reading 'off-load' (no current being supplied) may be indicated through a very high resistance circuit, that is, along the metallic spattering of the walls of a 'blown' HBC fuse. When the machine is switched on and current is required in the circuit, this voltage would collapse (IR drop) and the machine still would not operate satisfactorily. This may lead to faulty diagnosis of the problem.

Approved test lamp

This is another method of testing for the presence of supply or voltage although it does not indicate the actual value.

> ▲ Test lamps must be of the Standard-approved type which contain the necessary safety current-limited devices, such as resistors and fuses, so that in the event of a fault, there is no risk of an explosion. They are shrouded with insulation to prevent electric shock while in use.

Ammeter

This meter is used to check the value of the current in the supply conductors and in the various circuits

of switchgear and machines, to compare with manufacturer's data, nameplate details, etc. Ordinary ammeters do, of course, need to have the circuit disconnected and then be connected in series. This is where the **clip-on** type ammeter is of advantage (see Figure 10.14, Chapter 10).

> When checking current consumption of machines, in some cases the start current may be up to eight to ten times the full load value, so be sure of the ammeter range and allow the motor to run up to speed.

Multi-test instruments

Current, voltage, insulation and resistance continuity values can all be measured by one instrument which has all the necessary scales and ranges. These are selected as required by the use of a multi-position switch, or a set of outlet sockets. The instrument contains a battery to provide the current flow to measure resistance on the continuity range, plus a power-pack to step the voltage to 500 V d.c. for the insulation tests. It is known as the **Electrician's Universal Meter**.

Dismantling of standard electrical machines

1. Clean excess dirt, oil, grease, etc., from surfaces.
2. Dependent on the weight and size of the machine, place it in a suitable position on floor stand or work bench.
3. Any sign of rust on parts to be removed should be sprayed with release fluid.
4. Withdraw the key from pinion coupling pulley etc. and then withdraw pinion, etc.
   See Figure 8.10 for these operations.
5. Undo nuts from end cover bolts and mark the positions of covers relative to stator frame.
6. Examine for type of bearings, it may need removal of oil rings on the sleeve type.
7. Remove end covers which will leave ball or roller type bearings on the shaft.
8. Remove rotor or armature from stator. On large machines this may need lifting gear or two people, one at each end of the shaft.
9. If the motor is fitted with a commutator or slip rings, try to leave these in position on the shaft.

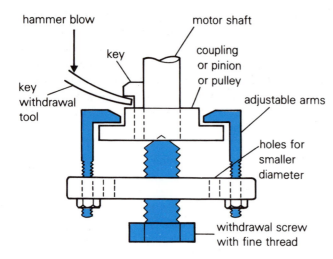

Note: When the withdrawal screw is fully tightened and there is no movement of coupling, etc., a sharp (shock) blow with hammer on the screw head will 'shock it' and should produce movement.

Figure 8.10 Motor coupling pinion or pulley withdrawal tool.

These operations now leave the machine available for cleaning, inspection and maintenance. To assemble the machine reverse the above steps.

Inspection of machinery and control gear

All electrical machinery and control gear should be inspected and tested at regular intervals. The frequency of the inspections will depend on the type of equipment and conditions under which it operates. A record of each inspection, together with test results should be kept for future reference.

The inspection of electrical machinery falls into two categories – mechanical and electrical.

Mechanical inspection

1. Visibly check the machine for mechanical damage.
2. Check the machine for correct alignment to en-sure that no undue stresses are imposed on the bearings.
3. Check the air gap (where possible) with feeler gauges.
4. Check the mechanical operation of switchgear and control gear, paying particular attention to contact condition and pressure.
5. If starters are fitted with dash-pots, check the grade and level of the oil.
6. In the case of any oil-immersed equipment, check that the oil level is correct and the oil is clean.

Electrical inspection

1. Check all connections on machinery and control gear, taking note of the condition of the wiring.
2. Carry out protective conductor continuity and insulation resistance tests.
3. Check fuses for correct rating and also check that any motor-overload current settings are correct.
4. Run machinery, listening for knocks, strange noises, etc., and check that all equipment in the circuit is functioning correctly.

D.c. machines – inspection and maintenance

Owing to their more complex construction, d.c. machines require more frequent maintenance than the common types of a.c. motors. On d.c. machines, the important points to check are the running condition, yoke and field windings, brushes, brush holders, brush springs, armature assembly, bearings, shaft, connection, wiring and insulation.

Running condition
With machine running, check for excessive noise and sparking at the brushes.

Yoke and field windings
With machine isolated from the supply, check that the yoke and field windings are in good condition.

Brushes and brush holders
Check that the brushes and brush holders are in good condition and that the brushes move freely in their holders. Brushes worn to half their original length should be replaced, and the new brushes properly bedded in with brush-bedding tape or fine sandpaper.

Brush springs
Check that the brush springs are in good condition, that spring pressure is adequate and even on all brushes. A small spring balance may be used for this.

Armature assembly
Check that the coils are in good condition and held securely at the commutator end by their bands. Check the commutator for concentricity, irregular-

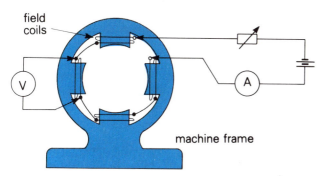

field
coils

machine frame

Note: Current is circulated around all the field coils which are connected in series.

Volts drop is measured in turn at each coil $R = \frac{V}{I}(\Omega)$. All drops should be equal.

High values denote open-circuit faults, low values short-circuit faults.

Figure 8.11 Location of 'short' or 'open' circuit faults on motor field coils.

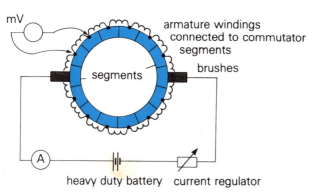

mV

armature windings connected to commutator segments

segments

brushes

A

heavy duty battery   current regulator

Note: The millivoltmeter is used to measure the volts drop across each coil.

$R = \dfrac{mV}{I}$ in milliohms (mΩ). All these readings

should be equal. Low readings denote shorted turns, while high readings denote open-circuit faults.

Figure 8.12 Location of 'short' or 'open' circuit faults on armature.

ities and cleanliness. Dirt may be removed with a commutator brush, and fine sandpaper will remove slight roughness. Emery cloth must not be used for this purpose as it leaves a greasy film on the commutator. If the commutator is badly worn or eccentric it must be skimmed on a lathe or on a special skimming machine, after which the insulation between the segments may have to be cut back.

Bearings
Check bearings as far as possible for condition and correct lubrication.

Shaft
Check the shaft for concentricity and general condition.

Connections and wiring
Check that all connections are tight and that wiring is in good condition with no signs of heat damage.

D.c. machine faults

Symptoms	Tests
Starter of the d.c. motor will not hold in 'ON' position, although the motor starts correctly.	1. Check that the overload trip is not stuck in the operated position and that remote 'stop' buttons, etc., are not operated. 2. Test 'no-volt coil' for short or open circuit. 3. In the case of series motors, or starters where the no-volt coil is not in series with a shunt winding, check the no-volts coil circuit for continuity.
Excessive sparking at commutator.	1. Check brushgear for correction tension, brushes sticking in holders, etc. 2. Check polarity of interpoles, if fitted. 3. Test the armature windings for short or open-circuits.
D.c. generator fails to excite.	1. May be due to loss of residual magnetism; 'flash' using a suitable battery. 2. Check that the rotation of the armature is in the correct direction and that field connections have not been reversed. 3. Check field and armature circuits for open or short-circuits. See Figures 8.11 and 8.12.

A.c. motor faults

Symptoms	Tests
Motor completely dead.	Check the voltage at the isolator and motor terminals.
Contactor starter does not operate, although supply at isolator is correct.	1. Check that overload trips, limit trips, interlocks and remote 'stop' buttons are not operated, and that the starter controls are correctly set to the start position. 2. Test continuity of the contactor coil and its associated circuits.
Fuses blow or overload trips operate when any attempt is made to start the motor.	1. Check that the motor is free to rotate. 2. Check that the starter is being operated correctly. 3. Test insulation resistance.
Three-phase motor buzzes or hums but refuses to start.	1. Check that the supply voltage is available at all three phases at the motor terminals. 2. Test each phase of the motor winding for continuity. 3. Test rotor circuits for continuity. See Figures 8.13 and 8.14.
Single-phase motor hums but refuses to start.	1. Check that the motor is free to rotate (particularly for small-sized motors). 2. Test continuity of main and starting windings and of the centrifugal switch or starting relay. 3. Test that the supply is actually reaching the starting winding via the capacitor, if fitted.

Insulation

Carry out a normal insulation test using a megger of twice the working voltage of the machine, up to a maximum of 500 V d.c. It is difficult to make hard and fast rules as to when worn items should be replaced. The chief consideration must be whether or not any items are likely to break down before the next scheduled inspection.

> It is much safer and cheaper in the long term to replace worn items if in any doubt, rather than risk an expensive breakdown. It is known as **preventive maintenance**.

Types of machine enclosures

Electrical machines are often subjected to adverse conditions such as dirt, moisture, excess heat, extreme weather, poorly ventilates areas, etc. To withstand these conditions, special types of enclosures have been designed.

Obviously, the more 'open' and ventilated a machine, the greater the heat dissipation from the losses within the machine and hence the frame can be smaller for a given power rating.

Open machine

The rotor is mounted on a pedestal with no end covers, so that there is free circulation of air through the frame and windings. This is usually the type used for larger machines, which are inaccessible to unauthorised persons, such as in substations and switchhouses.

Screen-ventilated enclosure

This is the more common type of enclosure where live and revolving parts are shielded against touch. The air is 'sucked' in through vents at the one end and 'exhausted' from the other end by a fan fitted to the rotor shaft.

Drip-proof enclosure

This is similar to the previous type, but with extended vents and slanted covers to prevent falling rain or water from other sources from entering the windings.

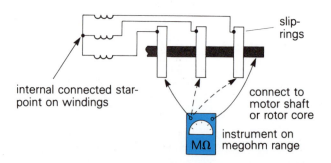

Figure 8.13 Insulation test of three-phase wound rotor.

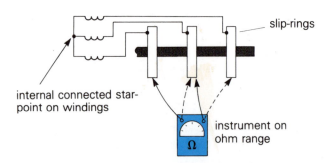

Figure 8.14 Resistance test of three-phase wound rotor.

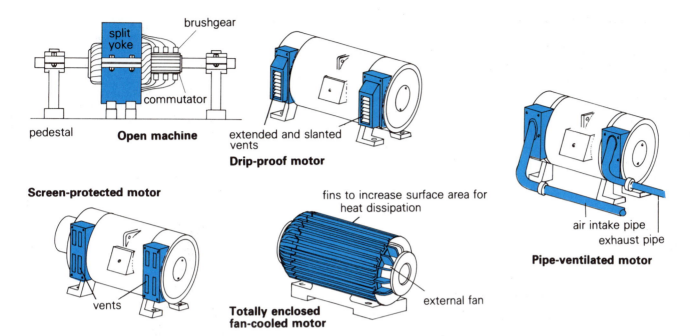

Figure 8.15 Types of machine enclosures.

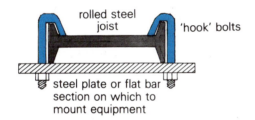

Figure 8.16 Fixing equipment to steelwork (R.S.J.).

occur under the particular operating conditions, without transmitting the explosion to the external atmosphere. It is similar in construction to the totally enclosed type, but the end covers, terminal boxes and bearing surfaces are very accurately machined and more bolts are provided to ensure that no leaks occur from any joints on the machine frame. See Figure 8.15.

Total enclosure

This is mainly used for motors used in conditions where there is a high concentration of dust and fumes. The protective enclosure has no openings. The outer frame is ribbed by fins which increase the surface area in contact with the atmosphere and hence provide better heat dissipation.

Pipe-ventilated enclosure

This is again used for dust- and fume-laden areas but where a clean and cool supply of air is close at hand, that is, where the motor is positioned near an outside wall. The air is circulated by an internal fan fitted to the rotor shaft.

Flame-proof enclosure

These enclosures are designed to withstand an internal explosion of an inflammable gas which may

Mounting of switch and control equipment

For high-power motors, the weight of the switch and control gear can be quite considerable. These require mounting in a vertical position close to the relevant motor. If a substantial brick or concrete wall is available, suitable mild steel brackets may be fabricated and secured to the wall and the switch-gear bolted to these brackets. Again, there may be steel supporting stanchions or columns nearby where suitable steel brackets may be secured.

Note: Structural load-bearing fixtures would be unduly weakened by excessive drilling. The alternative is to weld the equipment-supporting brackets to the fixtures. See Figure 8.16.

Floor-mounted framework

In areas where machines are located some distance from walls and supporting steelwork, the use of a floor-mounted framework on which to bolt the electrical distribution and control equipment will be required. See Figure 8.17. This is securely bolted to the floor foundation.

The framework is assembled from flat or angled sections in mild steel of suitable size, cut to the various required lengths and suitably shaped. On the heavier sections, this will require prior heating. The sections can then be bolted or welded together, dependent upon the facilities available.

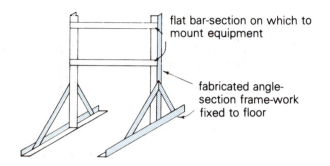

Figure 8.17 Free-standing framework.

Handling and transporting heavy plant

Where machines and switchgear are too heavy to lift manually, the electrician should always ensure that when handling, that is, unloading from a transporter, moving to site, erecting and installing, etc., the load is always under control.

In established buildings, factories and workshops, handling and lifting facilities are usually available. These will consist of overhead cranes, or chain blocks suspended from **rolled steel joists** (RSJ), which can be manually operated from the floor positions.

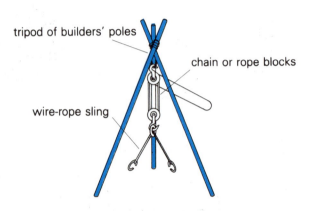

Figure 8.18 Method of unloading plant on site.

▲ It is always necessary to check that the lifting equipment to be used is of suitable capacity for the load.

On some sites, particularly on new installations in course of erection, such facilities may be unavailable. In this situation, the electrician will have to improvise, using any available resources.

Unloading from transporter

Assume that a heavy item of equipment has arrived on a transport vehicle, and is to be unloaded and moved into a building. If a chain of suitable capacity or rope lifting blocks are available, the problem is soon overcome. A suitable tripod can be assembled from builders' poles or planks lashed together firmly at the top to support the top

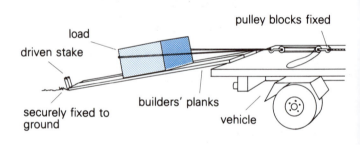

Figure 8.19 Method of lowering plant from a transporter.

blocks. The machine can be lifted a few centimetres, the vehicle moved and the machine then lowered. See Figure 8.18.

If suitable poles are not to hand, the builders' planks will have to be placed in position between the vehicle and the ground, using the longest planks available (they may require intermediate support) to reduce the gradient. The machine can then be moved by levers (crowbars) on to the planks and gently slid down the planks. See Figure 8.19.

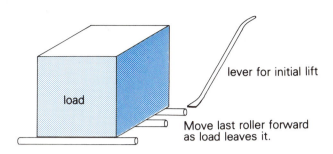

lever for initial lift

load

Move last roller forward
as load leaves it.

Figure 8.20 Movement of heavy plant using rollers.

The load should always be under control and no person should be in a potentially dangerous position should the load move unexpectedly.

Lateral movement

When the heavy load or machine is to be moved along the ground, the use of tubes or rollers may be employed. The load can be lifted sufficiently by levers to place the rollers under the machine feet. The load can then be moved forward on the rollers, taking the last roller and placing it at the front end and so on. See Figure 8.20.

Always ensure that the point at which the lever is placed will safely support the load weight, that is, it will not cause damage to the equipment. Also, the weight-bearing capacity of the approach road and floor finishes should be considered when making any decision regarding heavy equipment on a site.

Use of eye-bolts

Machines are normally fitted with 'eye-bolts' for lifting purposes. These are screwed into the top of the stator case and have a large circular hole to receive the crane or pulley-block hook.

Use of slings

Where a machine is fitted with two eye-bolts, a wire sling with a hook at each end is required. It is important to test for the best position between the

two eye-bolts for balance so that the machine does not tilt. Slings can also be used for moving equipment such as large distribution boards or switchgear, where no lifting points are provided.

Where there are no lifting points, wooden blocks or battens are required between the wire rope and the steel edge of the equipment to prevent slipping and also to protect the sling against 'fraying'.

Rectification

For some purposes, for example, the operation of d.c. motors, battery-chargers and electro-plating processes, the use of direct current (d.c.) is required. The supply brought into the consumer's premises is an a.c. supply, therefore when d.c. is required, the supply must be converted. This is known as **rectification**.

The rectifier

It has been found that when certain metals undergo special heat treatment and are placed in contact with each other, the junction will allow the free passage of current (low resistance) in one direction, called the **forward** direction. When the currents tries to flow in the opposite direction, the resistance will be very high and practically no current will flow. This direction is known as the **reverse** direction.

The single-element rectifier is referred to as a **diode** because it has two electrodes – an **anode** and a **cathode**. The direction of current flow is from anode to cathode.

A single diode will provide **half-wave rectification** only. **Full-wave rectification** can be obtained by the connection of four diodes in a bridge circuit, or two diodes connected to a **centre-tapped transformer**. See Figure 8.21. Early rectifiers were of two main types:

1. copper oxide,
2. selenium.

Modern rectifiers are made of germanium and silicon. These are physically much smaller than the earlier types for the same power rating. Because of their small dimensions, care must be taken to ensure that they have sufficient cooling. In many

1 Half-wave

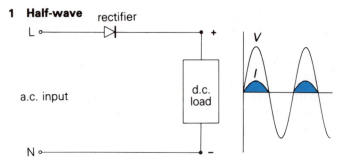

2 Full-wave (bridge circuit)

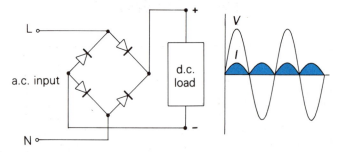

3 Full-wave centre-tap transformer

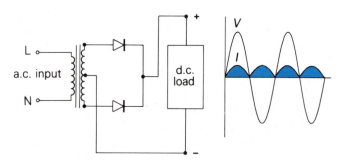

Figure 8.21 Rectifier wiring diagrams.

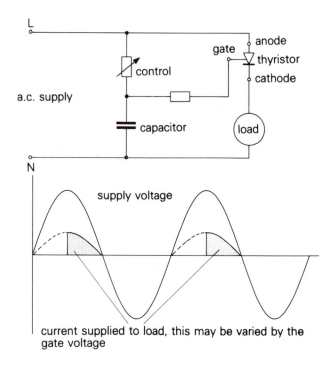

Figure 8.22 Thyristor control circuit.

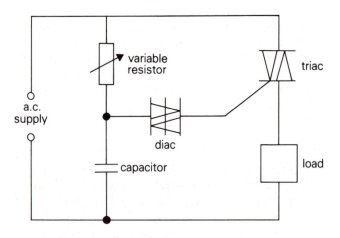

Figure 8.23 Triac control circuit.

cases, this means that they have to be mounted on **heat sinks** which present a much larger surface area to the atmosphere.

Rectifiers are sometimes referred to as **solid-state devices** since there are no moving parts in their operation.

The thyristor
This is a development of the silicon rectifier and is sometimes called the **silicon-controlled rectifier (SCR)**. It has the addition of a third electrode called the **gate**. The basic principle of the thyristor is that by varying the potential (voltage) on the gate electrode, the point at which current will commence to flow in the half cycle of the supply voltage can be varied. It means that the average amount of current and hence power supplied to the load in a given time, can be controlled.

This method of control is used in the dimming of filament lamps and for the speed control of d.c. and universal motors. It is a very efficient form of control since the power (I^2R) losses in the control device are practically nil. See Figure 8.22.

The triac
This is a more recent device in the semiconductor range. Its advantage over the thyristor is that because it has two anodes it will conduct on both half cycles of the a.c. input supply.

Like the thyristor it also has a gate electrode so

that the voltage on this can be adjusted to control the point on the input cycle at which conduction (current flow) takes place.

It is now used quite widely in domestic appliances and machines to control brilliance of lamps and speed of motors, it is also used on TV and radio power supplies. The triac control circuit is shown in Figure 8.23.

Tests on equipment fitted with electronic devices

For equipment which is fitted with an electronic device, for example, dimmer switches, some washing machines, variable speed drives, etc., care must be exercised when carrying out tests.

When using, say, a 500 V megger on circuits for insulation tests make certain these machines are disconnected.

If it is suspected that one of these devices is at fault, the most likely cause is a short circuit between electrodes. This can be checked by carrying out tests with a low voltage continuity tester or a universal meter on the resistance range.

On a rectifier diode if the tests leads are placed on the terminals it will read a low resistance from the anode to the cathode, but a high resistance from cathode to anode. If there is a low resistance reading both ways, the device is faulty.

The transistor test is a little more involved because the **transistor** has three terminals: **collector**, **base**, and **emitter**. There are two types of transistor: n-p-n junction and the p-n-p junction.

However, when testing there should not be low resistance both ways when testing between the same two terminals.

These tests will be sufficient to check for an insulation breakdown, which is the most common fault. A complete check means the replacement of the device.

Three-phase power rectification
The developments in silicon and germanium solid state rectifiers in terms of power handling together with smaller physical dimensions, has made the mercury arc rectifier obsolete.

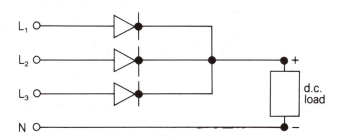

Figure 8.24 Three-phase half-wave rectifier circuit.

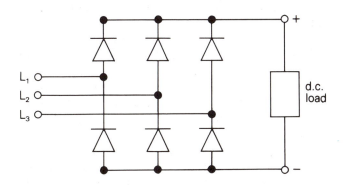

Figure 8.25 Three-phase full-wave rectifier circuit.

However, because of the small size of the latest rectifiers they do need to be mounted on heat shunts to present a large surface area to the cooler atmosphere.

The rectifiers can be connected to produce either half-wave or full-wave rectification of the three-phase supply. See Figure 8.24 three-phase half-wave, and Figure 8.25, three-phase full-wave.
Note: There is no N conductor required in the full-wave circuit. The full-wave circuit does produce a smoother d.c. output and therefore requires less smoothing on the output.

D.c. to a.c. invertor

By the interconnection of thyristors, an alternating current supply can be produced from a direct current supply. These are built as a unit to supply discharge lighting from emergency standby batteries in buildings or on public service vehicles for inside lighting. They can also supply three-phase emergency apparatus in the event of a power failure, using standby heavy-duty batteries.

■ CHECK YOUR UNDERSTANDING

● Motors are mounted on bedplates fitted with slide rails to tension belt and chain drives. The electric supply must be flexible to allow motor movement.

● Fluid and eddy current couplings are used to ease the starting load.

● Motor electric controls contain stop, start, excess current and no-volt devices, oil dash-pots delay operation of excess current to allow motor to start.

● Electrical tests include insulation and winding resistance values, checks on switchgear, on load currents by use of a 'clip-on' ammeter.
Mechanical checks – air gaps, brush gear condition and brush tension, alignment and bearings.

● Motor enclosure types must be suitable for the location, that is, screen ventilated, enclosed, drop proof, weather proof, flame proof or pipe ventilated.

● Fixing of switchgear to steelwork should be on a framework that is either free standing or 'clamped' to building structure rather than drilling or cutting of structure.

● For handling of heavy equipment use tripods supporting pulley or chain blocks, for lateral movement use levers and rollers.

● For rectification of a.c. supplies for d.c. equipment use diodes arranged for connection to 1 ph or 3 ph supplies, usually through transformers.

● Voltage and energy regulators use thyristors, or triacs. D.c. to a.c. invertors used for emergency and standby equipment employ the use of thyristors.

● Electronic devices may need disconnection when insulation tests using high voltages on equipment are being carried out.

REVISION EXERCISES AND QUESTIONS

1 A d.c. machine requires more periodical checks and maintenance than an a.c. cage type induction motor.
i) State the reasons for this.
ii) List maintenance items that would not apply to the d.c. motor.

2 i) Why is the air gap in an electric motor as small as is possible?
ii) How can this gap be measured?
iii) If the measurements of the gap vary, what does this indicate and how can it be remedied?

3 i) State the reasons that precautions should be taken when carrying out insulation tests on equipment where electronic devices are fitted.
ii) Explain a simple test that could be carried out if a breakdown of insulation (short circuit) occurred between the electrodes of (a) a rectifier, (b) a transistor, (c) a thyristor and (d) a triac.

4 A direction-on-line push button motor starter is to be modified so that an **inching button** (i.e., the motor will stop when the button is released) is provided.
i) Make a diagram of the existing control circuit and the alterations for the inching button.
ii) Four extra stop buttons are also to be provided; again make a diagram of the wiring to these from the starter.

5 Larger motor starters are fitted with a time delay on their excess current protection device.
i) Explain the necessity for this and, by the aid of a sketch, how it is achieved.
ii) Explain why the thermal protective devices are not fitted with time delays.

6 In an induction motor state:
i) how the power is developed in the rotor,
ii) (a) why the rotor conductors must be firmly fixed to the rotor core, (b) why the rotor cannot run at the synchronous speed.
iii) Why is the rotor voltage in a cage type motor lower than the wound type rotor?

7 It is required to carry out insulation and continuity tests on each phase of a large three-phase 415 V motor stator winding at the terminal block which has six terminals with three copper links.
i) Explain how these tests would be carried out.
ii) With the aid of a connection diagram, what equipment could be used for the very low resistance values?
iii) On disconnection of the test lead in (ii) a 'flash' was observed. State a reason for this.

8 A 415 V three-phase supply to a motor has become open-circuit on one phase.
Make a diagram of the motor windings and determine the voltage across each when connected in
i) (a) star and (b) delta.
ii) State the effect on the motor if the open circuit occurred (a) when the motor was running and (b) when it is switched on.

9 Explain with the aid of sketches the methods

and the devices used to carry out the following operations:

i) alignment of shaft coupling between two machines,

ii) alignment of two pulleys for a belt drive,

iii) withdrawal of a pulley from a shaft,

iv) checks on 'air gaps' between rotor and stator of a motor,

v) tensioning of belt drives.

10 A test is to be carried out on a single-phase motor of 3 kW output rating to determine its power factor and efficiency.

i) Draw a circuit diagram showing the instruments connected to measure the voltage, current and power.

ii) Which instruments will require protection against the starting current of the motor? State **one** method of protection.

iii) The readings obtained on the test were voltage 240 V, current 20 A, power 3600 W. Calculate (a) the power factor and (b) the efficiency.

11 A 1 kW, 240 V, 50 Hz single-phase two-pole motor is operating with 5 per cent slip, 75 per cent efficiency and 0.8 pf on full load.

i) Draw a labelled diagram of a push-button starter with overcurrent protection for the motor.

ii) State how extra STOP and START push-buttons may be connected in the circuit.

iii) Determine (a) the input power, (b) the current and (c) the speed at full load.

12 i) Describe, with the aid of sketches, **four** methods of mechanically coupling an electric motor to the drive machine.

ii) State **one** example where **each** of your methods would be most suitable.

13 State **one** application for **each** of the following motor enclosures:

(i) open, (ii) screen-protected, (iii) totally enclosed, (iv) pipe-ventilated, (v) drip-proof, (vi) flame-proof.

14 i) Draw the basic circuit diagram of a thyristor control circuit for an electrical load.

ii) Explain the function of the thyristor.

iii) Sketch the current waveform produced when it is arranged to trigger the thyristor one quarter of a cycle from zero voltage.

iv) What is the purpose of a heat sink?

v) State **two** applications of a thyristor control circuit.

15 i) Describe briefly the construction of the following parts of a three-phase induction motor:

(a) stator, (b) cage rotor, (c) wound rotor.

ii) Explain how the windings of a single-phase induction motor are arranged for starting.

iii) Make diagrams of **two** types of devices which operate when the motor speed increases.

16 i) Explain the reasons why the temperature of an electric motor rises when it is in operation.

ii) State **two** constructional features of a motor which help to reduce the temperature rise.

iii) What materials used in the motor construction are most affected by excess temperature rise?

17 Describe, with the aid of diagrams, how **each** of the following tests would be carried out on the three-phase motor, controlled by a star-delta starter, to find:

i) a phase-to-earth fault on the stator,

ii) a phase-to-phase fault on the stator,

iii) a short circuit between windings on the same phase of the stator.

(C & G 'C')

18 Having recently installed a 6 kW screen-protected cage motor with a normal direct-on-line starter to drive a line shaft for various machines on a farm, the electrician is called back because of a complaint that the motor is causing a smell and is tripping frequently, but is running normally. It is found that the farmer has built a small wooden enclosure which contains the motor, its starter and a hammer mill for grain milling with the object of minimising noise and dust pollution.

Describe briefly:

i) the probable cause of excessive tripping,

ii) the probable cause of motor smell,

iii) the likely effect of prolonged use,

iv) a remedy for starter tripping.

19 Draw a full circuit diagram for a three-phase **automatic** star-delta starter indicating the supply and motor connections. The following items are to be included in the diagram:

i) over-current protection,

ii) under-voltage protection,

iii) single-phase protection,

iv) local stop-start push buttons,

v) remote stop-start push buttons,

vi) two remote emergency stop push buttons.

(C & G 'C')

20 A wound rotor induction motor is causing the starter overloads to trip each time the operator attempts to start the machine.

State **two** possible causes of electrical defect in **each** of the following:
  i) the stator section of starter,
 ii) the rotor section of starter,
iii) the motor,
 iv) the wiring.

(C & G 'C')

21 Describe, with the aid of sketches, each stage of the following operations (i), (ii) and (iii). No crane is available but on site is (a) adequate labour, (b) a number of heavy timber scaffold boards, (c) scaffold tubing and fittings, (d) a 500 kg capacity rope block and ropes, (e) several strong steel tubes 5 m long, (f) a number of 1 m × 50 mm diameter solid steel bars.

  i) Offload a cubicle type switchboard weighing 300 kg from a flat platform truck.
 ii) Transport it 60 m along a bitumen asphalt pathway, and
iii) lower if through the roof of an underground substation.

(C & G 'C')

Special installations and batteries

Introduction

Special precautions must be taken in installing any electrical wiring or equipment in hazardous areas where there is a risk of fire or explosion, or where there is a risk of mechanical damage or corrosion that expose live conductors and could lead to electric shock.

Installations such as in hospitals, petrol stations, highways, farms and swimming pools have their own special problems.

Installations in hazardous areas

Three main types of hazard are considered here:

1. flammable liquids;
2. explosive gases and vapours;
3. explosive dusts, where flammable organic dusts (for example, sugar and flour) or metallic dusts (for example, magnesium, aluminium, titanium and zirconium) are liable to be present. Both the installation and the equipment should be dust-proof (Type VBS 587). Similar precautions should be taken where explosives such as cordite and gunpowder are used.

Flammable gases and vapours encountered within industry are classified into groups:

Group I	Gases encountered in coal mining, for example, methane.
Group II	Various gases commonly found in industry, for example, propane, butane, pentane, ammonia, carbon monoxide, etc. This group applies mainly to the petrochemical industry.
Group III	Coal gas.
Group IV	Acetylene, hydrogen.

Flame-proof equipment

Flame-proof equipment is so designed that it will withstand an internal explosion of the particular gas for which it is certified and also prevent any spark or flame from that explosion escaping from the enclosure and igniting the surrounding atmosphere. This is achieved by wide-machined flanges. See Figure 9.1.

There are two types of flame-proof apparatus:

1. mining gear, which is used with either special mining cables or armoured cable;
2. industrial gear, which may be used with solid-drawn conduit, MICC aluminium-sheathed, or armoured cables.

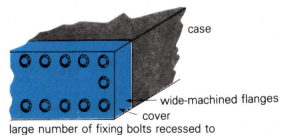

large number of fixing bolts recessed to avoid interference with ordinary tools

Figure 9.1 Typical design of flameproof equipment.

Buxton certified equipment

All flame-proof gear is 'Buxton' certified and is constructed in either grey or malleable iron. Each compartment is separated by integral barriers. Aluminium alloy is also used to reduce the weight of equipment.

Intrinsically safe equipment

▲ The basis of intrinsic safety in general is that the complete circuit and apparatus is so designed that the energy available is insufficient to cause a spark large enough to ignite the gas present.

Installations in flame-proof areas

Wiring systems

Conduit

1. All conduit must be solid-drawn.
2. All fittings and accessories must be Buxton certified.
3. Couplers must be of the flame-proof type with a minimum length of 50 mm.
4. The length of thread at fittings must be the same as the fitting plus a locknut.
5. Running couplers must not be used.
6. 25 mm and 20 mm conduit can screw directly into flame-proof enclosures.

Larger conduits must be sealed at the point of entry with plastic compound. Where the conduit passes from one flame-proof zone to another or to a non-flame-proof zone, the installation should be sectionalised. This is done by fitting a box between the two sections and filling it with compound. The same method can be used to prevent condensation within the enclosures.
Note: Flexible conduit is not flame-proof.

MICC cable

MICC cable is ideal for use in flame-proof areas. However, flame-proof glands, 50 mm thread and terminations must be used.

Armoured cables

Equipment

1. Flanges should be greased to prevent corrosion.
2. Care should be taken when tightening aluminium flanges to prevent distortion.
3. All external bolts must be of high-tensile steel.
4. Flame-proof equipment is not weather-proof.
5. Damaged flame-proof gear should be returned to the manufacturer for repair. Under no circumstances should any attempt to made to repair or modify equipment on site.

Potential danger areas

CP 1003 classified three areas in order of potential danger:
    Divisions 0, 1 and 2.

Division 0

This is an area in which flammable vapours etc. are continuously present. This is the most dangerous area and generally, it is recommended that electrical equipment should not be installed there.

▲ If it is necessary to instal electrical equipment, then a system of electrical enclosures could be pressurised above atmospheric pressure so that no explosive vapour would pass into the electrical system. An alternative method would be to install the electric motor and its control gear outside the area and have the drive shaft coupled to the driven machine (in the hazardous area) via a flame-proof seal in the dividing wall. See Figure 9.2.

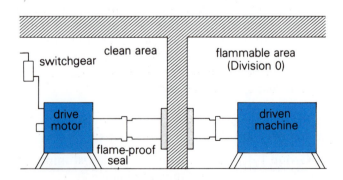

Figure 9.2 Drive shaft through a dividing wall.

Division 1

This denotes a less dangerous area than the previous category and flame-proof equipment can be installed as described earlier.

Division 2

Division 2 is still less dangerous than Division 1 areas where the equipment is unlikely to produce an arc or sparks during operation. It may be possible to install normal wiring systems with special attention to cable entries. See I.E.E. Regulations.

Regular testing must be carried out by competent personnel and only intrinsically safe test equipment be used. On mixed installations, where there are hazardous and safe areas, the electrical installation can revert from flame-proof wiring to normal wiring systems satisfactorily, provided that suitable sealing boxes are used as previously mentioned. For example, a conduit system could change from solid drawn to welded using a completely sealed circular through-conduit box (filled with a suitable compound).

Installations in hospitals

In some hospital areas, chemicals and vapours are used which are flammable. For example, liquid ether emits an explosive vapour. There are also other dangerous conditions, for example the sudden movement of a rubber sheet or nylon materials such as aprons can cause a static electricity flash which could ignite the gases.

All these factors contribute to potentially dangerous conditions which call for special requirements in the electrical installation. In more potentially dangerous areas, the equipment should be installed in accordance with Division 1 requirements, including the use of mercury-tilt switches for all lighting purposes. See Figure 9.3.

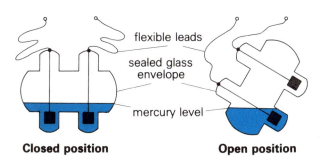

Figure 9.3 **Mercury-tilt switch.**

> ▲ In areas where there are dangers from static electricity, there are special requirements for earthing and bonding all metalwork. For mobile furniture and equipment, such as beds and trolleys, metal or electrical-conducting materials are required for at least one wheel.

Installations for petrol stations

The installation must be carried out in accordance with I.E.E. Regulations and, for Division 1 and 2 areas, as prescribed in CP 1003.

Wiring

Division 1 areas may be wired in:

1. armoured cable,
2. MICC cables with flame-proof glands and, for underground installations, a PVC oversheath, or
3. single or multicore cables enclosed in solid-drawn, heavy-duty conduit protected against corrosion. All conduit boxes and inspection fittings must be flame-proof.

Termination for any of the above systems must be with flame-proof boxes or cable glands.

Division 2 areas may be wired in:

1. MICC with a PVC oversheath for underground use, or
2. single or multicore cables in heavy-duty screwed and welded conduit.

Note: If sparking of apparatus occurs under normal operation, wiring must be as Division 1. For safe areas, normal industrial wiring systems may be employed. For conduit systems, the cables used must be PVC/PVC or rubber insulated with a sheath of PCP (polychloroprene) or HOFR (heat, oil, flame-resistant). A separate protective conductor must be used.

Equipment

In Division 1 areas, switchgear must be flame-proof or intrinsically safe (both cases for Group II gases) but in Division 2 areas, the standard of equipment need not exceed BS 4317. Switches in Division 2 areas, including kiosks, should be of the enclosed break-type, or hermetically-sealed mercury-in-glass switches. Enclosed break micro-switches are also acceptable for this purpose.

Lighting fittings (luminaires)

Lighting fittings on the top of pump houses must be installed to Division 2 requirements. Lighting fittings in kiosks can be of an enclosed design and provided with gaskets to resist petrol vapour. Fittings attached to a canopy above the petrol pumps may be of the standard industrial type with weather-proofing as required.

Master switch

In addition to the main switch, a master switch must be provided to isolate the supply to the pumps and integral pump lights. The master switch must be prominently positioned in case of emergency. A notice 'PETROLEUM SPIRIT PUMPS, SWITCH OFF HERE' should be sited adjacent to the master switch. If high-voltage or neon signs are installed, a separate fireman's switch is required.

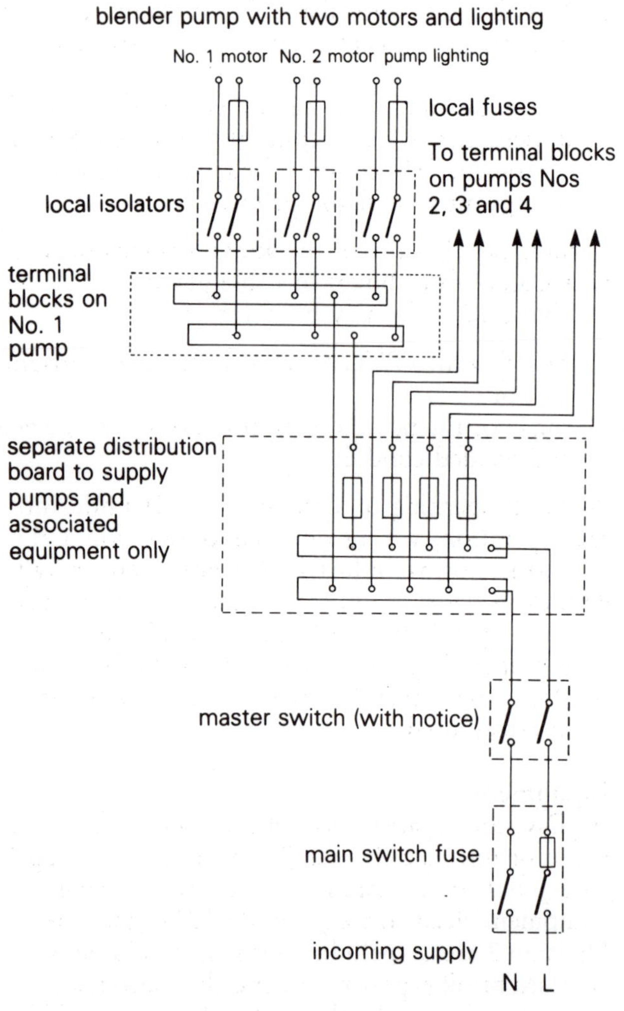

Pump circuits

Single delivery

Each pump must be connected to a separate circuit way in a fuse board to control both the pump and integral light. Also, a double-pole linked isolator or circuit breaker must be used for each pump.

Blender pumps

Each blender pump which has two pump motors must be connected to a separate subcircuit etc., as for single delivery pumps.

Dual delivery

The pumps must be connected to three separate subcircuits as follows:

Circuit 1 – Pump motor No. 1,
Circuit 2 – Pump motor No. 2,
Circuit 3 – Integral lighting.

Three linked isolators grouped together are required. See Figure 9.4.

Switches

All isolating switches (or **circuit breakers**) controlling pumps must be in one central position, accessible to the operator. Where switches are in Division 1 or 2 areas, they must be double-pole and capable of isolating all conductors to ensure safe changing of lamps.

Attended self-service stations

An isolating switch must be provided at the control position which is in addition to individual isolators. The recording and signalling circuits between the pump and control point need not be controlled by the isolating switch, provided that they are connected on extra low-voltage circuits and that intrinsically safe equipment is used.

Unattended self-service stations

The master switch control must be accessible and identified. The master switch must be a contactor with 'remote' stop buttons at appropriate points on the forecourt. To restore the supply, the 'ON' button should be accessible to authorised people only. The illumination at the top of each pump must not be less than 110 lux.

Earthing

▲ I.E.E. Regulations must be closely followed and regular tests and inspections should include earth-loop impedance, protective conductor tests and main earth connection.

Figure 9.4 Petrol (gasoline) station installation.

Where a direct earth cannot be obtained, ELCB must be installed and exposed metalwork should be bonded.

Testing and inspection
An annual test by a competent person is required.

Installations on caravan sites

The I.E.E. Regulations deal with both caravans and caravan sites and particularly with:

1. the wiring of caravan sites and terminations at caravans, where these are provided by the site operator;
2. installations within domestic residential (fixed) caravans, and
3. installations within domestic touring (mobile) caravans.

The termination of site wiring must include protection against excess current and earth leakage and have means of isolation. If the caravan site wiring is provided by the site operator, it becomes part of the consumer's installation. If the termination of the site wiring is external to, and not attached to the caravan, it must be contained in a weather-proof enclosure. The enclosure must have clearly marked terminals, or a non-reversible socket outlet including earthing means and be controlled by a switch or circuit breaker. The rating of the socket outlet should be at least 16 A.

For a mobile caravan, a notice is required giving the type of supply voltage, frequency and permitted load. Where the site termination is external and not attached to the caravan, a means of termination must be provided, which may be rubber-insulated, or PCP-sheathed flexible cable or flexible cord, or a cable in accordance with I.E.E. Regulations, which should terminate in the main switch of the caravan installation.

> The inlet to towing caravans must be a non-reversible socket outlet with means of earthing and preferably with a locking ring. The socket must be accessible from outside the caravan only.

A notice must be displayed in the caravan, giving procedural instructions before connection and disconnection of the supply. A test of the installation should be carried out annually.

The wiring inside the caravan must be suitably insulated to prevent contact with the metalwork or other services in the caravan. Lighting fittings must be mounted directly on to the structure of the lining of the caravan. Enclosed fittings must allow free airflow between the fittings and the body of the caravan. Flexible pendants are not permissible. Protective conductors must be insulated from the structural metalwork of the caravan and, if they are not enclosed in a composite cable, must be at least 4 mm^2. It is recommended that only insulated apparatus is used, otherwise protection against earth leakage is required in the form of double insulation, in accordance with I.E.E. Regulations. If the caravan has a compartment which contains electrical equipment with exposed metal parts and a fixed bath or shower which can be in metallic contact with earth, the metalwork and bath or shower must be bonded together.

> ▲ Caravan installations must be tested in accordance with I.E.E. Regulations on completion, and, if the caravan is disconnected for a period exceeding three months, the installation must be retested.

Earth leakage protection
Caravans and caravan sites are usually situated in areas where the electricity supply is by overhead cables and no earthing terminals are provided by the supply authority. This means that excess-current circuit breakers or fuses cannot meet the requirements for providing protection and the installation of earth leakage-type circuit breakers (RCDs) is therefore called for. Because of the close proximity of caravans on some sites, the use of a separate circuit breaker for each caravan would mean that the resistance areas (see Chapter 5) would overlap. Where these conditions exist, it is permissible for one earth leakage circuit breaker using one earth electrode to be installed to provide protection for up to six caravans.

Inspection and testing

> ▲ Caravan installations must be tested in accordance with the I.E.E. Regulations on completion, including the operation of the protection devices.

Farm and horticultural installations

Wiring systems suitable for use in other installations do not always give adequate protection on farm installations, because of the adverse conditions that are present. The installation will require specialised methods of installation and protection to guard against:

1. mechanical damage from movement of vehicles and livestock,
2. excessive vapours and moisture within buildings,
3. chemical vapours from milk-handling plant, fertilisers, animal and vegetable refuse,
4. exposure to weather since most of the installation will be in outbuildings or outside with continual exposure to extreme elements,
5. danger of shock to livestock. Very low voltages and current leakages can injure or kill livestock.

In potentially highly dangerous areas, the use of lower voltage supplies is advisable.

Switchgear

> ▲ All switchgear should be mounted out of reach of all livestock and suitably protected.

Each separate building must be controlled by its own main switch placed in an accessible position. Every wiring point must have a readily accessible switch with 'ON-OFF' positions clearly marked.

> All socket outlets must be provided with a switch. Non-switched socket outlets are not permitted.

Wiring
All-insulated wiring systems are the most suitable, provided that the wiring and accessories are positioned so as to avoid damage and interference from livestock.

1. Suitable systems would be vulcanised or butyl rubber-insulated and PCP-sheathed, since this sheath provides protection against oil, direct sunlight, weather, and is fire-resistant.
2. The cables can be drawn into PVC conduits where extra protection is required. This is pre-

ferable to steel conduits because of the danger of corrosive liquids and atmosphere.
3. Galvanised conduits or bright steel wire armour cable can be used if it is necessary to use metallic protection.

> The wiring system must have a separate circuit protective conductor, in addition to the metallic conduit and have suitable protection against mechanical damage. (See I.E.E. Regulations.)

All fixing materials such as clips and screws, should be corrosion-resistant. A good method is to use porcelain cleats which hold the cable away from the building surface.

> Flexible cords should be of the braided, non-kinkable kind, either circular or flat-sheathed. These should be kept as short as possible, so that an adequate number of socket outlets must be provided.

Wiring between buildings

Outside overhead
Overhead wiring between buildings may be done by catenary suspension using vulcanised rubber-insulated cable sheathed with weather-resistant compound (HSOS) type, or steel wire armour sheathed with PVC. The catenary suspension wire may be separately slung and tensioned at each end with straps suspended from it to supply the cable or the cable may contain its own steel catenary wire. See Chapter 4.
Note: The span should be kept as short as possible, by running the cables on the building surfaces to the shortest crossing point and high enough to avoid traffic.

> It should be noted that conduit cannot be used as an overhead run between buildings where the span is longer than one unjointed length.

Underground
This is a preferable method of wiring between

buildings where the ground is unlikely to be disturbed. PVC-armoured or PVA-sheathed MICC cable should be used, buried to a depth of at least 0.6 m and deeper where damage is likely.

Accessories
All switchgear, ceiling roses, lampholders and light fittings, should be of the all-insulated construction types, dust and moisture-proof. The use of cable couplers is not permitted.

In areas where any flammable dust is likely to be present, for example, where grain is processed, the equipment must be of a type which has enclosures suitable for these situations (BS 3807).

Electric fences
These have a controlling power-pack which supplies a high voltage, very low current pulse to the fence. The time duration of the pulse is such as to be non-lethal to livestock. If the power pack is supplied from the mains, it must be installed so as to avoid any risk of mechanical damage, interference and contact with wiring of any other system.

> Only one controller should be connected to each electric fence. If battery-operated, the battery must be disconnected from the fence when being charged.

Earthing
In an all-insulated wiring system, an earth terminal connected to the circuit protective conductor must be provided at every outlet point of the fixed wiring and at switches, ceiling roses and socket outlets.

> All earthing leads must be protected against damage and earth electrodes must be placed well clear of livestock.
>
> Where segregation from metal is unavoidable, the metal must be securely bonded to the protective conductor of the electrical system.

Testing and inspection
Because of the varying conditions to which outdoor installations are subject, it is recommended that regular tests be carried out to ensure compliance with the Regulations, particularly loop impedance tests on the protective earthing system.

Stand-by supplies
On farms where failure of the supply would be disastrous, for example on chicken rearing farms or for refrigeration equipment, it is necessary to install a stand-by generator with a power output sufficient to supply these loads. This could be an alternator of suitable power rating and voltage driven by a petrol or diesel engine (see later notes on standby plant).

Soil heating

> ▲ Where bare (uninsulated) elements are laid directly in the soil they must be supplied from the secondary winding of a double-wound transformer where the centre tap is connected to the earth mass.
>
> The maximum voltage to earth from the element should not exceed 30 V a.c.

Where insulated heating elements are used, they must be protected against damage in non-combustible enclosures in the soil. These can be supplied at mains voltage directly from the supply.

Swimming pools

Similar to other installations which present increased danger from electric shock, the installation is divided into zones according to the degree of that danger.

The areas in and immediately around the pool and the showers call for the use of insulated equipment and wiring systems, use of reduced voltage and RCDs.

Where accessories, equipment and lighting are immersed in water, they and the wiring must be water-tight and pumps must be of the submersible type.

In the recreation and dining areas normal types of wiring systems and equipment can be used. Section 602 I.E.E. Regulations deals with swimming pools.

> In all danger areas the costs of equipment and safety devices required increase the cost of the installation. This is the reason for dividing the area into zones.

Section 611 I.E.E. Regulations deals with highway power supplies and street furniture, where protection against mechanical damage from vehicles and against equipment being live after damage is required.

Isolation from mains supply

Where it is required to use equipment of the standard supply voltage, normally 240 V, in danger or hazardous areas, the dangers from electric shock can be reduced by the use of double-wound 1:1 ratio transformers, so that voltage is not changed.

The secondary winding of the transformer to which the equipment is connected has no connection to earth so that in the event of an insulation fault between the live parts and the case of the hand-held equipment there is no circuit for the current to flow through the operator's body.

The common example of this is the 'shaver unit' used in bathrooms, where the use of socket outlets connected to the mains supply is not permitted.
Note: This method of protection is confined to smaller low-powered devices because of the high cost of the transformer.

Corrosion

The basic cause of corrosion is the instability of metals in their refined state. They tend to revert to their natural (ore) state through the process of corrosion. This is an **electrochemical reaction** which involves moisture and oxygen, resulting in all or part of the metal being transferred back to its natural state by a flow of ions or the ionic state.

Corrosion sets up an electric current between the areas of the metal surfaces. This current flows through an electrolyte and, in effect, forms a simple electric cell. The electrolyte will be the liquid or moisture which is present. It may be water, salt water, acids, alkalis, soil, etc. If the metals are dissimilar, the action is greater. It is this passage of current which eventually eats away (**erodes**) the metal.

Cathodic protection

The metals are referred to as the **anode** and **cathode** of the circuit and the direction of current flow will be from anode to cathode. If a current was to be superimposed in the opposite direction to that leaving the corroding metal, it would be opposed and thus prevent the corrosion. In the protection of underground pipework, this auxiliary anode is buried close to the pipework so that the

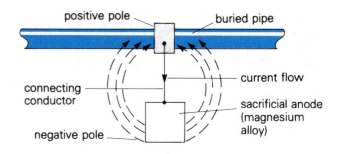

Figure 9.5 Cathodic sacrificial anode protection.

soil forms the electrolyte. Current will now flow from the auxiliary anode back to the pipe and prevent its corrosion. Eventually, the auxiliary anode is itself eaten away and must be replaced. Because of this, it is referred to as a **sacrificial anode**. See Figure 9.5.

Impressed current
This is another method of cathode protection which is used where a large number of buried pipes or metal sheath of cables occur near a building. A rectifier is installed in the building and connected to the pipework etc., in order to provide a negative potential with respect to the earth electrode. This minimises the possibility of the current flowing from the pipe or cable sheath to be protected and causing erosion.

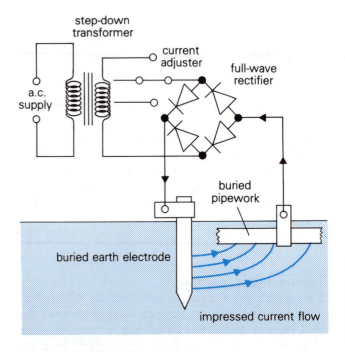

Figure 9.6 Cathodic impressed current protection.

To achieve this type of cathodic protection, no part of the protected metal must be at a potential greater than 8 V to the surrounding earth. The earth electrodes must be buried well away from metalwork of any other services or they will act as a sacrificial anode and be eroded.

In this method, the life of the earth electrode will be much prolonged because it is receiving current from the d.c. electrical supply. See Figure 9.6.

Installations in corrosive atmospheres

As previously mentioned, installations in buildings must be able to withstand the effect of any elements which are present, such as moisture, steam, chemical fumes, vapours, oils, grease, sulphur, etc., all of which lead to corrosion. Although it may be impossible to protect the installation completely, the following points should receive special attention where these conditions are present.

1. Ducts, trunking, metal sheaths, clips and all fixing devices must be of a suitable corrosion-resistant material. Metalwork components must not be placed in contact with other different metalwork, as corrosion will be speeded up through greater electrolytic action (dissimilar metal action).
2. Aluminium conductors should not be connected to brass, copper or other metals unless the surfaces to be joined have been plated or treated to prevent this action.
3. Iron or steel should be protected preferably by galvanising or similar plating treatment, or well painted with suitable paints such as bitumastic, anti-sulphuric and lead-based paint.
4. Cables should be installed in galvanised or PVC conduits or be PVC-sheathed.

Damp-proof installations

In damp situations, precautions are also necessary to prevent corrosion. Construction materials which cause corrosion to electrical installations are:

1. materials containing magnesium chloride, which are used in the construction of floors;
2. plaster containing corrosive salts;
3. lime cement and plaster;
4. oak and other acidic woods;
5. dissimilar metals, again causing speeded up electrolytic action.

Treatment with paints and corrosion-resistant finishes are again required. Special care should be taken when clipping or concealing cables in these materials.

Effective circuit protection in damp situations should be ensured by increasing the size and the protection of the protective conductor and the bonding of adjacent metalwork to it. Electric shock is much more severe in wet or damp situations.

High-temperature installations

These call for high temperature wiring systems such as:

1. MICC cabling, for temperatures up to 80°C with normal terminations, or up to 150°C using a glass fibre termination;
2. heat-resistant PVC compounded cables drawn into metal conduits or trunking, for temperatures up to 80°C, butyl cable up to 80°C and silicone rubber cable up to 145°C;
3. for higher voltages, paper-insulated lead-covered steel wire armours (PILCSWA) can be used for temperatures up to 75°C.

Flexible cables should be of butyl or silicone rubber insulation.

Note: General purpose PVC insulation will only withstand temperatures of up to 65°C.

Fungi and mould growth
This occurs in humid atmospheres such as in bakeries, breweries, greenhouses and food processing plants, which encourage growth of fungi and mould on materials.

Cables installed in humid atmospheres should always be enclosed in PVC or galvanised metal conduits. All metal equipment and accessories should be painted with effective fungicidal paint. All fittings should be of a type which can be completely and easily cleaned. Motors should preferably be of the totally enclosed type to exclude the atmosphere from the windings.

Lightning protection

Protection is obtained by providing a safe conducting path between the general mass of earth and the atmosphere above the structure or vice versa, so that lightning discharges can take place without producing dangerous potential differences (voltages) in, on, or near the structure.

The structure may be wholly or partly constructed of conducting material which could form its own lightning protective system, for example, a steelwork structure. If this is not the case, protect in accordance with C.P. 326.

Consider the following example.

Owing to the presence of a positively-charged cloud, the top of the conductor will acquire a negative charge by induction, with the result that air particles will be attracted towards the conductor. These will become negatively charged by contact, and will then be repelled into the space between the conductor and the cloud. It is probable that electrons will also be pulled from the conductor by the attraction of the positively-charged cloud. This stream of negative charges will tend to neutralise the positive charge on the cloud. The most likely result, however, is that the negative charging of the space between the conductor and the cloud will lower its electrical breakdown voltage to such an extent, that an arc (the lightning discharge) will take place and so form a conducting path between cloud and earth. There will be a stream of electrons from earth, through the conductor and through the arc to the cloud itself, the particles of which will acquire their normal complement of electrons and so become discharged.

Factors which determine whether lightning protection is required

The need for lightening protection depends on

1. the location of the structure to be protected and its size;
2. the purpose for which the building is being used, for example explosives factory, church, monument, railway station, spire, radio mast.

Zone protection

The zone of protection provided by a single vertical conductor fixed to a structure is considered to be a cone with an apex at the highest point of the conductor, and a base of radius equal to its height. This means for example, that a conductor 50 m high will protect that part of the building which comes within a cone extending to 100 m diameter at ground level. Care is therefore needed to ensure that the whole building lies within this cone. If it does not, two or more down conductors must be used.

Components of a lightning protection system

Air termination or termination network

1. For a spire or chimney, this will consist of one or more vertical conductors positioned just above the highest point.
2. For a small building, this will consist of a single

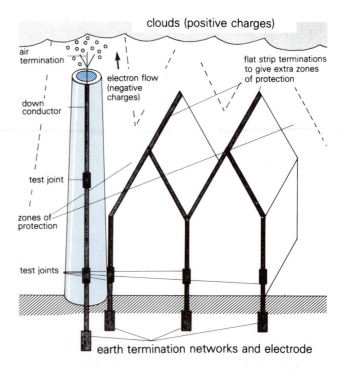

Figure 9.7 Components of a lightning protection circuit.

horizontal conductor along the ridge of the roof.

3. For roofs of larger dimensions this will consist of a system of horizontal conductors.

> No part of a roof should be more than 9 m from the nearest horizontal conductor and all metallic projections such as vent pipes, railing, gutters, etc., on or above the roof of the main building should be bonded to the conductor to form part of the air termination network.

Down conductors

The number of down conductors required is determined by the area covered by the structure. A structure with a base area not exceeding 100 m² needs only one down conductor. Base areas greater than 100 m² require one for every additional 300 m² or part thereof.

Test joints

These are provided in down conductors so that resistance measurements of the sections can be made.

Earth termination or termination network

This is the part of the lightning protection system intended to discharge current into the general mass of earth. All points below the lowest test point in a down conductor are included in this term. Figure 9.7 shows the components of a lightning protection system.

Earth electrode

This is the part of the earth termination which makes direct electrical contact with earth.
Note: Roof and down conductors are generally annealed copper strips, as are any interconnections. Down conductors are secured to the building by 'holdfast' fixings made from gunmetal. Earth electrodes can be copper rods or copper plates.

Testing

> ▲ All lightning protection systems should be inspected and tested after completion and at intervals of twelve months (six months if explosives are stored in the building). The tests should verify electrical continuity of the system and the resistance to the general mass of earth. This must not exceed 10 ohms using the electrode testing method. Records of tests should be kept on site by the person responsible for maintaining the installation.

Fire and intruder alarm systems

Fire alarms

In buildings to which the public have access and in those where the risk of fire outbreak is greater than normal, the installation of a fire-alarm system will be necessary. The system may vary from a very simple system, where a bell is sounded by means of a manually-operated push, to a much more advanced system where sprinklers and foam dispensers are operated automatically by fire detection units.

When the installation of a fire-alarm system is to be considered, consultation with the local fire authority should take place to determine the most suitable system for the particular circumstances. CP 1019 deals with fire alarm installations.

Basic alarm circuits

Open-circuit

See Figure 9.8. The closing of any detector point sounds the alarm bells.

Advantages

1. The circuit is simple.
2. No current is consumed on stand-by.
3. A broken connection or conductor will not result in a false alarm.

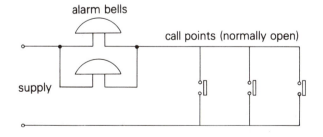

Figure 9.8 Basic open-circuit alarm system.

Disadvantages

1. No indication is given if there is a break in the circuit which makes part or all of the system inoperative.
2. A short circuit between conductors can produce a false alarm.
3. The detector points are not monitored for breaks in the cable.

Closed-circuit

See Figure 9.9. The opening of any detector point de-energises the relay and the closing of its contacts sounds the alarm bells.

Advantages

1. The circuit is simple.
2. The detector points are monitored.

Disadvantages

1. Current is consumed continuously on stand-by.
2. No indication is given of a short circuit between conductors which may make some parts of the system inoperative.
3. A broken connection or conductor can cause a false alarm.

In practice, variations and combinations of these two circuits are employed. Let us now look at alarm systems in more detail.

Sounders

These are devices in which electrical signals are converted into sound signals, for example, bells, hooters, sirens, etc. The types and the locations of the sounders should be such that alarms are clearly audible to people using the building. They must not have a similar sound to any other device on the premises.

Manual call points

Manual call points for fire only are usually of the 'BREAK THE GLASS' type and are coloured red.

> ▲ Call points should be located so that no person has to travel more than 30 m from any position within the premises in order to raise the alarm. They should be located on exit routes and, in particular, on floor landings of staircases and on exits to streets.

They should be fixed at a height of 1.4 m above

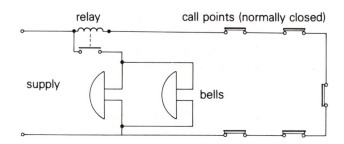

Figure 9.9 Basic closed-circuit alarm system.

the floor at easily accessible, well illuminated, conspicuous positions, free from obstruction.

Indicator boards

In large installations, one or more indicator boards will be required to show the location of the origin of the alarm. Suitable zones should be defined throughout the building and the alarm system designed so that all the detectors in any one zone are connected to an indicator exclusive to that zone. No zone should extend beyond one floor. In extensive installations, it may be desirable to divide the premises into sections, each comprising a number of zones and each sector having its own indicator board.

Silencing switches

Silencing switches may be provided for transferring an alarm or fault warning to a supervisory sounder installed at the control point. The operation of the silencing switch must not cancel the indications of the alarm on any indicator concerned.

> The restoration of the silencing switch to its normal position whilst an alarm (or fault) exists, should transfer the alarm back to the alarm sounders.

Wiring

Suitable systems are as follows:

1. mineral insulated metal sheathed cable (PVC-sheathed for damp and corrosive conditions),
2. PVC-insulated cables in metal conduit, duct or trunking,
3. PVC-armoured cables,
4. PVC-insulated cables in rigid PVC conduit (temperature range 0°C to 60°C),
5. Insulated and sheathed cables surface laid where continuous monitoring is used.

Automatic detection devices

Fire-alarm devices actually detect

1. air temperature change,
2. combustion products such as smoke,
3. radiation of electromagnetic waves either A) infra-red, where very slight changes of temperature are detected or B) ultra-violet rays.

Intruder detection devices use:

1. pressure pads placed in vulnerable areas such as under floor coverings etc.,
2. micro-switches fitted to entrance and exit points and windows,
3. proximity capacitor devices,
4. passive infra-red electromagnetic radiations which will activate when interrupted by movement or slight body heat.

Note: On electronic devices such as proximity devices and infra-red beams, data such as current and voltage ratings must be checked before installation.

Circuitry

Figures 9.10 to 9.12 show the cicuitry for alarm circuits, from the simple open circuits to the more sophisticated circuits with full monitoring of circuit faults. Indicator boards, diversion relays and supervisor buzzers, apply equally to both fire-alarm and intruder detection systems.

The power supplies and wiring systems also apply to both fire and intruder alarms, except that the wiring for the intruder system should, as far as is practicable, be concealed from view. On the diagrams all the detection device points are marked 'detector points'.

Power supply

It is preferable to operate a fire-alarm system at a voltage not exceeding 50 V between conductors, or 30 V a.c. or d.c. to earth. In no case should the voltage exceed 250 V nominal, whether between conductors or to earth.

> The power supply equipment for a fire-alarm system must be exclusive to the alarm system and usually comprises a secondary battery of ample capacity and charger.

There are numerous kinds of alarm circuits.

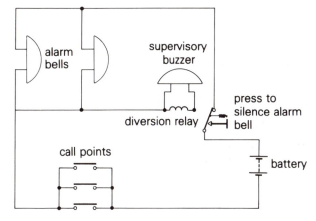

Figure 9.10 Open-circuit alarm system with diversion relay and supervisory buzzer.

Open-circuit system with a diversion relay and supervisory buzzer

Figure 9.10 shows an open-circuit alarm system with a diversion relay and supervisory buzzer.

Operation

The closing of the contacts of a call point sounds the alarm bells. To silence the alarm, the button of the diversion relay is pressed, which transfers the alarm to the supervisory buzzer. When all detector point contacts have been opened, the diversion relay will be de-energised, and its armature will spring back to its original position, thus silencing the supervisory buzzer and putting the alarm system in a state of readiness again.

Closed-contact alarm system with indicator board

Figure 9.11 shows a closed-contact alarm system with an indicator board.

Operation

If a detector point in Zone 1 is opened, the relay is de-energised and the closing of its contacts sounds the alarm bell in that zone only. In addition, the closing of the relay contacts drops the flag in the indicator board, which energises the main relay, and the closing of its contacts sounds the main alarm bell. A detector point, opened in Zone 2, will sound the alarm bell in that zone only and also the main alarm bell. The flag for Zone 2 will also be dropped.

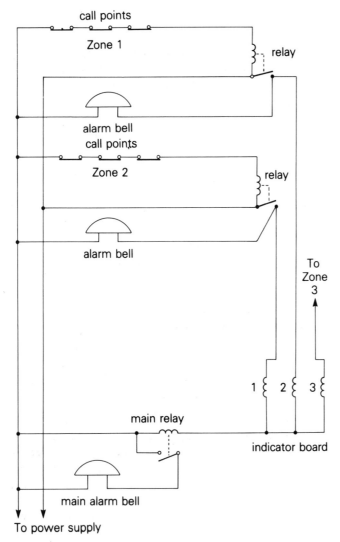

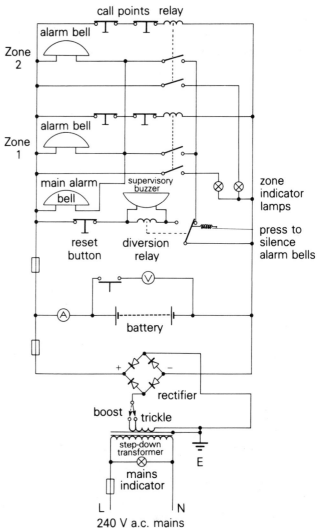

Figure 9.11 Closed circuit alarm system with indicator board.

Figure 9.12 Closed circuit alarm system with indicator board.

Note: This system would not be suitable for a multi-storey building, since in such buildings, all alarm bells would need to sound simultaneously.

Closed-circuit alarm system with indicator board, diversion relay and supervisory buzzer

Figure 9.12 shows a closed circuit fire-alarm system with indicator board, diversion relay and supervisory buzzer.

Operation

If a detector point is opened in Zone 1, the relay will be de-energised, and the closing of its contacts

sounds all the alarm bells and lights the indicator lamp for Zone 1.

Similarly, the opening of a detector point in Zone 2 will sound all the alarm bells and light the indicator lamp for Zone 2. To silence the alarm bells, the button of the diversion relay is pressed and the alarm is transferred to the supervisory buzzer. When all the detector point contacts have been returned (closed), both relays will be energised and the opening of their contacts will switch off the indicator lamps. The reset button is pressed, the diversion relay is de-energised and the supervisory buzzer silenced. The system is now in readiness should another alarm be raised.

Note: If the reset button is pressed before all the detector points have been closed, the alarm bells will sound again. As mentioned, this system is suitable for multi-storey buildings, since all the alarm bells sound simultaneously.

Circuit faults indication on open-circuit system

Figure 9.13 shows the detection of circuit faults on an open-circuit system.

Operation

When the supply is switched on, only L operates owing to the small current, which opens L_1. If an open circuit occurs in the detector point circuit, L is de-energised, L_1 closes and the open-circuit lamp lights. The operation of a detector point in a normal healthy circuit causes an increase in current which causes M to operate, closing M_1, M_2 and M_3. This results in the alarm bell ringing and the alarm lamp lighting.

Note that the closing of M_1 prevents excessive current from flowing through L. If a short circuit occurs on a previously healthy circuit (for example, between a detector point and the negative side of the supply), the heavy current causes H to operate, closing H_1, H_2 and H_3. This results in the short-circuit lamp lighting. Note that the closing of H_1 and H_2 prevents excessive current from flowing through L and M. The diversion relay and supervisory buzzer operate as explained previously. All the alarm diagrams will need careful study.

Inspection

All new installations should be inspected and tested to ensure that the work has been carried out satisfactorily and to the required standard. Earth connections should be tested in accordance with I.E.E. Regulations and the insulation resistance between conductors and earth tested with a 500 V tester, minimum resistance 0.5 mΩ. The test should be carried out with equipment disconnected to avoid possible damage to any of the equipment.

I.E.E. Regulations

> ▲ Fire alarm and emergency circuits must not be drawn into the same enclosures as other circuits.
> They must be separated by metallic barriers when placed in common trunking or ducting, or run in separate conduits. This is to ensure that the spread of fire does not put the circuit out of action.

Cables operating at extra low voltages such as those for bells, phones, signalling, etc., must run separately from mains (low) voltage circuits unless they are insulated to the same value.

Maintenance

Routine checks and tests should be made at inter-

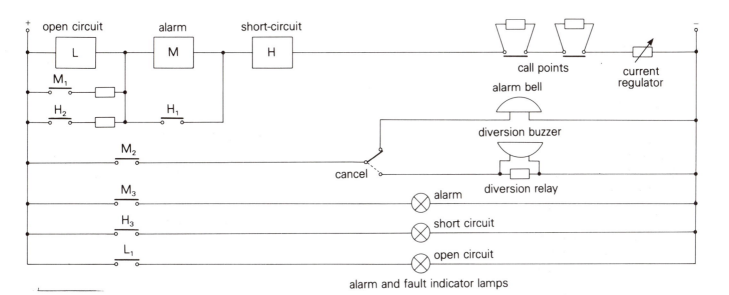

Figure 9.13 Diagram of circuit faults indicator on an open-circuit system.

vals as laid down in CP 1019 to ensure that the
alarm installation is kept in good working order.

Voltaic cells

Primary cells

See Figure 9.14 for the construction of the **Leclanché** primary cell.

Secondary cells

A secondary cell may be defined as a cell that can be
recharged electrically, its function depending upon
chemical action within the cell for the storage and
release of electrical energy. Secondary cells are
called **accumulators**.

There are two main types of secondary cell:

1. the **lead-acid** cell, and
2. the **alkaline** cell.

The lead–acid cell

This consists basically of two sets of lead plates
immersed in a solution of dilute sulphuric acid. If
an external electric current is passed between the
plates, a chemical reaction takes place. This process
is termed **charging** the cell. If the plates are disconnected from the external supply and reconnected to
a load, the cell will pass current to the load until it
is discharged. Repeating this charge–discharge cycle enables the cell to pass current for a longer
period and is termed the **Planté** or **forming process**.

To increase the maximum surface area and
mechanical strength, the plates are ribbed or corru-
gated as shown in Figure 9.15. This method of cell
construction is costly and is used only for heavy or
onerous duty cells.

Most plates for lead–acid cells are made by the
Faure or **pasted process**, in which a paste or active
material, red lead (Pb_3O_4) for positive plates and
litharge (PbO) for negative plates (both are oxides
of lead), is pressed into recesses in a grid of lead–
antimony alloy. See Figure 9.16.

The weight of the pasted or Faure plate is only a
third of that of the formed or Planté plate for the
same capacity. The plates are assembled as in Figure 9.17. An extra separator plate is always fitted
between the positive and negative plates to avoid
buckling of the plates which may be due to high
discharge rates. The plates are sited clear of the

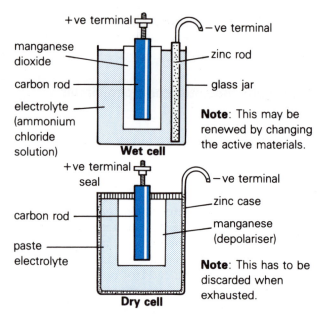

Note: The carbon has no part in the chemical action, it
simply conducts the current to the +ve terminal. It is the
chemical action between manganese and the zinc which
produces the e.m.f. (around 1.5 V). The manganese dioxide
removes hydrogen bubbles from the carbon rod.

Figure 9.14 Primary (Leclanché) cells.

Figure 9.15 Section through a solid 'ribbed' plate
of lead–acid cell.

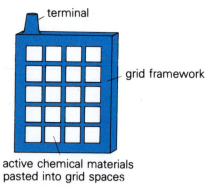

Figure 9.16 Section through a 'pasted' plate of
lead–acid cell.

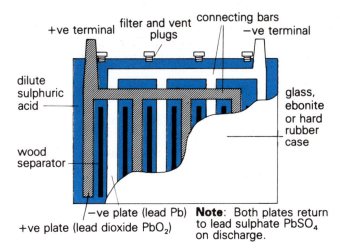

Figure 9.17 Lead–acid battery of four cells.

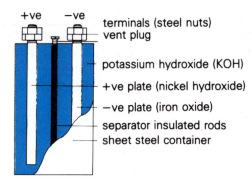

Note: Each cell is contained in its own steel case. Batteries are made up of cells placed in wooden crates to insulate the cell frames from each other. Terminals are joined with steel connecting straps.

Figure 9.18 Nickel–alkaline (Ni-Fe) cell.

bottom of the container to avoid silt or sediment shorting out the plates. Internal resistance of a cell is usually 1.0 ohm or less, hence it is important that the cell is not short-circuited.

A battery may be a number of cells connected in series for higher voltages or in parallel for heavier currents. Figure 9.17 shows a lead-acid battery of four cells.

The alkaline cell

The nickel–iron secondary cell

This consists of two sets of perforated steel tubes or pockets immersed in a solution of potassium hydroxide. The positive plate has a mixture of nickel hydroxide and a few flakes of nickel or graphite added to reduce electrical resistance. The tubes or pockets are assembled in a nickelled-steel support plate. The negative plate has a mixture of iron oxide plus the addition of a little mercuric oxide to reduce electrical resistance.

The plates are separated by insulated rods, the whole being assembled in a welded steel container. Unlike the lead–acid cell, the electrolyte does not undergo any chemical change on charge or discharge periods. See Figure 9.18.

The nickel–cadmium cell

This is identical to the nickel–iron cell with the exception of the negative plate, which is of cadmium with a little iron added to prevent the cadmium caking and losing its porosity. This type of cell has a lower internal resistance than the nickel–iron cell, making it more suitable for heavier current duties.

Characteristics of a lead–acid cell

Item	Discharging	Charging
Positive plate	Tends to change to lead sulphate ($PbSO_4$), colour whitish.	Changes to lead peroxide (PbO_2) (dioxin), colour reddish-brown.
Negative plate	Tends to change to lead sulphate ($PbSO_4$).	Changes to spongy (porous) clean lead Pb.
Electrolyte	Tends to change to water ($2H_2O$).	Changes to sulphuric acid ($2H_2SO_4$).
Specific gravity	Falls to approximately 1.1 at the end of the useful discharge period.	Rises to approximately 1.25.
E.m.f.	Remains steady at approximately 2 V until the end of the useful discharge period, after which it falls rapidly. It should be allowed to fall below 1.8 V per cell, to avoid sulphation when the $PbSO_4$ hardens.	Rises to approximately 2.3 V per cell.
Characteristic curves	See Figure 9.19.	

Characteristics of an alkaline cell

Item	Discharging	Charging
Positive plate	Tends to lose oxygen ($2Ni(OH)_2$).	Restored to original condition, hydroxide of nickel ($2Ni(OH)_3$).
Negative plate	Tends to oxidise giving cadmium hydroxide ($Cd(OH)_2$).	Restored to original condition, pure cadmium (Cd).
Electrolyte	Does not undergo any chemical change (KOH).	Does not undergo any chemical change (KOH).
Specific gravity	Remains constant at approximately 1.17.	Remains constant at approximately 1.17.
E.m.f.	Usually falls to 1.0 V at the end of the useful charge period.	Rises to approximately 1.4 V.
Characteristic curves	See Figure 9.20.	

Comparison of lead–acid and nickel–iron cells

Item	Lead–acid	Alkaline cell
Average e.m.f.	2.0 V	1.2 V
Ampere-hour efficiency* (A h)	85–90%	75–80%
Watt-hour efficiency* (W h)	70–75%	60–65%
Cost	An expensive source of electrical energy.	Even more expensive than the lead–acid cell.
Strength	Adversely affected by vibration and heavy currents.	Withstands vibration and is capable of heavy discharge currents.

* See battery efficiencies.

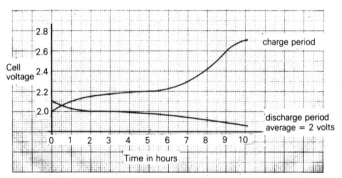

Figure 9.19 Terminal voltage graph of lead–acid cell.

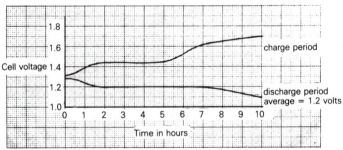

Figure 9.20 Terminal voltage graph of nickel–alkaline cell.

Internal resistance of cells and batteries

When a cell is supplying a current, the **internal resistance** causes the voltage at the terminals to fall.

The amount of the fall or the difference between (E) the e.m.f. (open circuit) and the voltage on load (V) is obtained from the formula

$$V = E - Ir$$
where I = current,
$\quad\quad r$ = internal resistance.

A battery with an open circuit e.m.f. (E) of 2.2 V and internal resistance 0.05 Ω supplies a current of 5 A.
Calculate the terminal voltage V.

$$\begin{aligned} V = E - Ir &= 2.2 - (5 \times 0.05) \\ &= 2.2 - 0.25 \\ &= 1.95 \text{ V} \end{aligned}$$

Similar to all resistance calculations, when the cells or batteries are connected in series

$$R_T = r_1 + r_2 + r_3 + \cdots$$

When they are connected in parallel

$$\frac{1}{R_T} = \frac{1}{r_1} + \frac{1}{r_2} + \frac{1}{r_3} + \cdots$$

EXAMPLE 2

Two batteries each of e.m.f. 10 V and internal resistance 0.5 Ω are connected (i) in series (ii) in parallel to supply a load which has a resistance of 4 Ω.

Make circuit diagrams of these circuits and calculate the current and voltage across the load in each case.

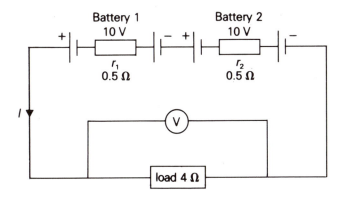

Figure 9.21 Diagram of Example 2 (i).

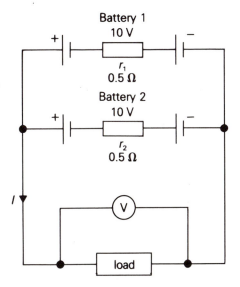

Figure 9.22 Diagram of Example 2 (ii).

Figures 9.21 and 9.22 show the circuit diagrams for series connection and parallel connection respectively.

i) Batteries voltage $= (B_1 + B_2) = 10 + 10 = 20$ V
   Batteries resistance $= (r_1 + r_2) = 0.5 + 05 = 1$ Ω
   Circuit resistance $=$ load $+$ battery r
   $$= (4 + 1) = 5\ \Omega$$
   Circuit current $I = \dfrac{E}{R} = \dfrac{20}{5} = 4$ A

   Voltage across load $= IR = (4 \times 4) = 16$ V

ii) Batteries voltage $=$ that of one battery $= 10$ V

   Batteries resistance
   $$\frac{1}{r_T} = \frac{1}{r_1} + \frac{1}{r_2} = \frac{1}{0.5} + \frac{1}{0.5}$$
   $$= \frac{1 + 1}{0.5} = \frac{2}{0.5}$$
   $$r_T = \frac{0.5}{2} = 0.25\ \Omega$$

   Circuit resistance (load $+$ battery) $= 4 + 0.25$
   $$= 4.25\ \Omega$$

   Circuit current $= \dfrac{E}{R} = \dfrac{10}{4.25} = 2.35$ A

   Voltage across load $= IR = 2.35 \times 4$
   $$= 9.4\ \text{V}$$

Battery charging

Figure 9.23 shows battery charging circuits.

Batteries are charged by passing a d.c. current in the electrolyte from the positive to the negative terminal. The cells are normally connected in series so that each cell receives the same charging current. If the cells were connected in parallel, it would be difficult to maintain the correct division between currents, since cells having a slightly higher e.m.f. would tend to discharge into those cells having a lower e.m.f.

There are two basic battery charging methods:

1. constant voltage, and
2. constant current.

Constant voltage method

When using the constant voltage method, the charging voltage is maintained at a constant value, slightly in excess of the e.m.f. of the fully charged battery. The charging current using this method depends upon the difference between the charging voltage and the total e.m.f. of the battery and its internal resistance:

Charging current (I)
$$= \frac{(\text{charging voltage} - \text{battery voltage})}{\text{resistance of battery circuit}}$$

EXAMPLE 3

A battery having a terminal voltage of 12 V and an internal resistance of 0.25 Ω is charged from a 14 V d.c. supply.
Calculate the charging current.

$$I = \frac{(14 - 12)\ V}{0.25\ \Omega} = 8\ A$$

Constant current method
When using the constant current charging method, the charging current is kept constant at a suitable value for the cells concerned. This may be done as shown in Figure 9.23 by using a **rheostat** (variable resistance) in series with the output of the charger. The current flowing through the rheostat depends on its setting and on the p.d. (**potential difference**) between its terminals. This p.d. is the difference between the output voltage of the rectifier and the voltage required to charge the cells. The rheostat resistance is adjusted (lowered) as the battery e.m.f. rises.

Floating battery charging
In this method, the battery is connected in parallel with the d.c. mains supply, hence it must have the same nominal voltage. The load is connected across both the mains and the battery. On a supply failure, the battery takes over, restoration of the supply recharges the battery until the e.m.f. is equal to the supply e.m.f., that is, the battery is again 'floating'. When a generator is being used for charging, a reverse current trip is necessary to prevent the generator **motoring** and discharging the battery should the generator fail.

Trickle charging
This system is an ideal method for maintaining healthy batteries by replacing 'open circuit loss'. The amount of charging current is small, in the region of the ampere-hour capacity divided by 1000, that is 40 A h = 40 mA (or 0.04 A), hence the term **trickle**. This method is used for emergency lighting and alarm and telephone stand-by systems,

Engine-driven generator

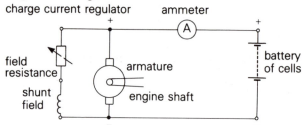

Rectifier constant voltage

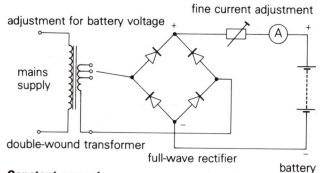

Constant current

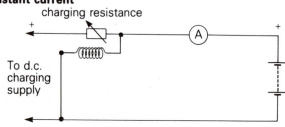

Note: The charging resistance would have to be automatically regulated to maintain current at a constant value (as the battery voltage rises, the resistance is reduced).

Figure 9.23 Battery-charging circuits.

where the battery is left standing for long periods and would eventually become discharged.

Battery efficiencies
Batteries receive electrical energy during charging and deliver it to external circuits during discharging. It is therefore useful to measure the efficiency with which batteries perform this function. The charging and discharging processes of a battery may be considered in terms of either charge (in ampere-hours) or energy (in watt-hours) so there are two ways of declaring the efficiency of batteries:

(QUANTITY) ampere-hour efficiency
$$= \frac{\text{ampere-hours given out during discharge} \times 100\%}{\text{ampere-hours received during charging}}$$

(ENERGY) watt-hour efficiency

$$= \frac{\text{watt-hours given out during discharge} \times 100\%}{\text{Watt-hours received during charging}}$$

EXAMPLE 4

A battery was discharged at 10 A for 6 hours and then brought back to its previous state of charge by charging at 3 A for 24 hours.

If the average p.d. during discharge was 1.9 V and during charging 2.15 V. Calculate (i) the ampere hour efficiency and (ii) the watt hour efficiency of the battery.

i) $\dfrac{(10 \times 6)}{(3 \times 24)}$ ampere-hours $\times 100\% = 83.3\%$

ii) $\dfrac{(1.9 \times 10 \times 6)}{(2.15 \times 3 \times 24)}$ watt-hours $\times 100\% = 73.6\%$

EXAMPLE 5

An alkaline cell is charged at 20 A for 6 hours, the average terminal voltage during charging being 1.72 V. It then supplies a load of 11 A for 8 hours, its average terminal voltage being 1.2 V.
Calculate (i) the watt-hour efficiency and (ii) the ampere-hour efficiency.

i) $\dfrac{(1.2 \times 11 \times 8)}{(1.72 \times 20 \times 6)}$ watt-hours $\times 100\% = 51.2\%$

ii) $\dfrac{(11 \times 8)}{(20 \times 6)}$ ampere-hours $\times 100\% = 73.3\%$

Maintenance of lead–acid cells

Lead-acid cells require regular maintenance if they are to be kept in efficient working order. The electrolyte must be maintained at the working level just above the plates by the addition of distilled water when required. Ordinary tap water should never be used for topping up, neither should concentrated acid, except under special circumstances dealt with later. Cells should be charged regularly; if a cell is allowed to remain discharged for a long period, the plates become covered with a hard, white substance which is a deposit of lead sulphate. This causes permanent damage to the cell and is known as **sulphation**. The state of charge of a cell can be checked either by using a **hydrometer**, which mea-sures the specific gravity of the electrolyte, or by using a voltmeter. The voltage of a cell should never be allowed to drop below 1.8 V, as this indicates that the useful charge of the cell is exhausted.

When sulphuric acid is mixed with water, a considerable amount of heat is generated. If distilled water is poured into concentrated acid, the heat produced is sufficient to cause dangerous spitting of the acid, but if the acid is poured a little at a time into the water, the heat is evolved more slowly and safely.

> ▲ When preparing the electrolyte, care must be taken always to add acid to water and never water to acid.

The electrolyte must be allowed to cool before its specific gravity is checked. It is not normally necessary to use concentrated acid when topping up cells. The principal loss of electrolyte is due to evaporation (gassing) of the water and so topping up with distilled water is usually all that is required.

Nevertheless, if there is reason to suspect that the acid in a cell is unduly weak, this can be checked by first charging the cell until it has been gassing freely for a long time, so ensuring that the cell is fully charged, and then testing the acid strength with a hydrometer. If a low reading is obtained, acid with a strength somewhat greater than that normally used in the cell may be added a little at a time, until the desired specific gravity reading is obtained. Care should be taken that thorough mixing of the electrolyte with the added acid takes place to avoid a false reading of specific gravity. Because of the heat that is evolved when adding acid to the electrolyte, acid should only be added to the cell a little at a time, sufficient time being allowed for the cell to cool before more acid is added.

Installation of lead–acid cells

Lead–acid cells tend to give off hydrogen gas when charging owing to the electrolysis of the water in the electrolyte. A mixture of hydrogen and air in certain proportions is highly explosive, so that the following precautions must be observed in all rooms where cells are installed or charged.

1. The battery room must be well ventilated so that the hydrogen may escape and not build up to a dangerous concentration.

2. No naked lights, or smoking must be allowed in the battery room.
3. All ventilator caps in the battery must allow gas to escape or be removed during charging period.

The fumes from lead–acid cells are very corrosive so that any metalwork in the vicinity of the cells should be protected by a coat of acid-resistant bitumistic paint. The terminals of cells should be kept lightly coated with petroleum jelly (or a suitable proprietary compound) in order to prevent corrosion. The outside of the cell should also be kept clean and dry.

In cases of burns or spills, the following neutralising agents should be available:

1. boric acid for accidents with alkaline cells,
2. washing soda and ample water for accidents with lead–acid cells.

Fire-fighting equipment must also be readily available.

Containers for mixing electrolyte must be of the non-corrosive type, all tables and stands should be lead-covered and suitable protective clothing, such as rubber aprons and gloves should be worn. In addition, separate hydrometers should be used for specific gravity tests on lead–acid and nickel–alkaline cells.

Emergency power stand-by supplies

Certain installations, such as cinemas, public buildings and hospitals have statutory regulations which state that in the event of a mains power failure, there must be a stand-by source of electric power.

This supply can be provided by:

1. an alternative mains supply from the supply authority, that is, it can be switched to another feeder cable direct from the substation;
2. a diesel, petrol or gas-fuelled engine to drive an alternator or a d.c. generator;
3. a battery system connected to a thyristor convertor to give an a.c. supply;
4. a battery system to supply d.c. only, where this supply is suitable;
5. lighting fittings which, for emergency lighting only, can be obtained with a built-in battery and thyristor-inverter and change-over switch, so that they automatically change over to this power pack on failure of supply. During the supply-on period, the battery is trickle-charged from the mains. These are known as **self-contained** luminaires and are quite expensive.

When a diesel, gas or petrol engine is used, the engine will take some time to run up to speed, so that there is a delay of two or three minutes before the supply is restored. The engine can be started automatically by the switching of a starter motor

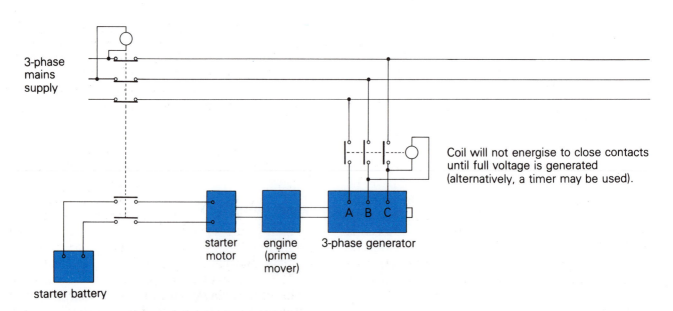

Figure 9.24 Engine (prime mover) stand-by supply.

when the supply fails, but there must be a delayed switching of the load to the generator until the engine is up to speed. It can, alternatively, be started manually, in which case the delay will be longer. See Figure 9.24.

With the stand-by battery system, the change-over will be almost instantaneous. During the supply-on period, it must be ensured that the battery is kept in a fully charged condition from a mains rectifier set.

Note: In all battery installations, good ventilation and acid-proof surfaces are necessary and there must be no naked flames (see 'Battery maintenance').

Emergency lighting

This is divided into two categories: maintained and non-maintained. See Figure 9.25.

Maintained

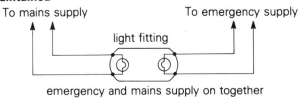

Non-maintained

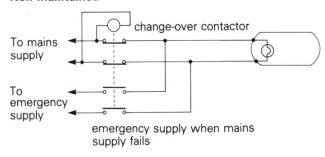

Separate emergency lighting

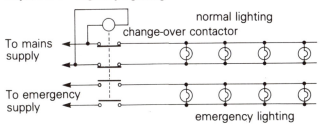

Figure 9.25 Emergency lighting systems.

Maintained lighting

This is an installation required for buildings such as cinemas and operating theatres, where the public are on the premises, and the emergency lighting is on all the time whether the mains have failed or not. It usually consists of two lamps in the same fitting, each connected to its own different supply.

Non-maintained lighting

This is used where the emergency lighting is only supplied when the mains supply fails.

■ CHECK YOUR UNDERSTANDING

● Hazardous areas include placed where flammable, explosive liquids, vapours or dusts are present.

● In hazardous areas, solid drawn conduit, MICC, armoured cables fitted with flameproof terminations should be used, where practicable switchgear should be installed in clean areas.

● Some hospital areas where ether vapours and rubber sheets (electrostatic) are present require the use of non-spark switches.

● Farms and horticultural premises need non-corrosive types of installations, mainly the use of PVC conduits and accessories, where possible out of reach of livestock and, where necessary, protected against damage.

● Electric fences use voltage pulses of very short duration that are non-lethal.

● Cathodic protection involves passing current in the opposite direction to that which caused the corrosion, mainly used for underground pipework using (a) sacrificial anodes or (b) impressed current.

● Lightning conductors provide a low resistance path to earth for the discharge or positively charged high voltages in the clouds, to avoid damage to buildings.

● Alarm circuits use open-circuit wiring or closed-circuit wiring systems with relays. Location indicators, supervisory buzzers and self-monitoring of faults are also used. Automatic fire detectors detect air temperature changes or combustion products and use infra-red or ultra-violet rays. Intruder detectors use pressure pads, micro-switches and proximity switches, PIR radiation.

● The wiring of alarm circuits should be separate from other wiring circuits, use of compartments in common trunking systems and preferably of low voltage.

● There are two types of secondary cells, (a) lead–acid (b) nickel–alkaline.

Charge current I
$$= \frac{V - E}{\text{(circuit + battery internal) resistance}}$$

1 For each of the following installations : (a) cow-shed, (b) petrol filling station, state:
  i) **two** harmful conditions that exist;
  ii) a suitable wiring system, giving reasons.

2 Compare, with the aid of diagrams, the advantages and disadvantages of the open-circuit alarm system over the closed-circuit type.
Draw a closed-circuit alarm system with an indicator board. Explain the working system of the circuit.

3 i) Compare the characteristics of the lead–acid cell with the alkaline cell.
  ii) What tests and observations would you make on a battery of lead–acid cells to determine their condition and state of charge?

4 With the aid of sketches, compare maintained and non-maintained emergency lighting systems.

5 Describe, with diagrams, the constant current and constant voltage methods of charging secondary batteries.

6 i) Describe a lead–acid secondary cell and state the changes in the cell during charging and discharge.
  ii) What are the effects of under-charge and over-charge of this cell?

7 i) Make a circuit diagram of a battery charging unit suitable to charge a 12 V battery from a 240 V 50 Hz supply. Label each component.
  ii) If the output from the charger is 16 V and the resistance of the charging circuit, including the internal resistance of the battery, is 0.5 Ω, calculate the charging current at:
    a) the beginning of the charge when the battery voltage is 10 V,
    b) end of the charge when the battery voltage has risen to 14 V.
  iii) What change in the circuit resistance would be required to maintain the charging current at its initial value?

8 A group of farm buildings situated some 40 m distant from a supply point are to be supplied with electricity.
  i) Name **two** systems of supply most suitable and the factors to be considered in making a final choice.
  ii) State the main requirements of the various regulations with reference to
    a) special precautions where livestock are present,
    b) control and isolation at each building,
    c) installation of socket outlets.

9 i) What is meant by cathodic protection?
  ii) Show, with the aid of a sketch, how this protection may be applied to **either** a dock-side pier **or** a cross-country pipe-line.
  iii) What maintenance is required on the system after installation?
                    (C & G 'C')

10 i) Explain, with the aid of sketches, the meaning of the term 'Zone of Protection' when referring to a single vertical lightning conductor.
  ii) Describe **one** method of providing lightning protection for a brick built chimney some 100 m high with top diameter of 2.5 m.
                    (C & G 'C')

11 Draw a diagram of an automatic control circuit which would effect a changeover on mains failure from the mains to a standby generator and return again to mains, after the mains had been restored for a period of two minutes. Provision should be made for a delay of 20 seconds in the changeover to the standby source in order to allow the diesel set providing the standby time to run up to full speed.
                    (C & G 'C')

12 Describe, with the aid of sketches:
  i) a method of cathodic protection for a long underground pipeline;
  ii) a different method suitable for the steelwork of quarry plant partly buried in the ground.
                    (C & G 'C')

13 It is decided to install a diesel engine standby a.c. generator for a multi-storey office block, the set is to be sited in a disused lift plant room on the roof of the building. The main switchboard is in the basement and a 75 mm × 75 mm cable trunking is to be run within the disused lift shaft which is to be floored at every second storey to form a storage area.
Explain:
  i) the reason why only part of the lighting and certain other circuits are to be supplied

by the standby set;

ii) why such sets often have a delay mechanism to allow them to reach full speed before the a.c. output is available;

iii) the precautions necessary when installing PVC cables within the duct;

iv) why such sets are often installed on the roof of the building.

(C & G 'C')

14 i) State **four** points to be considered when deciding whether a lightning protection system will be needed on a particular structure.

ii) List **four** of the principal components of a lightning protection system.

(C & G 'C')

15 i) Describe the process of electrolytic corrosion.

ii) Describe the following anti-corrosion processes, with the aid of sketches where applicable, and state **one** application for **each**:

a) zinc rich paint, (b) sacrificial electrodes, (c) impressed current cathodic protection.

(C & G 'C')

16 i) State **four** principal hazards to be guarded against in electrical installations on farms.

ii) Describe a system of wiring conforming to the I.E.E. Regulations which would be suitable for **each** of the following:

a) cowsheds, (b) grain drying areas, (c) storage area for heavy machinery (harvester, elevator, tractors).

(C & G 'C')

17 i) State **four** main requirements which must be observed in the wiring installation in a petrol service station.

ii) Draw the complete line diagram for a two-pump installation in a petrol service station where single-motor pumps are used.

(C & G 'C')

18 A pipe-ventilated three-phase motor and starter are to be installed in an explosive atmosphere.

i) Describe the installation.

ii) Sketch the installation to show the ventilation system and ancillary equipment.

iii) Draw a wiring diagram of the complete installation.

(C & G 'C')

Instruments, metering and tariffs

Introduction

Moving-coil and moving-iron instruments are used to measure current, voltage and resistance. Digital meters are used for measuring small values; these give a more accurate reading.

An oscilloscope is used to examine the wave forms of supply voltages and currents.

In order to calculate the cost of the electricity used by a consumer, the supply must be metered. There are a number of ways that the consumer can conserve costs, these include improving the power factor of his installation (and so reduce the kV A demand), taking advantage of off-peak tariffs, and ensuring that equipment is switched off when not in use.

Instruments

Moving-coil instrument

This consists of a coil of wire wound on an aluminium former and pivoted free to turn in a permanent magnetic field. When a voltage or current is connected to the coil it sets up a turning force or torque on the coil. This torque is controlled by two phosphor bronze coil springs which also supply the current to the coil. Attached to the coil former is a pointer which, as the former turns, moves over a calibrated scale and indicates the value of current or voltage supplied to the coil. The aluminium former has damping action and brings the pointer to rest more quickly. Figure 10.1 shows the basic construction of a moving coil instrument.

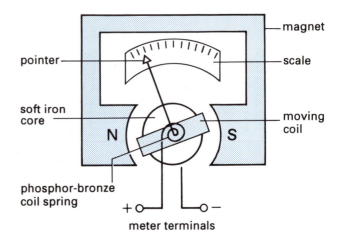

Figure 10.1 Moving-coil voltmeter circuit.

Use as a voltmeter

Since the coil is of very fine wire its current is limited to milliamperes (mA) or even micro-amperes (μA). This means that when higher voltages or currents are to be measured the instrument must be fitted with resistors so only a known proportion of it is fed to the coil.

When used as a voltmeter these resistors will be connected in series with the coil.

EXAMPLE 1

A moving coil instrument has a resistance of 8 Ω and gives full scale deflection with a current of

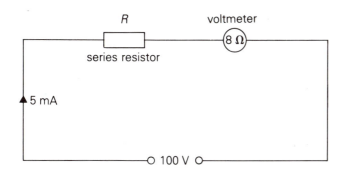

Figure 10.2 Moving-coil ammeter.

5 milliamperes. Calculate the value of a series resistor so that the instrument can measure up to a value of 100 V.

Figure 10.2 shows the circuit of a moving-coil voltmeter.

Maximum p.d. across the soil $= IR = 0.005 \times 8$
$$= 0.04 \text{ V}$$
so that p.d. across R $= (100 - 0.04) \text{ V} = 99.96 \text{ V}$

$$\text{Value} = \frac{V}{I} = \frac{99.96}{0.005} = 20 \times 10^3 = 20 \text{ k}\Omega$$

Note: By changing the value of the series resistor the range of the instrument can be changed.

Use as an ammeter

> To limit the current in the coil, the resistor is connected in parallel with it. It is referred to as a **shunt**.

Figure 10.3 shows the circuit of a moving-coil ammeter.

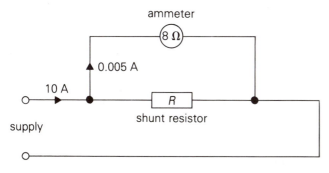

Figure 10.3 Construction of moving-coil instrument.

EXAMPLE 2

The instrument in the previous example is required to measure a current of up to 10 A. Calculate the value of the shunt resistor required.

Current in the resistor $= (10 - 0.005) = 9.995 \text{ A}$
Volts drop across R $= (0.005 \times 8) = 0.04 \text{ V}$

$$\text{Value of } R = \frac{V}{I} = \frac{0.04}{9.995} = 0.004 \text{ }\Omega$$

> As a voltmeter the series resistors are high. As an ammeter the shunt resistors are low.

See Figures 10.2 and 10.3.

Ohmmeter

The moving-coil instrument is also used for the measurement of resistance. A battery of a constant voltage is connected into the circuit so when the **test prods** are connected to an unknown value of resistance the current flow deflects the pointer across the scale.

$$R = \frac{V}{I}$$

so that if V is a constant of known value and I is measured, then R can be calculated. The instrument scale on the resistance range is calibrated directly in ohms.

There is an adjustment to compensate for the fall off in battery e.m.f.

> Multi-range instruments such as an AVO are available to read values of voltages, current and resistances on both a.c. and d.c. supplies over a wide range by simply switching the appropriate resistors into the coil circuit.

When a.c. values are to be measured a rectifier is switched into the coil circuit. This does affect the deflection of the pointer somewhat so that the a.c. values are indicated on a separate scale to the d.c. values.

Moving-iron instrument

This is more robust and can be used on a.c. or d.c. supplies. Its movement will depend upon the

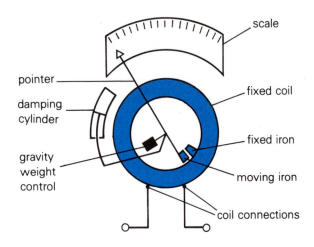

Figure 10.4 Construction of moving-iron instrument.

attraction or repulsion force between a fixed and a moving iron. The fixed iron is joined to the former on which the instrument coil is wound, while the moving iron is joined to one end of the pointer. See Figure 10.4.

> Both irons in a moving-iron instrument are magnetised in the same direction regardless of the current direction in the coil, this means that a repulsion between the two irons always occurs to move the pointer over the scale.

When these instruments are mounted vertically, as on a switchboard, the controlling force on the pointer is by means of a gravity weight attached to the pointer which simplifies the construction. The piston action of the cylinder forms a damping action as the piston compresses the air inside the cylinder.

Because the coil inductance causes errors, particularly when used on different frequencies, the extension of ranges of voltage or current is made by the use of an instrument transformer. See Figure 10.5.

Electronic digital meters

These are used for measurement of voltage, current and resistance by the use of transistorised circuits.

For voltage tests, the input is fed to a circuit which converts the volts into pulses, for example, if

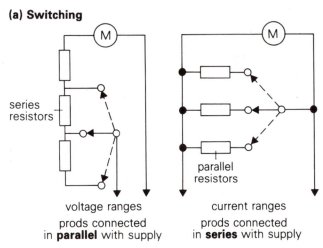

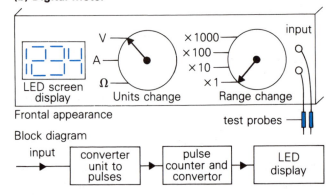

Figure 10.5 (a) Switching of ranges on moving coil instrument. (b) Digital meter: frontal appearance and block diagram.

the converter gave one pulse per volt, then 10 V would produce 10 pulses and so on. The same would apply for amperes or ohms.

These pulses are counted and converted into the value of the units under test which are displayed on **LED**s (light emitting diodes) which are arranged in the form of numbers or digits on the screen.

LEDs

These are small semiconductors which emit light when very small voltages or currents are applied to them.

An internal d.c. supply is necessary to power the circuits and LEDs.

Digital instruments are used mainly for very light current circuit measurements such as in radio or television equipment, because they draw a very small current when a test is being made, that is, they have a high input impedance which gives a more accurate reading than moving-coil or moving-iron type instruments.

Dynamometer type wattmeter

The voltage (moving) coil is situated in the centre of the fixed (current) coil, so that it is influenced by the field of the current coil. This ensures that only when the supply voltage and current are in phase the pointer moves in a forward direction (clockwise). See Figure 10.6.

The calibration of the scale and control of the moving coil is such that the scale reading is the mean value of the power in the a.c. circuit. See Figure 10.7.

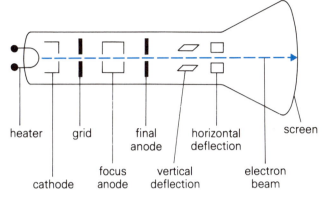

Figure 10.8 Construction of cathode-ray oscilloscope.

Cathode-ray oscilloscope

This is a development of the radio valve where the electrodes are placed in a vacuum envelope. It contains a cathode which is coated with a material rich in electrons which when heated are released. Plates (anodes) with positive potentials are placed further along the tube towards the screen.

These plates attract the electron beam (negative charges) and cause them to impinge on the fluorescent coating of the screen and produce a visible glow. This beam may be deflected across the screen vertically or horizontally by further plates to which the supply to be examined as a picture is connected.

It is used to examine wave forms of supply voltages and currents and can also be used for V and I measurements without taking current from the circuit under examination. See Figure 10.8.

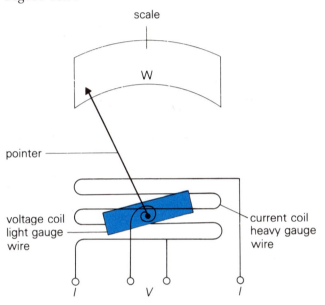

Figure 10.6 Construction of dynamometer wattmeter.

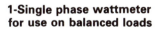

1-Single phase wattmeter for use on balanced loads

Total circuit power = 3 × wattmeter reading

Note: If a neutral conductor is available for the phase voltage there is no need for the artificial star box.

Figure 10.7 Measurement of power in three-phase circuits using single-phase element wattmeter.

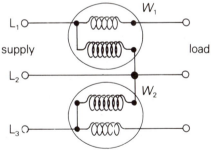

2 - Wattmeter method

Total power = $W_1 + W_2$

Note: If the pf of the circuit is less than 0.5 one of the wattmeters will indicate in the reverse direction. Then TOTAL $P = W_1 \sim W_2$.

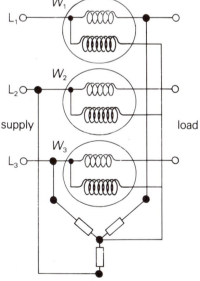

3 - Wattmeter method for use on unbalanced three-phase loads

Total power = $W_1 + W_2 + W_3$

Note: There is a **three-phase integrated meter** which is an interconnection of the above coils in one instrument.

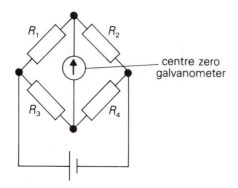

Figure 10.9 Wheatstone bridge circuit.

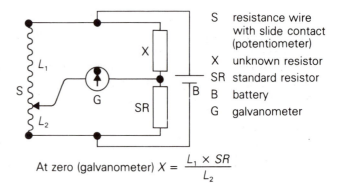

At zero (galvanometer) $X = \dfrac{L_1 \times SR}{L_2}$

S   resistance wire
    with slide contact
    (potentiometer)
X   unknown resistor
SR standard resistor
B   battery
G   galvanometer

Figure 10.10 Circuit arrangement for cable fault location on underground cable.

Wheatstone bridge

The wheatstone bridge consists of four resistors connected as shown. A centre zero galvanometer is connected between the junctions of R_1, R_3 and R_2, R_4. See Figure 10.9.

A p.d. (voltage) is connected between the junctions of R_1, R_2 and R_3, R_4.

When the galvanometer is in the centre (zero) position, that is, there is no current flow between the junctions R_1, R_3 and R_2, R_4.

Then the ratio $\dfrac{R_1}{R_2} = \dfrac{R_3}{R_4}$

This principle is made practical use of to locate a fault in a cable. See Figure 10.10.

In practice two of the resistors are replaced by a slide-wire resistance whose ratio of lengths may be varied. The other two consist of a standard resistance and an unknown value of resistance. By moving the contact on the slide wire until the point of the galvanometer is in the centre zero position, the unknown value can be calculated very accurately. See Figure 10.11.

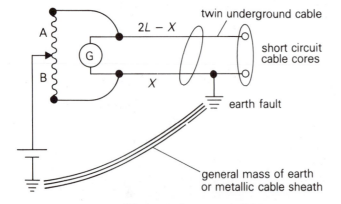

Figure 10.11 Wheatstone bridge to determine value of unknown resistance.

Metering of supplies

The installation electrician is mainly concerned with the alternating current instruments used on heavy current and domestic consumer supplies. Ammeters and voltmeters are of the moving-iron type and, because in the main they are mounted vertically on panels and switchgear, so the cheaper form of gravity control is employed in their movement.

Students should inspect the construction of moving-iron instruments.

Instrument transformers

These are used for the extension of the range on the moving-iron instruments, the current transformer for the extension of current range and the voltage or potential transformer for extension of the voltage range.

Current transformers (C/T)

The C/T is the reverse of a voltage transformer – a **step-down** C/T is a **step up** in voltage or potential. Normally, the full-scale deflection of a moving-iron ammeter is 5 A, hence this is the maximum current it will carry. The C/T is labelled as the ratio of the step-down current from the supply to the instrument. This means that a 100/5 A would be a step down of 20 to 1, a 500/5 A means a 100 to 1 step down.

The purpose of the C/T is to avoid the instrument windings having to be heavy enough to carry the full circuit current and hence being of huge dimensions.

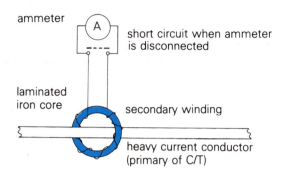

Figure 10.12 Bar-type current transformer (C/T).

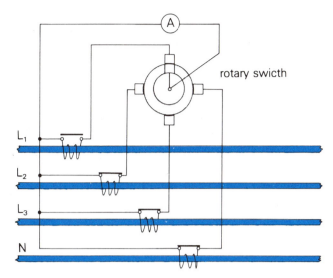

Note: When the switch is rotated it moves the short circuit link from the C/T, when the ammeter is connected to that C/T.

Figure 10.13 Ammeter switching.

Basic circuit

Most C/Ts used on power supplies are of the **bar** type. This consists of turns of insulated conductors wound on an iron core placed around the supply **busbar** or heavy-current conductor, in which the current is to be measured, or alternatively, the conductor is passed through the coil. Figure 10.12 shows a bar-type current transformer.

> The current-carrying conductor forms the primary winding and the coil the secondary winding of the current transformer, the greater the step down in current, the more the number of turns on the secondary coil. This is the reverse of the voltage transformer.

Protection

Note: When the ammeter is connected, it virtually puts a short circuit on the C/T secondary winding which forms the load or transformer burden and reduces the flux in the core and hence the induced voltage in the secondary to a safe value. If the ammeter is disconnected, the burden is removed then the flux and hence the induced e.m.f. would rise to a high value and possibly cause the transformer insulation to break down.

It is therefore important that the secondary terminals are short circuited when the ammeter is disconnected. See Figure 10.13.

Ammeter switching

It is normal practice on switchgear to have one ammeter on three-phase or three-phase four-wire supplies to read respectively the currents in the phase conductors and in the neutral. This is achieved by the use of a rotary ammeter switch because, as previously stated, it is necessary for this switch to include a short circuit connection for the secondary coil of the C/T which is not connected to the ammeter.

The **clip-on calliper** or **tong-test ammeter** is based on the current transformer principle. This is an instrument which can be used on a.c. supplies to measure the current in any conductor without disconnecting the circuit. The iron core on which the secondary coil is wound is hinged to open over the conductor and then closed around the conductor. Its ranges can be extended by the switching of tapped connections on the secondary coil, thereby altering the turns ratio between primary and secondary windings. See Figure 10.14.

This is a very useful instrument for checking the current taken by electrical equipment whilst on

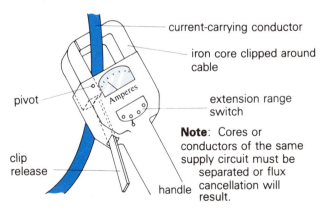

Figure 10.14 'Clip on' or clamp-type ammeter.

load. The readings can be checked against manufacturer's or name-plate data and any undue difference will indicate some fault in the equipment, or, in the case of rotating machines, possible overload due to the driven machine being overloaded.

Voltage or potential transformers (P/T)

These are used on high voltage supplies to reduce the voltage to the voltmeter. Generally, the full-scale deflection of the voltmeter is 110 V, so that if a voltage of 11 000 V (11 kV) needs to be measured, a step down P/T of 100 to 1 would be needed. Because of the high voltage on the primary side, a P/T must have a high insulation value and normally all the windings and the core are immersed in a metal tank containing the transformer-insulating oil.

The primary terminals are mounted on heavy porcelain insulators, the interiors of which house the high-voltage protection fuses, usually rated at 2 A. See Figure 10.15.

Wattmeter

For measurement of power in single-phase a.c. supplies, a two-element wattmeter is used. This consists of one current coil and one voltage coil which are arranged so that the pointer only moves in a forward direction when the current and the voltage are in the same phase or direction. This means that it indicates the power in the circuit.

For use on heavy-current, high-voltage supplies, the connection of a C/T and a P/T would be required. See Figure 10.16.

Measurement of power factor

A wattmeter indicates the **power** in a circuit, an ammeter the **current** and the voltmeter the **voltage** or potential.

The power factor (*pf*) is the ratio of the power in watts (W) to the product of the voltage and current (V A), that is

$$pf = \frac{W}{V\,A}$$

If, therefore, instruments are connected to measure these three values, the value of the pf can be obtained. See Figure 10.17.

Measurements in three-phase four-wire circuits

As previously mentioned, supplies on larger installations and to heavier equipment are of the three-phase or three-phase four-wire type, referred to as T.P. or T.P.N. supplies.

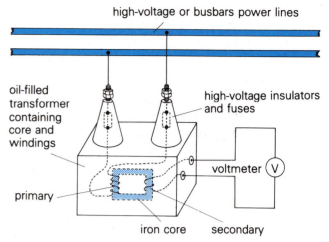

Figure 10.15 Higher voltage potential (instrument) transformer.

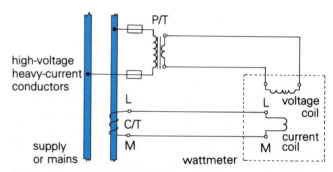

Note: For correct polarity C/T terminals are marked L for load side and M for mains side. It is essential that these are observed, particularly on T.P. and T.P.N. supplies. This also applies to the current coil terminals of the wattmeter.

Figure 10.16 Measurement of power using potential and current transformers in HV heavy current circuits.

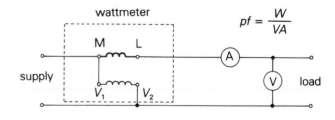

Figure 10.17 Measurement of power factor.

On these circuits, the total power (*P*) or the total volt-amperes (V A) is obtained by taking measurements in one phase only and multiplying the value by 3.

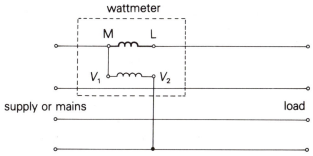

Total power for balanced load = 3 × wattmeter reading

Figure 10.18 Total power measurement in three-phase balanced load.

> For three-phase circuits, the phase and not the line voltage must be measured and the load **must** be balanced. See Figure 10.18.

For the measurement of total power (kW) and total kilovolt-amperes (kV A) on heavier current supplies, the use of integrated three-element type wattmeters and voltammeters is required. These are instruments which contain three sets of current and voltage coils. In the wattmeter they are physically arranged and integrated to indicate the total power reading on one scale in kW, in the voltammeter they are arranged to read the total volt-amperes on one scale in kV A for balanced or unbalanced loads.
Note: The pf of the circuit or installation can again be obtained.

$$pf = \frac{kW}{kV\,A}$$

Measurement of energy
For the purpose of electricity charges, referred to as **tariffs**, it is necessary to record the amount of electrical energy consumed over a given period of time, normally one month or one quarter (3 months), after which interval the meter is read and the charges calculated.

Energy is measured in joules (watt-seconds). But for tariff purposes, the larger unit, the **kilowatt-hour** (kW h) is used.
Note: 1 kW h = 3.6 × 10⁶ J.

The instrument used is an energy meter, known as the kW h meter. It is basically an induction-type wattmeter designed to rotate an aluminium disc which, in turn, is mechanically coupled to drive a series of pointers or numerals from which the kW h can be read. The speed at which the disc rotates is governed by the amount of energy being

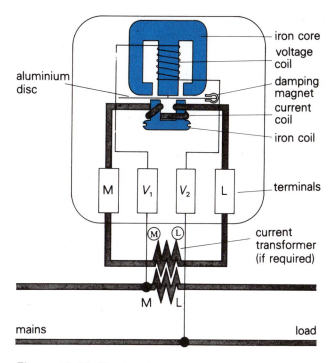

Figure 10.19 Single-phase energy meter.

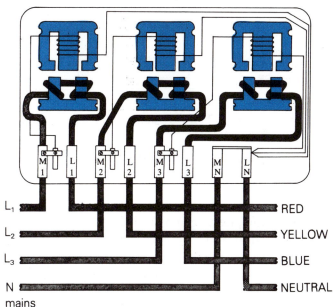

Note: Aluminium disc omitted for clarity (see Figure 10.19).

Figure 10.20 Three-phase energy meter.

consumed by the installation at any instant in time. A small permanent magnet is placed to 'damp' the disc so that it does not revolve when energy is not being consumed.

A single-phase type is shown in Figure 10.19. The three-phase four-wire integrated type in Figure 10.20.

Note: On the high-voltage heavy current supplies, the use of C/Ts and P/Ts would again be required.

Summation metering

When the total kW h, kV A h, or kvar h, transmitted by the number of feeders is required to be registered on one meter, it is essential that some arrangement be employed for their summation.

One method of summation metering is by using a **summation transformer**. See Figure 10.21.

Since the 'back' ampere-turns producing the flux in the secondary winding will be approximately equal to the total phase sum of the ampere-turns of the primary windings, it follows that the transformer will prove an effective medium for summation of current. It has the advantage of being suitable for use where several feeders supply a common load.

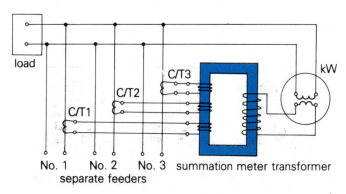

Figure 10.21 Summation metering.

Power factor
For lighting, heating and driving machinery, a consumer requires electrical power in watts or kilowatts. On a.c. circuits:

Power = volts × amperes × power factor

or, stated algebraically:

$P = VI \cos \phi$

where $\cos \phi$ is the power factor of the circuit and represents the cosine value of the phase angle between the voltage and current in the circuit. From the formula, it can be seen that if the value of the pf is zero, then no matter how much current is flowing in the circuit, then zero or no power is being transmitted.

Remember that cable sizes, conductors, windings and switchgear sizes of electrical equipment are based on the **current** they have to carry. Therefore, the higher the pf, the smaller the current for a given power load, which means that the above sizes can be reduced to handle the power requirements. Because manufacturers of electrical plant are unaware of the pf of the circuits and the installations in which their equipment will be operating, they cannot rate the plant in terms of power because the variation of current to be carried is dependent on pf. Therefore, they rate the plant in terms of V A, or the larger unit kV A, not W or kW.

EXAMPLE 3

A consumer has a power load of 20 kW operating at a pf of 0.5 on a 240 V single-phase supply. Calculate the load current: (i) at the present pf, (ii) when the pf is improved to 1 (unity).

i) $P = VI \cos \phi$

$$I = \frac{P}{V \cos \phi} = \frac{20 \times 1000}{240 \times 0.5} = 167 \text{ A}$$

ii) $I = \frac{20 \times 1000}{240 \times 1} = 83.3 \text{ A}$

This means that for the same power being delivered or utilised, the current demand has fallen to half, by improving the pf from 0.5 to 1.
Note: The pf cannot exceed **unity**.

Power factor improvement
In all electrical equipment which utilises the magnetic effect of current, that is, where inductive windings are employed and this means practically all a.c. equipment, transformers, motors, solenoids, discharge lighting, etc., the current in the circuit **lags** the voltage. This means that V and I are not always **in-phase**. This is best explained by a phasor diagram. See Figure 10.22.

Taking the supply voltage as the reference line on the horizontal, then the length of a phasor drawn to scale and the correct phase angle, can represent the current.
Note: The phasor rotates anti-clockwise, which means that the lag of the current arrow is behind the voltage reference in an anti-clockwise direction.

This total current can now be split into two component parts:

1. that which is 'in-phase' with the voltage and delivering power (unity pf) known as the **power component**; and
2. that which is out of phase with the voltage lagging by 90° and delivering no power, zero (0)

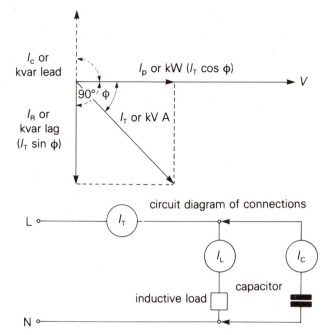

circuit diagram of connections

Note: Students are advised to connect ammeters with varying values of capacitors as shown and note the effect. It is possible to swing I_T from a lag value to a minimum at unity pf and then by increased capacitance increase I_T in a lead direction.

Figure 10.22 Power factor correction circuit and phasor diagram.

pf. This is referred to as the **reactive component** and, when multiplied by the voltage, as VAr or kVAr (volt-amperes reactive, unit: var).

If this lagging component of the current could be removed, then only the current required to deliver the power would remain. This means that the pf would be improved to unity and the current reduced in proportion. The improvement of the pf is known as **power factor correction** and can be obtained by the connection of **capacitors** in the circuit. See completion of Figure 10.22.

Use of capacitors
Capacitors are items of equipment which take a leading current from the supply. This means that the current **leads** the voltage by an angle of 90°. Hence this current directly opposes (180° apart) the lagging or reactive component of the load current and thus reduces its value and improves the pf.

By this means, a consumer can take the same power load with a reduction of current in his switchgear and cables, resulting in lower power transmission (I^2R) losses and enabling the use of smaller and more economic switchgear and cable.

Conversion of reactive kilovolt-amperes (kVA) to capacitance
The capacity of electrical capacitors is stated in farads (F) or the smaller unit, the microfarad (μF).
$$1 \text{ F} = 1\,000\,000 \text{ μF} = 10^6 \text{ μF}$$
The capacitance can be calculated when the kvar rating, working voltage and frequency of the supply are known.

$$\text{Capacitor current } (I) = \frac{\text{kvar rating} \times 1000}{\text{supply voltage } (V)}$$

so that when V is known, I may be calculated. The opposition to current flow by the capacitor is known as **capacitive reaction** (X_c).

$$X_c = \frac{V}{I}$$

hence when V and I are known, X_c may be calculated.

In terms of capacitance and frequency of supply:

$$X_c = \frac{10^6}{2\pi f C}$$

where X_c = capacitive reaction (Ω),
f = frequency of supply (Hz),
C = capacitance (μF).

$$C = \frac{10^6}{2\pi f X_c}$$

EXAMPLE 4

A certain capacitor has a rating of 20 kvar at 240 V 50 Hz. Calculate its capacitance.

$$I = \frac{\text{kvar} \times 1000}{V} = \frac{20 \times 1000}{240} = 83 \text{ A}$$

$$X_c = \frac{V}{I} = \frac{240}{83} = 2.89 \ \Omega$$

$$C = \frac{10^6}{2\pi f X_c}$$
$$= \frac{10^6}{2 \times 3.14 \times 50 \times 2.89}$$
$$= 1102 \text{ μF}$$

Note: The capacitor only improves the pf of the circuit up to the point where it is connected, i.e. when connected across the terminals of a motor, it reduces the current in the supply cables up to the terminals, not the current in the motor windings.

EXAMPLE 5

An induction motor operating at a pf of 0.6 lagging takes a current of 10 A from a single-phase 240 V 50 Hz supply.

Calculate:

i) a) the power component of the current and kW,
   b) the reactive component current and kvar.
ii) If the pf is to be corrected to (a) unity, (b) 0.8 lag, calculate the kvar rating and the current taken by the capacitor in each case.

From a study of Figure 10.22, it will be seen that:
Power component = 1 cos φ
Reactive component = 1 sin φ

i) a) I = 10 A × 0.6 = 6 A
      P = 240 × 6 − 1440 = 1.44 kW
   b) I = 10 A × 0.8 = 8 A lag
      P = 240 × 8 = 1920 = 1.92 kvar lag

For correction to unity, the leading value of current must equal the lagging value.

Therefore, the capacitor current must be 8 A lead and the kvar value must be 1.92 lead.

ii) **Note:** The power developed by the motor is unaltered by the correction of the pf. It is only the current value which changes. Therefore, when the pf is improved from 0.6 to 0.8, the power remains at 1.44 kW.

$$Now \ kVA = \frac{kW}{pf}$$

At 0.8 pf

$$kVA = \frac{1.44}{0.8} = 1.80$$

So that the new total current = $\frac{1800}{240}$
= 7.5 A
Power component of current = 7.5 A × 0.8 = 6 A (as before).
Power P = 240 × 6 = 1440 W = 1.44 kW (as before).
The sine of the phase angle is now 0.6.

ii) a) Therefore the reactive current component
      = 7.5 × 0.6 = 4.5 A
   b) Therefore the reactive kvar = 240 × 4.5
      = 1.08 kV A
      = 1.08 kvar
These will be the required capacitor values.

Students are advised to construct this example as a phasor diagram to scale, measure the values and calculate the capacitance of the capacitors.

On three-phase installations, three capacitors would be connected in **delta** to the supply, forming a three-phase capacitor bank. Each would receive line voltage.

Power factor correction can also be obtained by the use of auto-synchronous motors on a consumer's installation. Because these are made in larger sizes, they are used mainly for driving loads on heavy industrial installations. The rotor of these motors carries a d.c. winding and an increase of current in this winding will cause the stator windings to take current from the a.c. supply at a leading pf. By regulation of the d.c. current known as **excitation**, the pf may be corrected to the required value. These motors have an advantage over capacitors in that in addition to pf improvement, they can also be used to drive machines, providing the load characteristic of the driven machine is suitable.

Because these motors have a low start torque and must run at synchronous speed, the load must be of a steady nature. Any sudden overload would result in a **pull-out** of synchronism between the stator field and the speed of the rotor and the windings would be damaged by excessive current flow.

Suitable loads would be large fans, pumps and d.c. generators, which provide a fairly steady continuous load.

Electricity tariffs

It will be seen that it can be financially beneficial for a consumer to improve the value of the power factor of his installation.
Note: In order to reduce the current in the switchgear and cables on his own installation, the consumer must have the capacitors connected at the extreme ends of the circuits (see previous notes) mounted on, or near to the equipment and machine.

The electricity supply authorities also offer a reduction in charges to a consumer with a high pf, since it reduces the current in their switchgear and cables for a given power demand. A consumer can take advantage of this by installing the capacitors at the intake point of the supply, but this only reduces the current in the supply authority cables, not the consumer's own.

Financial incentives are also given to large consumers who can reduce their maximum electricity demand, since this means the installation of smaller generators, transformers, switchgear and transmission lines on the supply authority side.

One form of tariff combines the power factor correction and maximum demand operations. It is known as the **maximum demand (MD) charge**, and involves the use of a **maximum demand indicator** (MDI) instrument.

Maximum demand indicator (MDI)

This is an instrument which measures the maximum demand in kV A of the consumer's plant over a half-hour period of time. The combined tariff is a flat-rate charge per kW h of electricity used, plus a charge per kV A of maximum demand. **Note:** The improvement of pf reduces the kV A demand for a given power load and hence reduces the maximum demand charge. An improvement from 0.5 unity pf would halve the MDI charge and this is quite a considerable saving.

EXAMPLE 6

An industrial consumer has an annual electricity consumption of 1 000 000 (10^6) units (kW h) and the power factor of his plant is 0.65. In addition to this there is a maximum demand (MD) charge of £30 per kV A. If the units charge is 4p each and the MD is 1000 kV A, calculate the overall charge per unit.

The units used charge = $10^6 \times 4p$ = £40 000
MD charge   = $10^3 \times £30$ = £30 000
Total charge   = £70 000

Overall charge per unit = $\dfrac{£70\ 000}{1\ 000\ 000}$ = 7 pence

---

EXAMPLE 7

If the consumer in Example 6 installs capacitor equipment to improve the pf to 0.85 calculate the new cost per unit.
Note: There will be no change in the units charge.

Old power MD = 1000 kV A × 0.65 pf
              = 650 kW

New kV A MD = $\dfrac{650}{0.85}$ = 765

kV A MD charge = 765 × £30 = £22 950

Total charge = £40 000 + £22 950 = £62 950

Overall charge = $\dfrac{£62\ 950}{1\ 000\ 000}$ = 6.295 pence

In order to reduce maximum demand values, a consumer may install control devices to switch off non-essential equipment automatically when the demand exceeds a predetermined value. The control devices are operated from the MD indicator instrument. The consumer may also install switchgear for automatic operation of switching of capacitors in the circuit in order to maintain a predetermined value of pf. This is operated in conjunction with a kvar meter which energises relays.

Off-peak tariff

Because the running costs of generating stations are comparatively small compared with the overheads, the cost of operating when unloaded are not much lower than when fully loaded. This means that it is more economical to have a steady load demand. To encourage this, the consumer receives a reduction in charge for consuming electricity during off-peak periods. These periods are normally during the night around 11 pm to 7 am.

These installations require special metering techniques. There are two main systems.

Two-part tariff

This involves the division of the installation into two sections which are separately metered.

The essential supplies which are required at any time during the 24 hour-period, such as lights, socket outlets, central heating controls, are connected back to the normal meter and charged for at a higher rate. The second meter supplies equipment such as refractory material-filled storage radiators, water heaters and large capacity storage heaters (see Chapter 6) which can be supplied or 'charged' during the off-peak periods at night and give out heat and hot water the following day. See Figure 10.23.

White meter or economy tariff

In this system, only one meter is employed which contains two sets of dials. One set records the consumption during the peak (day-time) periods, while the second set records the off-peak (night-time) periods.

The complete installation is supplied through this meter. The dials are switched from one period

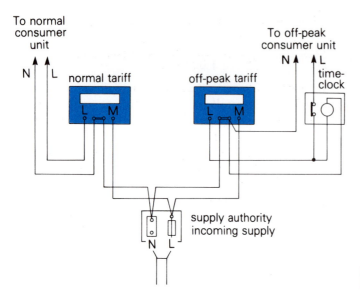

Figure 10.23 'Off-peak' two meter tariff.

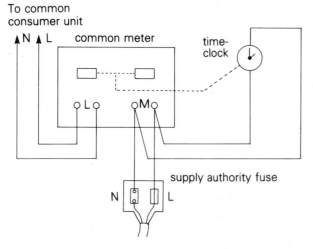

Figure 10.24 Single meter (two dials) economy tariff.

to the other at pre-set times from the authority's sealed time clock. See Figure 10.24.

Standing charge plus unit price

Because the transmission and installation costs to supply a consumer with a given power intake are the same regardless of the amount of units used, the supply authority makes a **standing charge** to recoup these costs in addition to a charge for each unit used.

Fuel adjustment

During any short period of time, the price of fuel to the generating stations may increase. In order to recover this from the consumer, an adjustment charge will be made to the bill at the end of each metered period. This charge mainly applies to the heavier industrial consumers. Students are advised to obtain a **Tariffs Sheet** from their local supply authority and study the tariffs that are available to the consumer.

■ CHECK YOUR UNDERSTANDING

● A moving coil instrument consists of a coil of wire which is free to turn in the field of a permanent magnet.
● Its voltage range can be extended by series (multiplier) resistors, its current range by parallel (shunt) resistors.
● Moving iron instruments employ the force between two magnetised irons. Their range is extended by the use of external instrument transformers.
● A wattmeter uses a fixed current coil in which a voltage coil which experiences a turning force is mounted. It moves in a clockwise direction when the current and voltage are in phase.
● A cathode-ray tube is an evacuated envelope with a phosphor screen. An electron gun emits rays which impinge on the screen and cause a luminous spot. This spot may be deflected by plates to which the supply under examination is connected.
● A Wheatstone bridge is an arrangement of four resistors, usually two of which form a potentiometer slide wire which is adjusted until balance is obtained and the value of an unknown resistor may be obtained.
● High voltage, heavy current consumers are metered using kV A, kW and kW h meters supplies through instrument voltage and current transformers. Energy meters are fitted with an aluminium disc which revolves to give a record of units used.
● Maximum demand indicators show the consumer's maximum demands in kV A over a period of time, usually half an hour, on which a separate charge is made.
● Improvement of power factor will reduce kV A demand for a given power demand and hence reduce cost.

REVISION EXERCISES AND QUESTIONS

1 i) Explain the difference between electrical power and energy.

   ii) A wattmeter having one voltage and one current coil is to measure the total powers in a three-phase four-wire supply. Make a diagram of this and state the total power in the circuit.

   iii) A three-phase balanced load takes a line current of 30 A at 415 V operating at 0.8 pf. Calculate the energy consumed over a 24 hour period.

2 i) State two reasons why current transformers are used in the metering systems of large installations.

   ii) Why are tong-testers (clamp) ammeters preferred to other types of meter for current measurement?

   iii) A load of up to 200 kV A is balanced on a three-phase 415 V 50 Hz supply. The current is indicated on a 5 A meter in one line, using a current transformer.
      a) Determine the ratio of the C/T.
      b) Show a circuit diagram of the arrangement.

3 A 50 kW a.c. motor operates at 0.65 pf lag and an efficiency of 83 per cent. A 40 kV A capacitor is connected in parallel with the motor terminals. Determine by phasor diagrams or calculation:
   i) full load input (kV A) to the motor without the capacitor.
   ii) supply kV A and pf when motor is on full load when the capacitor is connected.

4 State how and give reasons a consumer can reduce the following:
   i) power loss in cables supplying equipment operating at a low pf,
   ii) kV A charges for the consumption of his overall energy,
   iii) maximum demand charges over a short period.

5 Give reasons for the following types of tariff charges by the supply authority:
   i) standing charge plus units used,
   ii) off-peak reduction per unit,
   iii) maximum demand cost plus units used,
   iv) sliding-scale reduction per unit.

6 Describe with the aid of a sketch the instrument most suitable for the measurement of a.c. voltage or current, to be mounted on a vertical switchboard. State how the controlling torque and the damping are obtained.

7 Make a diagram of the internal switching and circuitry to produce three ranges each of voltage and current on the scale of a moving coil instrument.

8 i) If the coil of a moving coil instrument has a resistance of 10 Ω and a full scale deflection (f.s.d.) of 20 mA, list to the nearest round figure the values of resistors required to enable the instrument to indicate up to (a) 10 V, (b) 20 V, (c) 50 V, (d) 1 A, (e) 2 A, (f) 5 A.

   ii) State how the resistors would be connected to the instrument.

9 i) Make a sketch of the construction of a dynamometer type of wattmeter. Show the connection to the supply.

   ii) Explain the technical reasons why the instrument indicates the mean power of the supply.

10 A wattmeter is connected in each of the following three circuits, one of a
   i) pure inductance of 1 henry (H),
   ii) pure capacitance of 1 farad (F),
   iii) pure resistance of 20 Ω.
   If the supply is 100 V 50 Hz, determine the reading on the meter in each circuit.

11 i) State the additional components to be connected in the circuitry of a moving coil instrument to enable it to measure: (a) resistance values, and (b) a.c. values of current and voltage.
   Show how they are connected to the instrument.

   ii) Before carrying out a resistance test, the instrument should be zeroed. State the meaning of this and why it is necessary.

12 Compare the measurement of power with the measurement of energy. Explain the working principles of all the instruments used in the process.

13 i) What is tariff? Describe various ways of charging for the energy used in your area.

   ii) Describe, giving reasons, one method by which the consumer could reduce the cost of his power while taking the same number of units.

14 For what purpose would you use the following? Illustrate by sketches their connections when used to measure the input to a single-phase motor:
   i) voltmeter,
   ii) ammeter,
   iii) wattmeter.

15 With the aid of circuit diagrams, describe the

operation of the off-peak tariff employing two meters. How does it differ from the white meter tariff?

16 i) Draw a diagram showing the internal and external connections of high voltage metering equipment for a maximum demand tariff.
   ii) How is the cost of the maximum demand included in the tariff?

(C & G 'C')

17 Draw a circuit diagram of the following instruments on an 11 kV three-phase three-wire system serving a balanced load:
   i) a voltmeter to indicate line voltage,
   ii) an ammeter and selector switch to indicate any line current,
   iii) a wattmeter (showing the connections to the current and voltage coils).
The diagram should show all necessary protection.

(C & G 'C')

18 i) Make a diagram of a Wheatstone bridge arrangement using a slide wire potentiometer.
   ii) If the bridge is balanced when the ratio of slide wire R_1/R_2 is 4:1 and R_3 the standard resistor is 60 Ω, what is the value of the unknown resistor R_4?

Contract planning

Introduction

Once the design of an installation has been completed and agreed, the electrical contractor must estimate the total cost including materials, labour and overheads. He must then prepare a programme of work that fits in with all the other contractors on the site.

A contract which includes the final sum and method of payment can then be drawn up and agreed upon. Penalty clauses for a delay in work may be included.

Once the work is underway the contractor must monitor it carefully; materials must be ordered and arrive on time in good condition, and variations and extra costs must be recorded.

Design of an installation

The design may be prepared for Government departments, local authorities, public and private companies, consultants or, in some cases, by the electrical contractors themselves. These designs are used as a basis for obtaining a tender for the client to select a contractor to carry out the work.

Installation design by the contractor

The electrical contractor may be asked to design the installation for the client on payment of a fee, or some guarantee that he will eventually get the contract and carry out the work. Such an arrangement should be on a formal basis to avoid wasting time and money.

Planning the installation

The designer must translate the client's requirements into the most suitable installation within the constraints of time and cost. He must extract all relevant information and requirements either verbally or in written form from the client. All the electrical services must be skillfully incorporated into the building fabric without undue obtrusion. Initial installation and subsequent running costs must be compared and thought must be given to future extension. Common location symbols for installation drawings are shown in Figure 11.1.

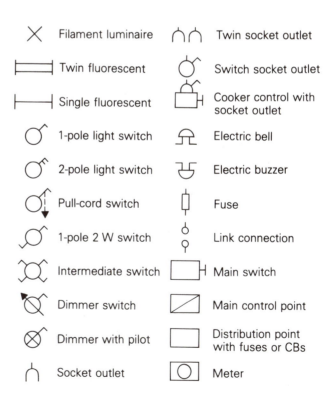

Figure 11.1 Location symbols for installation drawings.

Preliminary design

When the requirements are fully analysed, a first or preliminary design should be prepared and fully discussed with the client. The design must fulfil all the statutory regulations, relevant codes of practice and I.E.E. Regulations. On agreement, the client is now committed to the design and any change which results in delay and extra cost is therefore his responsibility.

Types of contract

On completion of the design, the contract documents may now be drawn up and a decision made as to which type of contract is to be adopted: **measured work, lump sum, fixed price** or **fluctuation price**.

Measured work (or Bill of Quantities)

This details all the estimated materials which are required for the installation. The estimator's function is to submit rates for the supply of these and the labour costs to install them. A final figure is thus obtained from these breakdowns which is quoted to the prospective client.

Lump sum

This is the most common type of contract. The estimator has to take all the quantities from the drawing and/or specification submitted to him. He then submits a lump sum total for the cost of these materials and labour costs to install them.

Firm or fixed price

With this contract, the contractor is not allowed to claim for any later variation in costs, either materials or labour. It is therefore the estimator's responsibility to make provision for any likely variation in the quotation. There must obviously be a time-limit clause (normally not more than one year) mainly because of inflation in prices.

Fluctuation price

Here, the contractor may claim for increases in the costs of materials or nationally agreed labour awards. Wage award dates and manufacturer's list price changes are normally required as evidence of the price change.

Specialised installations
When the contract calls for these, for example, lifts, alarms, neons, high-voltage cable jointing, etc., the contractor must make early contact with the appropriate firms who specialise in this work.

Installation programme

When the contractor is appointed and accepted, he should prepare a proposed programme of work in consultation with the main contractor and other trades at site meetings etc. A **critical path analysis** programme should then be set out. The availability of capital and consumable equipment, together with the labour requirements, should be carefully checked so that target dates can be met.

Principles of estimating for electrical contracts

Estimating involves:

1. a study of the specification or brief,
2. a knowledge of site conditions,
3. a knowledge of building construction,
4. measurement of the quantity of materials required from the drawings using a **scale rule** for wiring-run measurements,
5. a study of the time required to complete various operations,
6. a knowledge of the statutory requirements, codes of practice and I.E.E. Regulations,
7. noting any unusual features of the contract, such as excessive working heights, transport and communications difficulties and requirements for specialised equipment.

Costing

Material estimate

This is usually more simple than estimating labour requirements. The drawings are studied, equipment located, cable runs are marked out and careful measurements are made.

When the Bill of Quantities is prepared, it can be priced either from current price lists or by forwarding to the suppliers of the materials.

Labour costs

These are more difficult to estimate. The installation should be sub-divided and each sub-division considered separately. It is possible to obtain a national average time factor for most common operations, for example the installation of various wiring systems, switchgear and accessories. One such publication is '*Mechanical and Electrical Services Price Book*' which is published annually by 'SPON'. These times can be adjusted in the light of experience, and when an estimator has established some reliable times, either in man-hours or pair-man-hours, he should keep a library of these for future reference.

Sub-division of the installation

This will depend upon the nature of the installation, but for general buildings such as offices, schools, etc., a suggested method, starting at the intake position, would be in order:

1. high-voltage distribution,
2. low-voltage distribution,
3. subcircuit distribution feeders,
4. subcircuit distribution boards,
5. lighting installation,
6. socket outlets and machine power circuits,
7. special rooms,
8. boiler house,
9. detector systems,
10. alarm systems,
11. emergency lighting,
12. heating controls,
13. clocks,
14. earthing,
15. lightning conductors if required,
16. neon signs if required.

An industrial installation would have, say:
No. 1 machine shop, No. 2 machine shop, press shop and so on.

Since all installations will have a lighting sub-division which covers the whole of the building, it is helpful if the estimator starts on this to get the 'feel' of the layout and size of the installation.

Price take-off sheet

One of these is prepared for each sub-division. Where labour, man-hours or pair-hours are required, these can be entered and priced at current rates of pay as a total cost (obviously this sheet includes material costs as well).

Final costing

When all the total price sheets for each sub-division are completed, so that all material and labour costs can be calculated, all other expenses and work involved must be considered, these include

1. overheads – these are normally based on annual turnover to fixed overheads as a percentage to be added,
2. tools and accommodation on site,
3. supervision of non-productive labour,
4. out allowances – payment to employees away from home overnight,
5. insurance,
6. prime cost sums (PC) – sums for the basic cost of capital items to client's choice,
7. provisional sums (PS) – sums set aside for capital items, provided these are required on the contract,
8. main contractor's discount – usually $2\frac{1}{2}$ per cent of the contract price; selling price is obtained by adding 1/39 of the contract price to the contract price thus providing the $2\frac{1}{2}$ per cent discount,
9. contingency risks – to allow for unforeseen necessary costs which arise on the contract,
10. production of an 'as fitted drawing' for the client.

Recapitulation sheet

On this, individual price sheet totals are entered on separate lines and the totals are then added to produce a **net total** cost of materials and labour times. All the other costs and contractor's profit are then added to produce a final quotation price.

Interim payments

These are payments made to the electrical subcontractor by the main building contractor for materials and labour costs at various stages in the project. The work completed will normally be measured by a quantity surveyor and amounts to be paid will be agreed with the subcontractor.

Penalty clause

This is a penalty which may be imposed on a subcontractor if his progress is delayed to an extent where it causes the work of other contractors to be held up. If there is a delay men may be idle and the main contractor cannot complete the project on time, therefore his payment will be held up. Normally, the penalty is a set amount for each day or week of the hold up.

Variations

These are alterations during the course of the construction which will affect the work for which the subcontractor has tendered. Before any alteration or extension of the original contract is carried out, the subcontractor should have specific written authority from an authorised person, such as the **Clerk of Works**, architect or the main contractor himself. The extra work is then measured and the payment rate is related to the charges for similar work in the original tender and payment is agreed.

Site diary

This is the diary kept up to date by the subcontractor's foreman or supervisor on-site. He will enter in the diary all variations and extra costs incurred and any instructions which are given to him by authorised persons for later submission to his head office.

Material deliveries

In order to reduce storage space and to prevent breakages and materials going missing, it is preferable that only those materials required for use within a few days or so are delivered on site. Care should be taken, though, to ensure that any special equipment or materials for which there will be longer deliveries times are ready for despatch to site when required.

Materials delivered should, wherever possible, be examined and checked against the delivery note contents. Any discrepancies or damage or breakages should then be reported to the vehicle driver and noted in **Material Records Books**. The contractor's main office will also have to be informed so that payment can be withheld if necessary.

If it is not practicable to examine goods on delivery, the delivery note must be signed '**packages unexamined**' and the contents should then be checked as soon as possible and the delivery firm or supplier notified of any shortage or breakages. Normally, the supplier will allow three days for this notification.

Bar charts

These are charts which show the various operations in the project programme. Each chart will show the dates and length of time allocated for each operation and how each 'fits in' with the other trades on site.

For a given project, it would be normal for the main contractor or architect to produce a master chart to co-ordinate all the various operations required for the completion of the project. From this, each subcontractor will see the date on which he can begin his part of the overall project and the date on which he will be expected to finish. He can also see whether or not he is going to be delayed by other trades. From the master chart dates, the subcontractor can then produce his own bar chart showing the stages in his programme with dates and the duration of each operation. He can then arrange for the necessary labour and material to be available. Once he has commenced his work, he can check the progress of each stage on the bar chart and see if any stage requires speeding up to meet his completion date. It may be that unforeseen snags have arisen and more men will be required than he anticipated.

See bar charts in Figures 11.2 and 11.3.

For some projects, it may be necessary to produce a critical path analysis of the various stages in the programme.

Critical path analysis (CPA)

All projects are made up of individual tasks or jobs which start and finish at a certain time during the course of the overall project. Some of these jobs or activities must be completed before others can start to run **consecutively**. Some can be carried out at the same time or run **concurrently**.

The project planner's task is to sort out all the start and finish dates and durations of the individual jobs. The process is called critical path analysis (CPA) and when it is completed, the planner can see how long it will take to complete the project. The total overall time it will take to complete the project is the added times of the longest sequence of jobs or events in the CPA. This longest path through the CPA is known as the **critical path** (CP).

Any alterations for any reason, which shorten or lengthen this CP, will obviously shorten or lengthen the overall time required to complete the project. The shorter paths can be varied without affecting the overall time duration, unless of course one of these shorter paths is considerably lengthened or delayed, when it may exceed the original CP in duration. In this case, the extended path now becomes the new CP and the whole duration of the project will be increased to that amount.

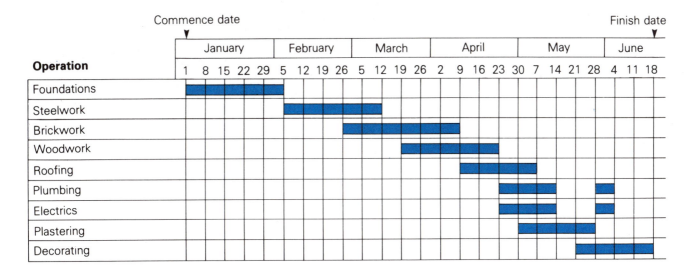

Figure 11.2 Building construction programme – main contractor's bar chart.

| Operation | First fix | | | Second fix | |
| | Week 1 | Week 2 | Week 3 | Week 6 | |
	1	2	3	4	5	1	2	3	4	5	1	2	3	4	5	1	2	3	4	5		
Installing PVC/SWA main and submain cables	2p	2p	2p																			
Erecting switchgear and distribution boards	2p	2p	2p																			
Terminating of above				2p	2p																	
Erecting of main trunking and conduit runs				2p	2p	2p	2p	2p														
Wiring and connecting above						2p	2p	2p														
Conduit runs to lighting subcircuits									2p	2p	2p	2p										
Conduit runs to power subcircuits									2p	2p	2p	2p										
Wiring of above												2p	2p	2p								
												2p	2p	2p								
Fixing and connecting of lighting fittings																1p	1p	1p	1p	1p		
Fixing and connecting of power outlets																1p	1p	1p	1p			
Testing																			1p			
Number of pairs of men required on site	4	4	4	4	4	4	4	4	4	4	4	4	4	4	4	2	2	2	2	2		

Figure 11.3 Electrical construction programme (complied from main contractor's bar chart).

Compiling a critical path analysis

The basic methods and terminology used in compiling a critical path analysis are outlined in the following sections.

Arrow diagrams
These are constructed by using three symbols.

1. **Full arrows** by which the individual jobs are represented. These show the direction of the job in time. 'End of job' is indicated by the arrow head. The duration time can be marked on the arrows.
2. **Nodes**. The start and finish of a job are events. These are represented by circles known as nodes.

3. **Numbers.** These are placed in the nodes to indicate the sequence of events.

Concurrent events

Concurrent events

Events 1 and 3 finished. Jobs M and N can start.

Events 2 and 4 must finish before other jobs can start.

Event 1 only finished. Jobs M and N can start.

Events 2 and 3 must finish before other jobs can start.

Events 1 and 2 finished. Jobs M and N can start.

Event 3 must finish before other jobs can start.

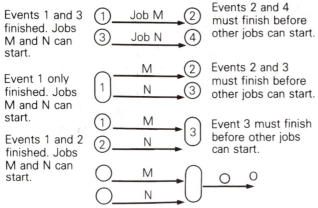

The start of Job O depends on Jobs M and N being finished.

Figure 11.4 Arrows diagram of concurrent events.

Dummy activities

In preparing a CPA, there is the possibility that two or more jobs which involve different firms or craftsmen on a given project can:

1. start at the same point,
2. finish at the same point.

These jobs would therefore run concurrently between the same two events. The jobs which do not directly concern the firm compiling the CPA are referred to as **dummy activities** and are represented by dotted arrows.

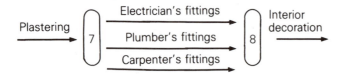

Figure 11.5 Arrows diagram of dummy activities.

Any reference to events 7 to 8 would not indicate whose job was under consideration – the electrician's, plumber's or carpenter's.
Note: As far as the contractor's firm is concerned, the dummy activities can be regarded as:

1. being of zero duration, and
2. consuming no materials.

EXAMPLE 1

i) Draw an arrow diagram to represent JOB A which immediately follows JOBS B and C.
ii) JOBS B and E immediately follow JOB D.

i)

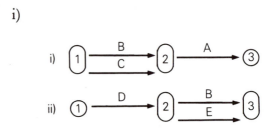

Figure 11.6 Arrows diagrams of 'following on' events (Example 1).

ii)

EXAMPLE 2

Draw an arrow diagram to show the following jobs:
JOB L and M cannot start until K is complete.
JOB L must be completed before JOB N can start.
JOB M must be followed by JOB Q.

Both N and Q must be completed before JOB P can start.

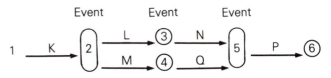

Figure 11.7 Arrows diagrams of events sequence (Example 2).

EXAMPLE 3

The following layout shows the network analysis of a contract about to be undertaken by an electrical firm. The length of time required to complete each activity is shown in days.
i) Determine the activities (jobs) forming the critical path and draw the bar chart for this network on the graph paper provided.
ii) State:
  (a) the activity days on the critical path,

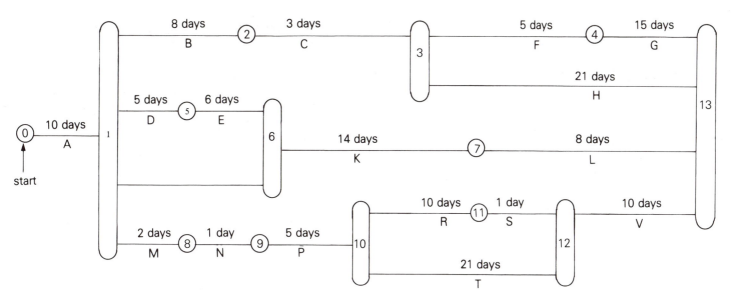

Figure 11.8 Network analysis of an electrical contract.

(b) the length of time needed to complete the contract,

(c) the effect of activity E taking 7 days longer than expected.

i) A, M, N, P, T, V.

ii) (a) 10 + 2 + 1 + 5 + 21 + 10.

(b) 49 days.

(c) Activities A, D, E, K, L become the critical path which total 50 days. This means that the length of time required to complete the contract is extended by one day.

Site management

Every site supervisor who has charge of a group of workmen and the work in progress has the following responsibilities:

1. site safety,
2. legal responsibilities,
3. responsibilities for his fellow men,
4. responsibility for working to construction regulations,
5. responsibility for maintaining the required progress of the work at the correct costs.

He should have knowledge of the construction site regulations which include:

1. supervision over the safe methods of carrying out the various work operations;

2. the safety provisions for working places and means of access;
3. methods of transportation and handling of goods;
4. first aid boxes and room, ambulance, accommodation for clothing and meals, washing and sanitary conveniences;
5. The Electricity (Factories Act) Regulations;
6. Mines and Quarries Act;
7. Petroleum Regulations.

Records

The following registers should be kept in the site office:

1. General Register (FORM 36),
2. Prescribed Register for Reports (FORM 91),
3. Certificate of Test for Lifting Appliances on Site,
4. Employer's Insurance Company and Accident Book.

Notifications to Health and Safety Inspector

The inspector should be notified of

1. accidents or dangerous occurrences (form 43B),
2. absences (caused by accidents) exceeding three days,
3. deaths, fires and explosions,

4. employment of a person under 18 years within seven days of his taking up employment.

Appointment of Safety Supervisors

> ▲ Where any one sub-contractor employs more than 20 people on a site, he should appoint a safety supervisor whose name and whereabouts should be posted up.

The supervisor need not be full-time and can be a joint supervisor with other sub-contract employees.

■ CHECK YOUR UNDERSTANDING

● The designer translates the client's requirements into the most suitable installation within the constraints of cost and time.

● Estimating involves a knowledge of site conditions and the building construction, measurement for material costs and a study of operation times for labour costs.

● An estimator should note any unusual features or equipment so that advanced warning for obtaining special plant or equipment can be given.

● In addition to materials and labour, the final costing will include overheads, insurance, accommodation, supervision, transport. A contingency risk may also be added for unforeseen costs.

● A bar chart compiled from the main contractor's programme of the electrical content showing dates and durations of operations will be produced so that labour and materials are available.

● A critical path analysis (CPA) uses arrows to show the start and finish times of individual operations in conjunction with those of other trades.

● Site management involves knowledge of legal aspects, employees' welfare and safety, sanitation and first aid facilities.

● A materials record book shows dates, shortages and breakages of deliveries.

● Material deliveries should be kept to those required for work in operation, to avoid theft and reduce storage space.

● A site diary shows details of any variations to the original contract. These variations can only be authorised in writing by the client or his agent.

1 Explain what is meant by 'time is money' when workmen are employed.
How would you ensure that precious time is not wasted when carrying out installation work?

2 The I.E.E. Regulations are framed to ensure that your work is of an acceptable standard. It protects the life of the consumer and his property. Bearing this in mind, what would you consider to be the qualities of a good foreman in charge of the electrical installation of a building?

3 i) Outline the features of the following type of contract:
   a) lump sum, (b) measured work or bill of quantities, and (c) fixed price.
   ii) State **six** considerations in the preparation of a tender for an electrical contract.

4 Labour and material costs form the major part of the costs on any contract.
List **six** other costs to be calculated before the total cost is prepared.

5 An existing building with an obsolete electrical installation is to be rewired, the job consists of the operations listed below. Completely free access is available throughout the building, but work on the sub-main distribution cables cannot commence until all the existing installation has been removed.
   i) On graph paper draw a bar chart of the programme needed to complete the job in the least time.
   ii) Show by means of the chart the number of men required on the job each week.

Item		Time (pair-men-weeks)
A	Removal of first floor wiring	1
B	Removal of ground floor wiring	1.5
C	Install conduits, first floor	2
D	Install conduits, ground floor	3
E	Install sub-main cables	3
F	Install main switchgear	2
G	Install wiring, first floor	0.5
H	Install wiring, ground floor	1
I	Install light fittings, first floor	0.5
J	Install light fittings, ground floor	1
K	Install accessories, first floor	0.5
L	Install accessories, ground floor	0.5
M	Test and hand over	0.5

(C & G 'C')

6 Imagine you have been placed in charge of an electrical installation work force. Describe your actions and state the reasons for them when you:
   i) first arrive on site some days in advance of your work force,
   ii) discover that the drawing contains a possible error,
   iii) realise that the drawing does not show the position of emergency lighting fittings other than exit signs,
   iv) receive a wooden case containing light fittings which has obviously been damaged in transit by the carrier.
                                                        (C & G 'C')

7 i) A technician electrician on a large construction site is required to implement the safety precautions to be taken by the group of electricians for whom he is responsible. List **six** measures which should be taken to ensure satisfactory safety standards on the site.
   ii) Draw a labelled diagram to show how a suitable supply for portable electrical tools may be obtained from a 240 V supply on a construction site.   (C & G 'C')

8 Briefly explain the action that should be taken by a technician electrician in charge of the electrical work being carried out on a building site in the event of **each** of the following labour problems arising.
   i) A group of electricians request that a meeting be held to discuss an alleged grievance.
   ii) The daily work output of a particular group of electricians is much below that of other groups on the site.
   iii) An electrician alleges that the standing scaffold provided by the main contractor is unsafe.
   iv) An electrician is persistently late in reporting for work.   (C & G 'C')

9 i) Explain clearly the difference between an electrical contract being carried out as a 'lump sum contract' compared with a contract carried out on a 'bill of quantities'.
   ii) Describe the administrative actions that should be taken by a technician electrician in charge of electrical installation work on a site if the contract is being conducted on a bill of quantities.   (C & G 'C')

10 Draw a critical path network for the installation of lighting, block storage heating and power services in a new house showing such items of other trades' work as are relevant to the electrical installation. Assume that the construction is traditional with solid ground floor, timbered first floor and plastered walls.   (C & G 'C')

11 Prepare notes for guidance to be given by a site foreman to a job/shop representative (shop steward) in order to ensure good labour relations on a site. The areas to be covered should include:
   i) clocking on and off routines,
   ii) tea and meal breaks,
   iii) washing and changing facilities,
   iv) grievance and disputes procedure,
   v) meetings of men,
   vi) redundancy procedure.   (C & G 'C')

12 Variations frequently occur during the progress of an electrical contract for a new building.
   i) Explain fully what is meant by the term 'variation'.
   ii) List the details which should be forwarded to the electrical contractor's office from the site giving all relevant information regarding a variation that has been verbally requested on site.   (C & G 'C')

13 A standby generating set is to be installed in a building in which some reconstruction work is required. The estimated time for each activity involved is shown below.

Activity detail		Time (days)
A	Clearing site prior to laying foundations	1
B	Completion of site clearing	2
C	Foundation work	2
D	Construction of walls	2
E	Cabling to existing switchgear	3
F	Installation of set	2
G	Installation of ancillary apparatus	2
H	Electrical connections	1
I	Testing and commissioning	1

The cabling work cannot be started until all the site is cleared and the set cannot be installed until all constructional work has been completed.
   i) Draw a network diagram for the programme.
   ii) Determine the minimum time necessary for completion.
   iii) State what effect, if any, there would be on the total programme time, if the time taken to carry out the cabling to the existing switchgear were increased to five days.
                                                        (C & G 'C')

Projects (with answers)

1 Village hall

The building is of brick construction with plaster finish in the larger room and wall tiles in the kitchen. The floor is floor boards on supporting timber joists. Access is available into the gabled roof space. A 240 V single-phase a.c. supply is brought into the kitchen by means of two core metal sheathed cable.

Assignment
Figure 11.9 shows the electrical layout of the hall, drawn to scale.
State:
1 i) the length and width of the larger room (m),
   ii) the area of the kitchen (m²),
   iii) the total floor area of the complete building.

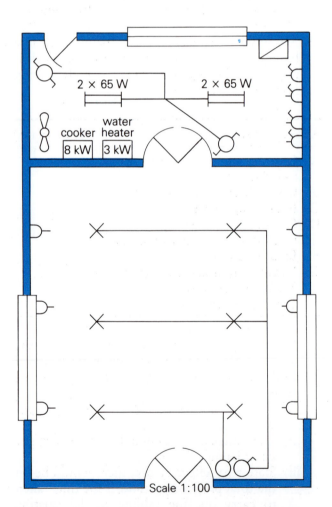

Figure 11.9 Electrical layout of village hall with kitchen. Scale 1:100.

2 State briefly, giving your reasons, the type of wiring system that could be used, bearing in mind cost and finished appearance.
3 Draw a schematic wiring diagram of the complete installation showing the incoming supply cable, supply authority fuse and neutral link, meter and the consumer's control unit, including the number of outgoing circuits and their current ratings.
   Show the earthing arrangements and conductor sizes if it is a PME system.
4 State what each symbol on the plan represents.
5 State the tests that should be carried out in accordance with the I.E.E. Regulations in the recommended sequence.
6 It was found that when an electric fire was plugged into one of the sockets in the kitchen, the fire element was still 'live' to earth when the socket was switched off. Give the most likely reason for this and state the remedy for it.
7 State briefly the work to be carried out at the 'first fix' and the stage of the building work at which this would be done. Also state the work to be carried out for the second fix and again at what stage of the building work.

Answers
1 i) 8.5 m × 7.5 m.
   ii) 7.5 × 3 = 22.5 m².
   iii) 11.5 × 7.5 = 86.25 m².
2 Since there are no adverse conditions such as high temperature, mechanical damage, oil, grease, etc., a PVC insulated and sheath cable would be in order. It would be advisable to give further protection where liable to damage, that is, through brickwork or when buried in walls. This system would lend itself to being installed in the roof space for the lighting and under the floorboards for the socket outlets. It would also keep down the overall costs of the installation.
3 The total floor is less than 100 m² so that the socket outlets can be wired on one circuit.
   The lighting would be on one circuit.
   Water heater on one circuit.
   Cooker on one circuit.
   It would require a four-way consumer unit and since they are conventional circuits and there are no extenuating circumstances, the protection and the cable current ratings can be calculated from the ratings.
   i) Lighting load is less than 1200 W, so that a 5 A fuse and 1 mm² cable would suffice.
   ii) Socket outlets wired on open ring circuits with 2.5 mm² cables. The extractor fan could

be connected to the ring via a fuse-spur unit.
iii) Water heater would require a 15 A fuse with 1.5 mm² cable.
iv) With diversity the cooker current would be 22.5 A so that a 30 A fuse with 6 mm² cable would suffice.
The supply authority would normally 'bring in' the standard small consumer supply with 100 A fuse 'cut out'. This means the 'meter tails' would be 25 mm² phase and neutral conductors, 16 mm² for the earth conductor which would be connected to main earth terminal and linked to the incoming neutral at the supply point. The bonding conductors to other service pipes would be 10 mm².

5 i) Continuity of all c.p.c.s and bonding.
ii) Continuity of all ring circuit conductors.
iii) Insulation between phase and neutral and these to earth.
iv) Polarity of all switches, sockets and screw lampholders.
v) Earth loop impedance.
vi) Earth electrode resistance.
vii) Operation of RCDs.

6 The polarity of the wiring to this socket is incorrect. The live or phase conductors have been connected to the neutral terminal so that they are not switched. It is only a single pole switch. The L and N conductors need changing over. No. (iv) test above should have diagnosed this fault!

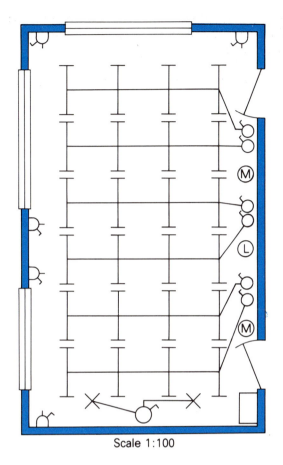

Scale 1:100

Figure 11.10 Plan of a general office. Scale 1:100.

2 Small general office

The drawing shows the electrical layout of an office. There is access to the roof space above the ceiling. The lighting is to be supplied by three final circuits. The luminaires are rated at 80 W each and have an efficiency of 60 lumen per watt.
The socket outlets are to be supplied from the skirting trunking which is fixed around the perimeter of the office.
There are two photocopiers, each rated at 250 W. Figure 11.10 shows a scale plan of a small general office.

1 i) State the length, width and area of the room.
ii) List what each symbol represents.
2 Make a theoretical wiring diagram for the installation.
3 Make a complete list of all the materials required for the installation including:
i) cable size and approximate lengths of each,

ii) the number of ways and the current rating of the protection devices in the distribution board.
4 From the information given, calculate the general luminance in the room if the utilisation factor is 0.65 and the maintenance factor is 0.8.

3 Domestic dwelling

A house is to be built in a garden and is to have an electricity supply. The supply authority have notified the owner that it will be a 100 A single-phase and neutral supply brought by overhead conductors to the boundary of the ground which is some 50 metres from the house and that the owner must provide a suitable enclosure at that point.
Use sketches and diagrams for the following.

1 Give a brief description of the construction of the suitable enclosure.

2 Describe the switchgear which is to be installed in the enclosure, marking the authority and consumer property.

3 Describe the type and size of cable for underground supply, means of protection and depth.

4 State the means of earthing, distribution and excess current protection at house intake point. State cable and c.p.c. and earth conductor sizes.

5 Give details of preparing and terminating underground cable.

Answers to questions and answering hints

Introduction

This section provides you with the answers to the variety of questions and exercises given in the book. Always try a question or exercise yourself before you look at the answer. This will increase your understanding of the topic and give you practice in answering questions. If you are not sure of a particular answer, re-read the relevant section or chapter in the book to revise the work. You need to understand why a question has a particular answer, so that you can apply your understanding to similar types of question or exercise in your examinations and course assignments.

The book contains a variety of types of question and exercise. Find out the types of question that you will be expected to answer and their pattern. If possible, obtain past papers to support your work and revision. Some of the questions in the book require longer answers. We have provided hints on how to tackle these questions, and on the range of topics that you should include. Practise giving full answers to these questions and then check the answering hints to see that you have included all the relevant topics.

To revise a topic quickly you can also refer to the 'Check your understanding' sections given at the end of each chapter, and the list of key words with definitions given at the end of the book.

Most of the questions set in *Electrical Installation Technology and Practice* call for descriptions, explanations, sketches and diagrams. Questions at the end of each chapter are typical of these, some have been taken direct from past papers, while others are based on them.

The answers given are brief pointers and guidance as to where fuller information can be found in the appropriate chapter and figures, plus numerical answers when required. Bear in mind around

twenty minutes is allowed to answer each question.

In questions where precise values are called for such as current ratings, voltage drop, conductor resistance, disconnection time, enclosure capacities rating factors and so on, the question would state letter and figure number in the I.E.E. Regulations in order to enable the candidate to extract the required information to solve the question.

Hints to answering questions in examinations and course work

- Read all the questions carefully before you try anything. Make sure that you understand what each question is asking you to do.
- Plan the time that you will spend on each question. Use the marks as a guide: the more marks a question is worth, the more time it is worth spending on it.
- If you have a choice of questions, try to make your choice and stick to it. Don't change your mind half-way through the examination.
- Make sure that you earn all the 'easy' marks. Do not spend too long on a question you find difficult. Leave it; if you have time, you can try it again later when you have finished all the other questions.
- Keep an eye on the time. Make sure that you try all the questions you are required to answer.
- Always present your work as clearly as you can, whether you are writing or drawing. Make your work easy to follow for the examiner or assessor.
- Try and allow some time at the end to check your answers and improve them.

- In practical work, make sure that you understand what you are being asked to do by rereading the question before you start. Follow all instructions carefully.

Chapter 1

1 i)   Isolate, resuscitate, call for help.
   ii) Date, place, time, name, details, type of injury and aid.
   iii) Withdraw from use, holding for enquiry.
2 i)   See Figures 1.34, 1.35, 1.36.
   ii) Secure against movement.
        Do not stretch or overbalance.
3 i)   They are hollow walls. See Figure 1.37.
   ii) See Figure 1.37.
4 Use existing tubes, channels, voids where possible.
   Use existing old cables to draw in new ones.
5 i)   Do not cut or remove any load-bearing fabric.
        Remove only sufficient to accommodate cables etc.
   ii) See Figure 1.38.
6 i)   Ensure the circuit is not carrying current.
        Danger from excessive arc or flash as the current is broken.
   ii) (a) CO_2, (b) funnel shape of nozzle,
        (c) cooling with clean water.
7 i)   Moving parts, transmission by chains, belts, gears.
   ii) See Figures 1.1 to 1.4.
   iii) Use of mushroom head emergency buttons.
8 i)   On higher voltage circuits or when under supervision.
   ii) To ensure it is safe to carry out the work.
9 i) See Figure 1.16.
10 Push or pull away by clothing or dry material.
   Check for breathing, start resuscitation.
   Call for help and medical assistance.
11 See Figures 1.6–1.16, 1.25–1.30.
12 See Figure 1.24.
13 See Figure 1.20.
14 Isolate, ensure that it cannot be made live without your knowledge.

Chapter 2

1 $S = 12 \times 10^6$.
2 See Chapter 2, Figure 2.20 and Figure 2.21.
3 See diagram.

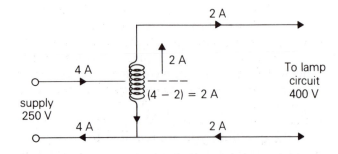

4 0.404 tesla.
5 0.00428/°C at 0°C.
6 i)   Eddy currents, hysteresis.
   ii) (a) Practically nil, (b) as the square of the load current.

7 See Chapter 2.
   i)   See Figure 2.10.
   ii) (a) Directly proportional,
        (b) inversely proportional.
   iii) $\dfrac{800}{3}$ = 270 V.

8 Resistance at 2000°C = $\dfrac{V^2}{W} = \dfrac{(240)^2}{60}$ = 960 Ω.

   $\dfrac{960}{R_2} = \dfrac{1 + (0.005 \times 2000)}{1 + (0.005 \times 20)}$

   $R_2 = \dfrac{960 \times 1.1}{11}$ = 96 Ω

   Current at 20°C = $\dfrac{240}{96}$ = 2.5 A

9 iii) (a) Maximum, (b) 0.707 × maximum,
        (c) 0.637 × maximum, (d) 2 × maximum.
10 0.7 tesla. See sketch.

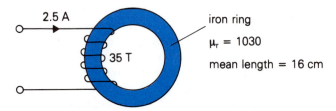

11 Initial resistance of coils = $\dfrac{V}{R} = \dfrac{500}{2}$ = 250 Ω at 15°C

   $\dfrac{R_1}{R_2} = \dfrac{1 + \alpha + 1}{1 + \alpha + 2}$

   $\dfrac{250}{R_2} = \dfrac{1 + (0.0043 \times 15)}{1 + (0.0043 \times 45)}$

   $\dfrac{250}{R_2} = \dfrac{1.0642}{1.1926}$

   $R_2 = \dfrac{250 \times 1.1926}{1.0642}$
      = 280 Ω

   Current at higher temperature = $\dfrac{500 \text{ V}}{280 \text{ Ω}}$ = 1.786 A

12 i)   (a) Z = 2000 Ω, (b) 6.3 H.
   ii) 988 Ω.
13 i)   Storing of an electric charge (shock danger).
   ii) A high value resistor is connected internally across the terminal to discharge the capacitor slowly.
14 i)   (a) 20 Ω, (b) 12 A, (c) 144 V, (d) 192 V.

   ii) $pf = \cos \phi = \dfrac{R}{Z} = \dfrac{12}{20}$ = 0.6 lag
        ϕ = 52°
   See diagram.

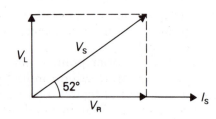

Chapter 3

1 C.p.c. not connected in consumer unit – capacitance between cable cores of live and c.p.c. conductors.

2 i) Ease of stepping up and stepping down voltage and switching.

   ii) (a) Current at 240 V = $\dfrac{100 \times 1000}{240}$ = 417 A

   (b) Current at 33 000 V = $\dfrac{100 \times 1000}{33\,000}$ = 3.3 A

   (a) Power loss = I^2R = 17.4 kW
   (b) Power loss = I^2R = 1.09 W

3 i) 0 A.
   ii) 150 A.
   iii) 318 V.
   iv) See chapter notes.
   v) Nil, unless the load becomes unbalanced – then the phase voltages would be upset.

4 i) Dual Vs 415 and 240, smaller cables, balancing of loads.
   ii) (a) 0.75
   (b) Connection of wattmeter, voltmeter and ammeter,

   $pf = \dfrac{W}{VA}$.

5 ii) (a) Sum total current in all conductors = 300 A.
   (b) Sum total current in all conductors = 150 A.

6 i) None.
   ii) (a) They would be upset, (b) none, (c) none.
   iii) The one conductor would carry the whole of the circuit current causing overheating and possible fire risk.

7 iii) (a) 0.0833 A, 48 V, 192 V; (b) 0.512 A, 240 V each.

8 i) Reduction in size of long transmission conductors.
   ii) 400, 275, 132, 33, 11 kV down to 415/240 V.
   See Figure 3.1 and key to diagram for further information.

9 28 A.

10 $\dfrac{\text{Normal load}}{\text{Total connected load}}$; cooker and socket outlets

11 i) See Figure 3.5.
   ii) 1.732:1.
   iii) 17.32 A.

12 See Figure 3.28.

13 42.

14 a) (i) Ambient temperature = 0.94, grouping = 0.8,
   (ii) 39.89 A, (iii) 6 mm², (iv) 5.75 V.
   b) (i) temperature = 0.97, grouping = 0.8, fuse = 0.725,
   (ii) 53.3 A, (iii) 10 mm², (iv) 3.45 V.

15 See Figure 3.11.

16 300 A.

17 1. To create the high start voltage. 2. To limit the circuit current.

18 See notes and tables in Chapter 3.

19 See Figure 3.28 and chapter notes.

20 See Figure 3.24 and chapter notes.

21 See Figure 3.30 and chapter notes.

22 See Figure 3.28 and chapter notes.

23 See Figure 3.26 and chapter notes.

24 i) 20 customers only would lose supply.
   ii) Nil.
   iii) Phase voltage would be unequal, damage to appliances.

Chapter 4

1 See Figures 4.7 and 4.17.

2 i) Plugs on flexible cables, lampholders, ceiling roses. To support weights and secure cable sheaths.
   ii) Excess heat and inductive effect.

3 i) Cracking and softening of sheath and conductors.
   ii) Able to withstand higher conductor temperatures.
   iii) 0.1 Ω.

4 i) Where metal sheath is used as return conductor, usually with MIMS cables.
   ii) Saving of conductor material, has a neat appearance, etc.
   iii) When fed by private generating plants where there is isolation from the public supply.

5 i) (a) 32 mm, (b) it only carries the out of balance I.
   ii) 75 × 38 mm.

6 i) (a) Ease of rewire, (b) cancellation of fluxes.
   ii) (a) To draw in cables on long or difficult runs.
   (b) Neater appearance, less likelihood of damage to insulation.
   (c) $2\frac{1}{2}$ times diameter of conduit.

7 i) See notes in chapter.
   ii) (a) MICC with PVC sheath and flameproof terminations, (b) conduits with skirting and underfloor trunking for office machines, (c) PVC conduits, (d) PVC SWA cables, (e) overhead bus-bar trunking.

8 Joints should be made by 'looping in' at accessories and available for inspection.
   Bonding (see notes).

9 See Figure 4.8.
   Where more and larger cables have to be installed.

10 See Figure 4.13.

11 See Figure 4.27 and 4.28.

12 See Figure 4.28 and enlarge on it.

13 See Figure 4.10 for (i) and (ii).
   iii) Should be free to expand and contract fitting of expansion joints on longer runs.

14 See Figure 4.22 and notes.

15 See Figure 4.13 for (i), (ii) and (iii).
   iv) Barriers fitted at floor levels to prevent updraught concentration of heat.
   v) Equal number of floors or room on each phase.

16 i) Flexible where frequent movement of equipment is involved.
   ii) Similar to permanent installation, with extra protection against movement of equipment and plant.
   iii) Similar to permanent, with extra earth monitoring of flexible cables.
   iv) Three-monthly intervals.
   v) In high risk and wet areas.

17 i) Barriers fitted at floor levels.
   ii) Slope on floor to soakaway area in case of oil leak.
   iii) Sealed flameproof fittings.
   iv) Termination against ingress of vapours.

18 Chemical action from soils and atmospheres
   i) Use PVC sheath on cable and sleeve at termination.
   ii) Suitable paintwork, sited or shielded against extreme weather conditions.
   iii) Use of cathodic protector.

19 See Figure 4.14 and expand to joint box.
   See Figure 4.7 with the use of high temperature seals.

20 i) Make provision for inspection places so that cables can be withdrawn and replaced.

ii) Suspension from main ceiling.
iii) Short length of flexible conduit to be inserted.
21 i) and (ii) See Figure 4.20.
iii) Smeared with bitumen type covering where the outer cover is stripped back at termination.

Chapter 5

1 See Chapter 5. See Figure 5.1; intake position, bathrooms, kitchens.
2 i) To ensure that disconnection operates within the disconnection time.
$$I = V_0$$
where $Z_s = V_E + \dfrac{R_1}{Z_s} + R_2$.
R_1 = phase conductor, R_2 = c.p.c.
ii) (a) Risk of shock and fire.
(b) Fit r.c.d. or lower Z_s.
3 i) Three electrode method with ammeters and voltmeters $R = V/I$.
ii) Deeper, extra electrode outside area of earth R.
iii) Below ground level with cover, notices.
4 i) Authority cut out, meter, consumer unit, r.c.d., E terminal, earth electrode.
ii) Causes unbalance in the sensitive r.c.d. (around 30 mA).
iii) Outside which the R cannot be practically measured.
iv) 0.45s.
5 i) E and N connected by a link from main earth terminal to neutral by authority.
ii) See in Chapter 5.
iii) (a) Better Z_E, less cost and maintenance.
(b) Earth faults become s/c faults, less cost in earthing equipment. See earthing methods Figure 5.1.
6 i) (a) 40 A, (b) 6.4 kW, (c) 160 V.
ii) It would not operate for a very long time.
Danger of shock and fire.
7 i) For full details see information in the chapter.
ii) C.p.c., earth conductor, earth electrode.
iii) Protect against mechanical damage, mechanical clamp, label, protect against corrosion.
iv) Criss-cross grid framework, horizontal plate, length of metallic tapes. See Figure 5.1 and Figure 5.12.
8 i) Short-circuit conductor at one end, instruments at other.
ii) (a) 20 mV, (b) 16.67 m.
iii) 80 MΩ.
9 i) Operating current against the time for operation.
ii) Fuse to BS 3036
HBC BS 88 or BS 1361
CB to BS 3871.
iii) (a) 0.4 s, hand-held appliances and machines.
(b) 5 s.
iv) $S = \dfrac{\sqrt{I^2\,t}}{k} = \dfrac{\sqrt{(200)^2 \times 0.42}}{115} = 1.127\ mm^2$
10 i) (a) Conductor between consumer E terminal and electrode.
(b) Conductor joining together all equipment to be earthed.
(c) Total impedance of consumer earth circuit.
(d) Final connection to general mass of earth.
(e) Connecting of all metal work required to be earthed to common conductor.
ii) That outside which it is not practicable to measure.

11 See Figure 5.2 and Figure 5.17.
12 i) See Figure 5.14.
ii) (a) and (b) See Figure 5.14.
iii) 500 V d.c., 0.5 MΩ.
13 i) (a) 24 A, (b) 4.624 kW,
(c) insufficient current to operate fuse, conduit would be 'live'.
ii) (a) 120 A sufficient to melt fuse.
iii) Zero.
14 i) Common E–N return to supply transformer.
ii) See Figure 5.1.
iii) (a) Lower Z_E, quicker and safer operation of excess current device, no need to provide separate electrodes.
iv) Consumer's earthing could become live if a break in the E–N conductor occurs. Earthing at multiple points.
15 i) More sensitive and quicker-acting in the event of earth leakage circuit faults, particularly in areas where no E terminal is provided.
ii) and (iii) See Figure 5.10 and 5.11.
16 i) See Figure 5.7.
ii) 192 A.
17 i) Time delay between fault and operation of excess current device results in excessive heating of cable conductors.
ii) The slower acting devices need to have a lower c.p.c. resistance to operate within the time limit.
18 i) See Figure 5.20 and chapter notes.
ii) 75 MV A, 104 kV A.
19 Size of c.p.c. $S = \dfrac{\sqrt{(If) \times t}}{k}$
where S is in mm^2, If = fault current (A), t = time (s), k = temperature factor.
20 $S = \dfrac{\sqrt{(175)^2 \times 4}}{143}$
$= 2.45\ mm^2$

Chapter 6

1 (i) 500 lux, (ii) 358 lux, (iii) ratio lumens per watt.
2 See Chapter 6, (i) zero current point, (ii) see Figure 6.22, (iii) see Figure 6.23.

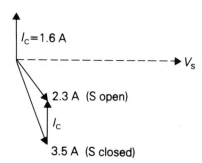

3 $\cos\phi\ (pf) = \dfrac{W}{VA} = \dfrac{440}{240 \times 3.5} = 0.521$
$\phi = 58°C$
$A_1 = 2.3\ A$

4 i) (a) Higher efficiency than filament lamps, (b) long

restart period up to full brilliance after switch on or interruption of supply; higher cost.
ii) Losses in ballast equipment.
iii) Light meter using selenium cell with micro-ammeter (lux).
5 i) Moving parts appearing to be stationary.
ii) Danger of being caught in revolving machines.
iii) See Figure 6.13 and notes.
6 See Figure 6.16.
7 See Figure 6.26.
8 Tap on the water outlet side. Tap on inlet side.
9 i) Discharge resistors.
ii) 'Off' position at the top, clearly marked position, etc.
iii) Should be contained within fitting or shrouded.
iv) Correctly protected against excess current, earthed, cord grips, flexible cables.
v) Calculated current × 1.8.
10 See Figure 6.27.
11 See Figure 6.21.
12 i) See Figure 6.11.
ii) 100 lumens per watt.
iii) 0.81, 0.288.
iv) Dangerous radiation.
13 See Figure 6.9 and notes.
14 i) See Projects. (a) 36 tubes, (b) six rows of six per row.
ii) (a) 17.55 A, (ii) 75 pence.
15 i) See Figure 6.16.
ii) Back to a consumer unit controlled by a time clock.
16 i) Possible strengthening of floor construction or spreading the weight over a larger area.
ii) Flexible cable to a fused outlet unit.
17 See Figure 6.14.
18 See Figure 6.19.
19 122.5 cd. See Figure 6.4.

Chapter 7

1 See chapter notes and Appendix A.
2 i) Low resistance would result in excess current.
ii) Loss of back e.m.f. causing excess current.
iii) Very low current in field coils which causes armature to race.
Possible damage from centrifugal forces.
3 i) Small poles placed between the main poles of the machine.
ii) To compensate for the distortion of the main flux which would cause a shift in the neutral axis.
In series with the armature.
4 i) $W = 2\pi NT$ where N is r.p.s., T is torque (N m).

$$T = \frac{W}{2\pi N} = \frac{20\,000}{6.28 \times 15} = 212 \text{ N m}$$

$$\text{Power pinpoint to motor} = \frac{20\,000}{0.9} = 22\,222 \text{ W}$$

$$I_L = \frac{P}{\sqrt{3}V_L \cos\varnothing} = \frac{22\,222}{1.732 \times 415 \times 0.8} = 38.6 \text{ A}$$

5 iii) (a) 240 V, (b) 415 V.
6 i) copper, (ii) brass, (iii) carbon, (iv) iron lamination, (v) copper.
7 i) (a) Reverse either winding connection.
(b) Reverse any two line of supply line connections.
ii) Autotransformer, Star–Delta.

iii) $\dfrac{\text{Synchronous speed} - \text{actual rotor speed} \times 100\%}{\text{synchronous speed}}$

8 i) 14.18 A, (ii) 19.16 Ω, (iii) 270 V, (iv) 15 A.
9 i) V and A meters, 2 wattmeter method, brake test rig.
ii) (a) $2\pi NT$, (b) $W_1 + W_2$,

(c) $\dfrac{W}{V A} = \dfrac{P_{\text{in}}}{P_{\text{out}}}$

iii) Current coils in series (two conductors) voltage coil ends to conductor without current coil.
10 i) High start I_s.
ii) Flux cancellation.
iii) Tapping connection and secondary coil.
11 i) To ensure that the magnetic flux are phased to assist each other.
ii) See Star and Delta connections in chapter and Appendix A.
iii) (a) 40 A, (b) 24 A.

Chapter 8

1 Inspection of brushgear, commutator segments, extraction of carbon dust and deposits.
2 See Chapters 2 and 8. To reduce reluctance of magnetic circuit.
ii) Worn bearings.
3 i) High voltage causes damage to devices.
ii) Resistance reverse polarity test.
4 i) Two sets of contacts on 'inch' button.
5 To allow heavy start current. See notes.
Build up heat is a natural delay.
6 i) Induced from stator.
ii) (a) Magnetic force, (b) zero voltage.
iii) Higher turns ratio.
7 i) Disconnect the links, test for insulation with 500 V megger.
ii) Either a ductor or heavy duty battery, A + V meter

$$R = \frac{V}{I} \Omega$$

iii) Collapse of flux inducing high e.m.f.s.
8 i) (a) 207.5 V, 207.5 V, (b) 425 V, 207.5 V, 207.5 V.
ii) (a) Motor continues to run with excess current in windings. (b) It would not start.
9 i) Straight edge and feeler gauge.
ii) Straight edge or string.
iii) Use of a pulley drawer.
iv) Use of feeler gauge at four points.
10 i) Voltmeter in parallel, ammeter in series.
Wattmeter with I and V coils.
ii) Current coils to be shorted out.
iii) 0.75, 83%
11 1.3 kW, 8 A, 2850 rev/min.
12 Coupling, gears, belts, chains.
13 i) Clean atmosphere, restricted access.
ii) Clean atmosphere, general purpose.
iii) Dirty conditions, metallic dusts, oils present.
iv) High temperature, dirty location to clean and cooler atmosphere.
v) Outside in sheltered location.
vi) Flammable or explosive liquids or vapours present.
14 See chapter notes and diagrams Figure 8.22.

15 (i) and (ii) See Chapter 7 figures, (iii) centrifugal switch and relay.

16 (i) Iron and copper (I^2R).

17 See Figures 8.13 and 8.14.

18 Grain dust entering motor, getting into air gap, reducing ventilation.

19 Normal star delta with protection devices.
See Appendix A
Automatic would require a relay which operates when the motor current falls and cause change over to delta position.

20 i) Excess current delay device operating too quickly.
ii) Short circuits on rotor resistance.
iii) Breakdown of/or low insulation resistance on windings.
iv) Possible short circuit, insulation check required.

21 See Figures 8.17, 8.18 and 8.19.

Chapter 9

1 i) (a) Chemical action due to excretion from animals, ammonia, etc; excessive water due to hosing, damage to installation by cattle. (b) Petrol vapours (flammable), possible damage from vehicles.
ii) (a) All insulated systems using PVC conduits or PVC sheathed cables, if metallic protection is necessary it must be protected against corrosion and out of reach of cattle. (b) MICC or PVC armoured cables using flameproof fittings near pumps.

2 See Figure 9.11.

3 i) See Figures 9.19 and 9.20.

4 See Figure 9.25.

5 See Figure 9.23.

6 See Figures 9.19 and 9.20.

7 i) See Figure 23.
ii) (a) 12 A, (b) 4 A.
iii) 0.167 Ω.

8 i) Overhead catenary system or underground PVC PVC SWA cable dependent on obstructions etc.
ii) (a) Out of reach of livestock, use of mainly PVC systems, (b) switchgear and distribution at incoming supply point.

9 See Figures 9.5 and 9.6 and notes.

10 See Figure 9.7 and notes.

11 See Figure 9.24 and notes.

12 See Figures 9.25 and 9.6 and notes.

13 i) Emergency only circuits to reduce load and hence size of standby set.
ii) To ensure the correct supply voltage is present.
iii) Use of staggered cable support pins to prevent excess strain on cable.
iv) Diesel fumes.

14 See Figure 9.7 and notes.

15 See Figure 9.5 and notes.

16 i) Animal excretion, ammonia etc., cattle, farm machinery, weather conditions.
ii) (a) PVC conduits, MICC with PVC cover, (b) galvanised steel conduit out of reach or PVC PVCSWA cables.

17 See Figure 9.4.

18 See motor enclosures and possibly Figure 9.2.

Chapter 10

1 i) Energy is the product of power and times, i.e. kW h.
ii) Current coil in one line conductor.

Voltage coil between line and neutral to read phase V. $P = 3 \times$ the wattmeter reading.
iii) $P = \sqrt{3}\ V_L I_L \cos \varnothing = 1.732 \times 415 \times 30 \times 0.8 = 17.25$ kW
Energy = $17.25 \times 24 = 414$ kW h

2 i) Reduce size of instrument, cut down Vs and Is to meter.
ii) No need to interrupt the supply.
iii) $I_L = 278$ A, C/T 300/5 A.

3 i) 92.68.
ii) 67.5 and 0.89.

4 i) Pf correction on the load itself.
ii) Pf correction at income point on his installation.
iii) Switch off non-essential loads when demand is rising too fast.

5 i) To pay towards the authority's outlay for the supply.
ii) Taking of supply when the supply plant is not fully loaded.
iii) Initial cost of supply – heavy cables and switchgear for intermittent loads.
iv) To make the small consumer pay higher charges per unit, the fair share of cost of initial outlay by authority.

6 M.i.; gravity weight, piston and cylinder compression.

7 See Figure 10.5.

8 i) (a) 550 Ω, (b) 1 kΩ, (c) 2.5 kΩ (series), (d) 0.2 Ω, (e) 0.1 Ω, (f) 0.04 Ω (shunts).

9 See Figure 10.6 and notes.

10 i) Zero, ii) zero, iii) 500 W.

11 i) Adjustment of the battery voltage to its standard value for accurate R measurement.
ii) Battery, rectifier in the coil current.

12 Energy depends on time.
See Figures 10.19 and 10.20.

13 i) Improvement of power factor.

14 See Figure 10.17.

15 See Figure 10.23.

16 See Figure 10.16.

17 See Figures 10.13 and 10.16.

18 i) See Figure 10.9.
ii) $\dfrac{R_1}{R_2} = \dfrac{\text{Standard } R_3}{\text{Unknown } R_4} = 15\ \Omega$

Chapter 11

1 All the time that workmen are idle whilst being paid, money is being lost. Ensure that the work and the materials are available to keep them fully occupied.

2 Good working knowledge of all aspects of the work and able to organise the labour force fully.

3 See chapter notes regarding types of contracts.

4 See chapter notes regarding overhead, transport, insurance, profit, etc.

5 See diagram and procedure for bar chart construction.

6 Examine working conditions, facilities, storage, security available, check with main contractor or client.
Report to supplier and head office.

7 Refer to chapter notes.

8 Advance details of grievance notice to head office.
To be held in duty or off duty time?
See if there are unforeseen difficulties in the work.
Is there a 'troublemaker'?
Examine and discuss with main contractor.

9 See chapter notes for information on these contracts.
Ensure that no quantities have been omitted, that the quantities listed are available when required.

10 Ensure that the carpenter lays 'plinths' of sufficient strength on the first floor.
All cable and protective covers are in position before plastering.

11 This question calls for local knowledge of employment conditions and trade union procedure.

12 Any work outside the original contract agreement.
It must be received **in writing** from the client or his agent. It can then be 'costed' and details forwarded to head office for sanction.

13 i) Make a bar chart showing duration of all operations, the ones which can run concurrently and those consecutively.
ii) Completion time 12 days.
iii) Increased by an extra 1 day.

Electrical symbols and abbreviations

Quantity	Symbol	Unit	Unit symbol
Capacitance	C	farad	F
Capacitive reactance	X_c	microfarad	μF
		ohm	Ω
Charge or Quantity of electricity	Q	coulomb	C
Current	I	ampere	A
		milliampere	mA
Current density in a conductor	J	amperes per metre	A/m
Potential difference (p.d.)	V	volt	V
		millivolt	mV
Electromotive force (e.m.f.)	E	volt	V
Energy	W	joule	J
Force	F	newton	N
Frequency	f	hertz	Hz
Impedance	Z	ohm	Ω
Inductance	L	henry	H
Inductive reactance	X_L	ohm	Ω
Magnetic flux	Φ	weber	Wb
Magnetic flux density	B	tesla	T
Permeability			
free space	μ_o	henry per metre	H/m
relative	μ_r	—	—
Permittivity			
free space	ε_o	farad per metre	F/m
relative	ε_r	—	—
Power	P	watt	W
Reactance	X	ohm	Ω
Reactive volt-amperes	Q	VAr	var
Reluctance	S	ampere per weber	A/Wb
Resistance	R	ohm	Ω
Resistivity	ρ	ohm metre	Ω m
Temperature coefficient	α	ohm per degree centigrade	Ω/°C
Torque	T	newton metre	N m
Illumination	E	lux	lx
Luminous flux	Φ	lumen	lm
Luminous intensity	I	candela	cd

Key words

Accepter circuit one which accepts maximum current at resonant frequency.

Accessory a device other than current using equipment associated with the wiring of an installation.

Alternating current (a.c) current which reverses direction at a regular rate.

Ambient temperature temperature of air where equipment is installed.

Anode a positive electrode.

Appliance an item of current using equipment other than a light fitting or separate motor.

Armature moving parts of apparatus due to electro-magnetism.

Autotransformer transformer with a single winding with tapping off connections.

Ballast equipment to stabilise the current in a fluorescent or discharge lamp circuit.

Bar chart a chart showing the times and dates of the various operations on an installation.

Bonding applies to pipes and other exposed metal work connected to form a common earth potential.

Bridge circuit a circuit of four resistors arranged to measure an unknown resistance.

Brush spring a spring to tension carbon brushes on d.c. or a.c. machines.

Busbar a copper bar which forms a common connection between several circuits.

Busbar trunking heavy copper conductors, usually bare, fitted in a metallic enclosure erected either horizontally or vertically to supply different floors or machines from tap-off points.

Cable, armoured a cable protected by steel wires or tape against damage.

Capacitor equipment which stores an electric charge.

Catenary a wire for supporting the suspension of an overhead cable.

Cathode a negative electrode.

Circuit an arrangement of conductors for the purpose of carrying current.

Circuit breaker a device for automatically opening a circuit under abnormal conditions.

Circuit protective conductor (c.p.c.) a conductor connecting exposed metal work of equipment to the main earthing terminal of an installation.

Commutator revolving device fitted to the shaft of a machine for reversing the current at the correct instant.

Conduit a tube for enclosing cables to protect against mechanical damage.

Continuity test a test to ensure there is no break or high resistance in a conductor.

Crimping a method of securing connection and termination of a conductor by compression.

Critical path analysis (c.p.a.) a study of the logical sequence of tasks on an installation.

Current transformer apparatus for reducing current to be measured by an ammeter.

Dash pot a device for delaying the operation of a circuit breaker mechanism.

Dead circuits disconnected from a live supply or at earth potential.

Delta a method of connecting the ends of the phases of a three-phase winding.

Detector a device for automatically opening or closing a circuit when conditions change, that is, detection of fire or intruders.

Diode a device with two electrodes for rectification.

Direct current (d.c.) current which does not change direction.

Discharge lamp a lamp where the light is produced by the passage of current through a gas.

Discrimination relates to the time–current characteristics of protection devices.

Distribution board a board from which connections are taken off for the distribution of electrical circuits, usually through fuses or circuit breakers.

Diversity relationship between the normal and the total connected load.

Duct a passage in which cable may be drawn.

Earth concentric wiring a system where one or more insulated conductors are surrounded by a common return conductor.

Earth conductor joins the main earth terminal to the earth electrode.

Earth electrode final connection with the general mass of earth by rods, tapes, etc.

Earth fault abnormal passage of current to general mass of earth.

Earth leakage circuit breaker a device which operates when excess current to earth flows.

Earth loop impedance impedance of the earthing circuit of a consumer's and/or the supply authority's installation.

Eddy current current induced in metals by the alternating magnetisation.

Electrode conductor carrying current into or out of a liquid, gas, or to another solid conductor of a different material.

Electrode boiler equipment for the heating of water by the passage of current through it.

Energy product of power and time measured in kilowatt-hours.

Excitation production of the magnetic flux of a machine.

Extraneous metalwork to be bonded but not part of the installation proper.

Face plate starter device to control the start current of a d.c. motor and provide electrical protection.

Farad unit of capacitance.

Feeler gauge set of calibrated blades for the measurement of gaps.

Field winding the winding which produces the magnetic flux in the yoke or stator of a machine.

Final circuit circuit which supplies current direct to the termination at the appliance or machine or its switchgear.

Flameproof equipment will not cause ignition of gases.

Frequency the number of complete cycles per second of an a.c. supply, measured in hertz.

Fuse factor relationship between the current rating and the current at which it operates (melts or blows).

Gate electrode the electrode which regulates the flow of current in a thyristor, transistor or triac.

Grid high voltage transmission system.

Grouping related to the number of cables contained in an enclosure or in close contact with each other.

Hazardous relating to areas in which there are potential dangers to the installation of equipment and wiring.

High voltage systems over 1000 V.

Immersion heater heater where the elements are immersed in the liquid to be heated.

Impedance total opposition to the current flow in a circuit.

Indicator board device to indicate the origin of a call or detection of fire or intrusion.

Induction motor a motor where the stator only is connected to the supply and induces the current in the rotor.

Intake position point on a consumer's installation where the supply is brought in.

Invertor device for converting direct into alternating current by the use of thyristors.

Isolator a device for manually opening or closing a circuit on no-load or low currents.

Live points on an installation which are above earth potential.

Lumen unit of luminous flux produced by a luminaire.

Lux unit of illumination on a surface in lumen per square metre.

Main earth terminal terminal or bar provided for connection of all c.p.c.s and earthing conductors.

Maximum demand the maximum current or kV A in a consumer's installation.

Micrometer instrument for mechanical measurement to a fine degree of accuracy.

Neutral conductor common return wire of an a.c. supply system which is connected to earth at the supply transformer.

P.M.E. a method of earthing where the neutral conductor is connected to the earthing conductor.

Point (in wiring) termination of the fixed wiring to supply luminaires and appliances.

Power factor ratio of the power in a circuit to the volt-amperes.

Primary cell a source of electrical energy which cannot be renewed by passing of current in the opposite direction (charging).

P.V.C. a polyvinyl chloride compound used for the insulation and/or sheath of a cable.

Radial circuit a distribution system where the circuit cable radiates from the distribution centre to the apparatus.

Rectification conversion of an alternating to a direct current.

Rejector circuit one which rejects current at resonant frequency.

Residual current device device to disconnect a circuit where there is an unbalance of current in supply conductors.

Ring circuit a circuit in the form of a ring which starts from and returns to its point of origin.

Rupturing capacity the kV A rating of switchgear above which it will rupture or break down.

Secondary cell a cell whose energy may be renewed by charging, that is, passing of current in the opposite direction.

Shaded pole of a motor a copper band placed on the poles of a single-phase motor to produce a starting torque by phase shift.

Short circuit a connection caused by breakdown of insulation or otherwise to allow a very heavy current to flow.

Simmerstat a device used for power control of heating appliances.

Slip rings brass rings fitted to the shaft of a machine to provide a connection to the revolving windings.

Slip speed difference in speed between the rotating magnetic field of the stator and the rotor actual speed in an a.c. motor.

Smoothing the levelling of the ripple on the d.c. output to a rectified a.c. supply.

Solenoid a coil used for producing a magnetic flux.

Space factor ratio of the total cable area and the overall area of the enclosure in which they are placed.

Squirrel cage rotor of an induction motor which has copper bars as its winding.

Star connecting the three ends of a three-phase winding to a common point.

Stroboscopic effect interaction of light from fluorescent or discharge lamps and the speed of revolving parts, making them appear stationary.

Suspended ceiling a ceiling suspended from the main ceiling to hide engineering services.

Switchgear apparatus for the controlling, protecting and distribution of electrical energy.

Thermocouple a junction of two dissimilar metals used for temperature measurement.

Torque turning power or effort of an electric motor.

Transformer apparatus for the transforming (changing) of voltages and currents.

Trunking a square or rectangular enclosure with a hinged or removable cover for the enclosure and protection of cables.

Wound rotor the rotor of a motor whose windings are coils of wire as opposed to copper bars, usually connected to slip rings.

Further definitions of words and terms are given in I.E.E. Regulations.

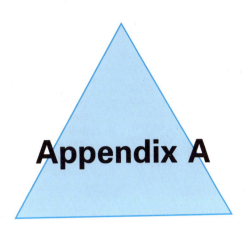

Appendix A

Machine control diagrams

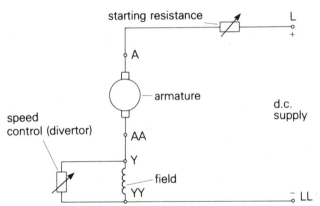

Note: To reverse direction interchange A for AA or Y for YY.

Figure A.1 D.c. series motor.

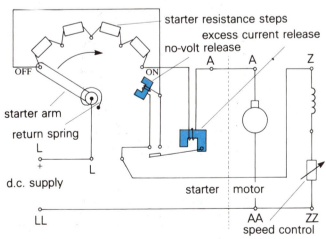

Note: To reverse direction interchange A for AA or Z for ZZ.

Figure A.2 D.c. shunt (face plate).

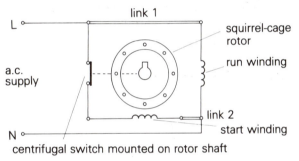

Figure A.3 A.c. single-phase – centrifugal switch.

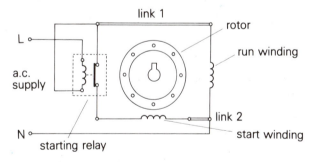

Figure A.4 A.c. single-phase – relay.

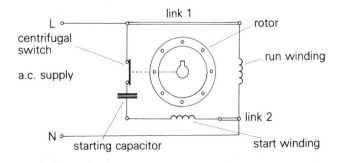

Figure A.5 A.c. single-phase – capacitor start.

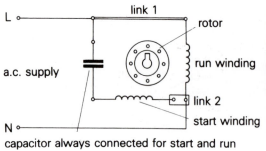

Figure A.6 A.c. single-phase – capacitor start and run.

Note:
For reversal of direction in 3, 4, 5 and 6 motors, interchange the ends of **either** the start **or** the run windings. Windings may be identified by disconnecting links in terminal box and testing for continuity.

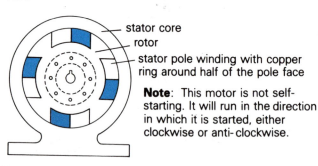

Figure A.7 Shaded pole.

Note: This motor is not self-starting. It will run in the direction in which it is started, either clockwise or anti-clockwise.

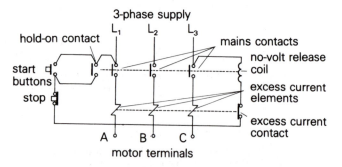

Figure A.8 Three-phase direct-on-line (DOL) with push-button control.

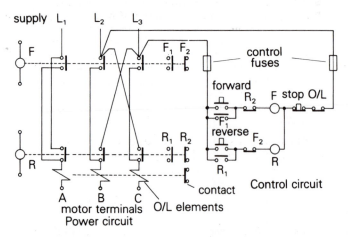

Figure A.9 Push-button forward–reverse control with safety interlocks.

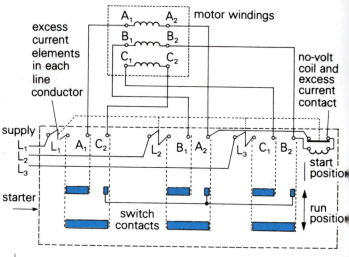

Figure A.10 Star–delta starter.

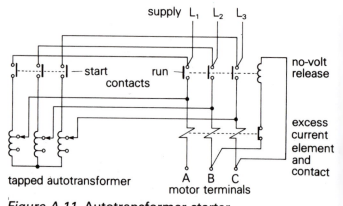

Figure A.11 Autotransformer starter.

Figure A.12 Three-phase commutator motor.

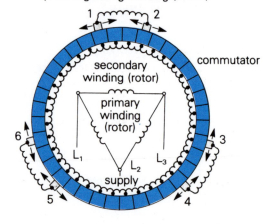

Note: The primary winding is supplied via brushes and slip-rings. Both primary and secondary windings are in slots on rotor core. The speed-regulating winding is in slots on the stator core. Brushes 1, 3 and 5 are connected to one common insulated spindle and 2, 4 and 6 are connected to another common spindle so that the brushes connected to the regulating winding either move towards each other **or** away from each other, thus varying the d.c. current in the speed-regulating winding and hence the speed of the motor.

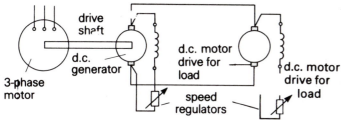

Figure A.13 Ward–Leonard speed control system.

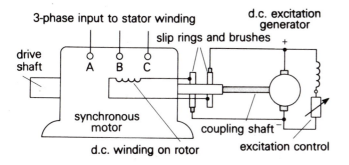

Figure A.14 Three-phase synchronous inductor motor.

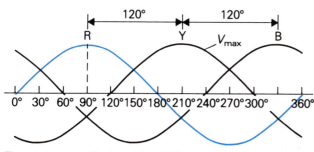

The phases are displaced by 120°.

Note: This is spacing between the R, Y and B winding on alternator stator. Maximum voltage is only produced when the revolving magnet is passing directly under the pole of the winding. The voltage at any other instant (instantaneous V) = V_{max} × **sine** of the **angle** at which magnet is at.

The stated supply voltage = V_{max} × 0.707. On, say, a 240 V supply

$$V_{max} = \frac{240\,V}{0.707} = 340\,V.$$

Figure A.15 Phasor diagram of output voltages from three-phase alternator.

R_1, R_2, Y_1, Y_2, B_1, B_2 are field coils in which the e.m.f. (voltage) is generated. The opposite coils R_1, R_2, etc., are connected in series to double the voltage.

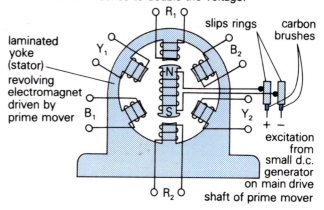

Figure A.16 Construction of three-phase alternator. See Figure A.15 for output voltages.

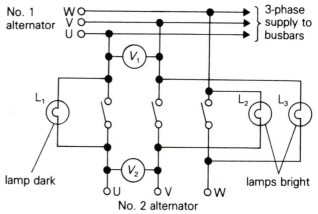

Two lamps (L_2 and L_3) are **cross-connected** as shown to the supplies of each machine, while the third L_1 is **connected** to the **same** phases. No. 2 **alternator** is run up to speed and the voltage adjusted until $V_2 = V_1$. From a study of three-phase waveforms it will be seen that when two such waveforms are in **synchronism** opposite phases will have quite an appreciable p.d. between them, so L_2 and L_3 will be **bright**, while L_1 will have none or very little p.d. across it. The speed of the prime mover is adjusted very carefully until these conditions are obtained, at which point the switch is closed. Any slight error and the larger machine will **pull** the smaller into step. An instrument called a **synchroscope** can be used, but is not always available.

Figure A.17 Synchronising of alternator by use of lamps; lamp bright, lamp dark method.

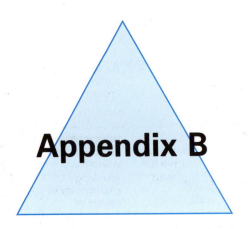

Appendix B

Electric motor data

Motor	Characteristics	Uses	Method of starting
D.c. series	High start torque. Increase of torque/fall of speed on load. Motor will 'race' when load removed.	Traction, cranes hoists.	Direct-on-line (DOL). Series resistance. Face plate.
D.c. shunt	Speed almost constant – current and torque increase to meet increase of speed. Fine-speed control by field regulator.	Machine tools, pumps, fans, etc. Variable speed drives on d.c. supplies.	Face plate.
D.c. compound	Differing speed/torque characteristics can be obtained. Can operate at constant speeds.	Machines of intermittent loads, shears, presses, rolling mills, etc. Fitted with fly wheels.	Face plate.
A.c. single-phase series universal (a.c./d.c.)	Series characteristics (as above).	Portable tools, vacuum cleaners, lawn mowers, etc.	Direct-on-line. Series resistance.
A.c. single-phase induction split phase capacitor	Shunt characteristics. Speed remains constant regardless of load variation.	Domestic fans, pumps refrigerators.	Phase-shift devices necessary. Relays or centrifugal switch disconnecting start winding at speed.
Shaded pole		Clocks, recording tapes, turn-tables.	Copper shading ring on stator poles. Direct-on-line.
3-phase induction	Shunt characteristics. Speed fall slightly on load. $n = \dfrac{f}{p}$ (1% to 4%) rotor slip.	Most general industrial uses for machines drives	Direct-on-line (DOL) for motors up to 8 kW rating. Start current up 8 times F/L current.
Squirrel cage rotor Double cage rotor	Low starting torque. High starting torque.	Where no speed required and motor can start off-load.	Star–delta or auto-transformer for higher power ratings.
3-phase slip-ring wound rotor	Starting torque increased by external resistance connected in rotor windings circuit. Speed variable within limits.	Machines required to start against heavier loads. Cranes, winches, etc.	3-phase rotor resistance starters reduced in steps until at full speed.

210

Motor	Characteristics	Uses	Method of starting
3-phase commutator (synchrage motor)	Precision control of speed from standstill to full speed by movement of brushes around the commutator.	Cotton looms, printing machines, where speed may be varied over wide range by foot pedal moving brush gear, or by hand wheel.	Start in minimum speed brush position brushgear movement.
3-phase synchronous induction	D.c. excitation of rotor winding causes stator to take a leading pf current from the a.c. supply.	To drive heavy steady loads. Motor generators, large pumps, fans, compressors, etc. Improvement of pf on installation.	Damping case winding on rotor in addition to d.c. winding. Pony motor. **Note**: These motors are NOT self-starting.
Ward-Leonard	Gives a wide range of speed control with constant torque.	Main steel and paper rolling-mill drives.	A.c. motor started with auto transformer or rotor resistance method.

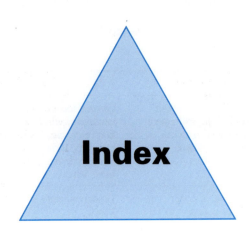

Index